ORGANISED CRIME

ORGANISED CRIME

Editor
Prafullah Padhy

ISHA

ISHA BOOKS

DELHI-110033

Organised Crime

Rs. 750

ISBN: 81-8205-348-X

Published in 2006 in India by
Isha Books
D-43, Prithviraj Road,
Adarsh Nagar, Delhi-110033
e-mail : ishabooks@hotmail.com

Laser Typesetting at : Shiva Infosystem, Delhi
Printed at : Mehra Offset Press, Delhi

Preface

Organised crime is crime committed by criminal organisations whose existence has continuity over time and across crimes, and that use systematic violence and corruption to facilitate their criminal activities. These criminal organisations have varying capacities to inflict economic, physical, psychological, and societal harm. The greater their capacity to harm, the greater the danger they pose to society.

During the past quarter century, organised crime has become a more complex phenomenon, spreading to less developed and/or more centralised societies previously untouched by it. Today's crime groups blend illegality with legitimate business. Major crime groups have rather evolved into complex networks, with activities in many countries, taking advantage of open markets and of governments' different levels of commitment to combat them. They are more pervasive and dynamic, having broadened their scope of operations, geographically and by sector. They are not merely trans-national and specialised: crime groups are now trans-continental and diversified, part and parcel of globalisation.

The pervasive nature of organised crime in legitimate global and domestic commercial markets has a widespread impact to all areas of the society. Areas such as our healthcare, safety systems, and financial security are at the forefront of those adversely impacted by the far reaches of organised crime. Economic crimes committed by organised crime groups cost millions of dollars every year. The impacts of organised crime also go far beyond monetary effects. Violence, intimidation, and corruption are mainstays of many organised criminal groups. They affect public confidence in most fundamental sources of solace and security. Organised crime also affects the basic rights to peace, order and good governance.

The threat posed by transnational organised crime to the political, economic and social fabric of societies was recognised by the international community beginning in the mid-1990s. The subsequent negotiation of an International Convention against Transnational Organised Crime was a historic step forward in countering this threat. The Convention provides the normative framework and orientation for the global programme.

This book provides a comprehensive introduction to organised crime. It analyses various types of organised crime and their adverse impact of the society. The diverse legislative and law enforcement efforts to control organised crime are also discussed. While primarily a book for students and scholars, it will be of interest to the educated public also.

Editor

Contents

1

Introduction

Crime is not new. It started with mankind's second generation, as Cain raised his hands against Abel. Criminal organisations keep their illicit actions secret, and members communicate by word of mouth. Many organised crime operations have substantial legitimate businesses, such as licensed gambling, building construction, trash hauling, or dockloading enterprises, which operate in parallel with and provide cover for drug trafficking, money laundering, prostitution, extortion, hijacking, fraud, and insider trading, among many other possible criminal activities.

In order for a criminal organisation to prosper, some degree of support is required from the society in which it lives. Thus, it is often necessary to corrupt some of its respected members, which is most commonly achieved through bribery, blackmail, and the establishment of symbiotic relationships with legitimate businesses. People in the judiciary, police forces, and legislature are especially targeted for control by organised crime via bribes, threats, or a combination.

Financing is made easier by the development of a customer base inside or outside the local population, as occurs for instance in the case of drug trafficking. In addition, criminal organisations also benefit if there is social distrust of the government or the police. As a consequence, criminal organisations sometimes arise in closely-knit immigrant groups who do not trust the local police. Conversely, as an immigrant group begins to integrate into the wider society, this generally causes the organised crime group to weaken.

Lacking much of the paperwork that is common to legitimate organisations, criminal organisations can usually evolve and reorganise much more quickly when the need arises. They are quick to capitalize on newly-opened markets, and quick to rebuild themselves under another guise when caught by authorities. Globalization occurs in crime as much as it does in business. Criminal organisations easily cross boundaries between countries. This is especially true of organised crime groups that engage in human trafficking.

The newest growth sectors for organised crime are identity theft and online extortion. These activities are troubling because they discourage consumers from using the Internet for e-commerce. Furthermore, e-commerce was supposed to level the playing ground between small and large businesses, but the growth of online organised crime is leading to the opposite effect; large businesses are able to afford more bandwidth (in order to resist denial-of-service attacks) and superior security.

Characteristics of Organised Crime

During the past quarter century, organised crime has become a more complex phenomenon, spreading to less developed and/or more centralized societies previously untouched by it. Today's crime groups blend illegality with legitimate business. UNODC has probed into the key characteristics of these groups (Fig. 1).

To a large extent, the earlier hierarchical structures of crime (the families, the cartels, the cupolas and the like), specialized in violence and therefore easily cast to the margins of society, are gone. Major crime groups have rather evolved into complex networks, with activities in many countries, taking advantage of open markets and of governments' different levels of commitment (and readiness) to combat them. They are more pervasive and dynamic, having broadened their scope of operations, geographically and by sector. They are not merely transnational and specialized: crime groups are now transcontinental and diversified, part and parcel of globalization.

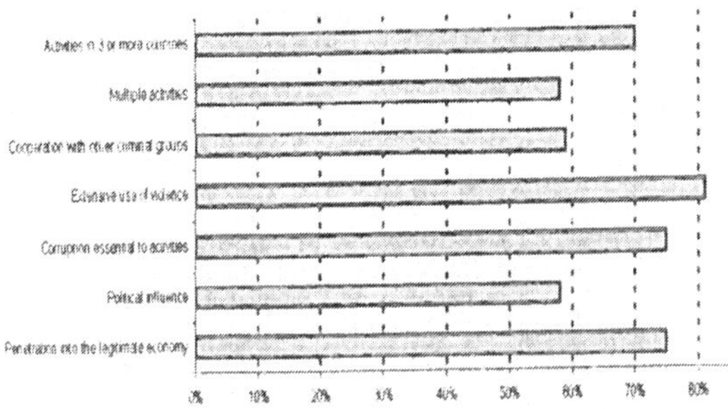

Figure 1: Characteristics of organised crime groups

In other words, criminal organisations today are not simply creatures of the underworld. Their business (bloody as it may be) uses legitimate trade networks: for example, they ship goods (merchandise, money, currency etc) by means of the same containers, the same commercial liners, scheduled air-carriers, postal systems and couriers as honest businesses. Figure 1 also shows that, like legitimate business, organised crime today pursues multiple activities. While drug trafficking remains a key specialization, illegal traffic deals with whatever is available for large-scale profit - from nuclear waste and firearms to protected species, cultural artefacts and, most tragically, human beings and their organs.

Cyber-links have opened greater, and even more sophisticated opportunities, especially as illegal profits are in most cases invested in the legal economy. Above all, Figure 1 shows that crime weighs heavily on its victims: think of the women and children trafficked for sexual exploitation, or of the male adults enslaved in suburban sweat-shops or remote countryside.

Trafficking in these human beings is quite remunerative: commodities, once sold, are gone, while human bodies can be sold over and over again, until they are consumed by disease. Criminals do not always bend victims' resolve at gun-point. They bribe and pamper public officials to gain acquiescence. They court and payoff next-of-kin. But they also threaten illness, or refuse medical treatment (in brothels and at the work-place) if this is necessary to achieve their aims. They take away identity papers. In short, crime knows how to adapt.

The intangible aspects of crime have today become very prominent, for example, their penetration of governments, media and the economy at large. Crime groups bribe governments, rendering law-making unfair and to the advantage of the few. They keep journalists on the pay-roll, to disseminate the kind of news they wish - and their opponents hate. The resulting corrupt behaviour undermines investment, and therefore development. Few legitimate (international) firms wish to top investments with kickbacks or bribes. Moreover, the danger to society is not always openly visible, or palpable: public suspicion that the system of governance is corrupt weaken democratic legitimacy, the market system and the rule of law.

With the likelihood of democratic retaliation weakened, illegal activities become viciously more and more rewarding. Crime has also learnt how to put on a mantra of purposefulness. In Afghanistan and Colombia early on — and more recently in many other countries —

the bloodiest attacks on innocent civilians have come from terrorist groups, namely from criminals pretending to justify their acts on the basis of ideology. Paraphrasing a famous statement, we can call "terrorism as crime conducted in a different form": as on earlier occasions, the recent terrorist attack in Madrid was paid for with crime money.

Crime and terrorist groups do cooperate: terrorists run illegal activities (they smuggle drugs or people) to raise cash, while criminals trade forged papers and clandestine weapons for security cover and free transit (offered by insurgents).

Spreading of Crime

While organised crime first developed (in the 1950s) in rich countries, the phenomenon has now reached global proportions. Mafia-style behaviour and, more recently, corporate crimes are increasingly present in transition (former communist) and developing (third world) countries. Given the scarcity of resources to fight the problem and cushion the consequences, the impact of organised crime on these countries is, of course, great.

The rapid growth of organised crime in new regions has been greatly facilitated by weak, even collapsed governments, wars and ethnic strife, growing poverty and wealth inequality, forms of privatization gone wild, and high levels of corruption. At times it is difficult to discern whether such factors are the cause or the consequence of organised crime because illicit activities, like the licit ones, are driven by market forces.

Rich countries are the main consumers of drugs, counterfeits and natural resources (including, sadly, people) illegally trafficked from poor, corrupt or conflict areas. On the other hand, motor vehicles, appliances and firearms stolen in rich countries make their way to poorer countries, where people are unable to buy these commodities at market prices. A good example is provided by trafficking in humans beings (Figure 2). Countries of origin are mainly Central and Eastern European, African and Asian states. Countries of destination are mainly the rich ones. A similar pattern also characterizes the smuggling of migrants.

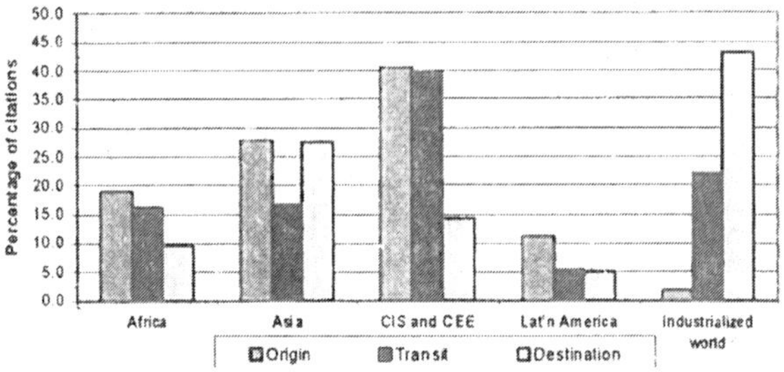

Figure 2: Global human trafficking patterns

The global nature of today's organised crime, corruption and terrorism, therefore, calls first and foremost for increased international governance. Civil society cannot surrender to the notion that these social malaises are unavoidable because so widely spread and part of modern world. Hence the legitimate question: at the United Nations, which lies at the heart of international cooperation, are we doing enough about these social evils?

International Governance

In this section we can see the issue of international governance like (i) peace, (ii) development, and (iii) rule of law and democracy.

Peace

Today's conflicts, even when civil and political in the origin, are closely linked to the formation and growth of criminal networks. Conflicts and instability in the Andean region; in West, Central and Southern Africa; in Central Asia and South Eastern Europe have all been intimately associated with the growth of powerful criminal organisations as well as corruption. War not only generates instability, in which organised crime thrives; war also provides opportunities for illicit enrichment, through the creation of profitable new trading opportunities (most typically, natural resources for weapons). Criminal networks have often constituted an important interface between legitimate commercial operations and dishonest groups within conflict zones.

Common features of conflicts that have taken place in the past half century are:

— conflicts have tended to repeat themselves in the same regions. It is as if the earth in these areas quakes periodically, causing death and destruction;

— even before international peace-keepers intervene, the foot soldiers of organised crime have parachuted into war-torn lands, ready to exchange money and weapons for the right to exploit the resources and make fast money;

— therefore conflicts, even those which start on identifiable political/religious/ethnic grounds, inevitably tend to turn into large scale humanitarian crises if and when the land has something valuable to offer: natural resources above ground (forests in Congo, coca in Colombia and opium in Afghanistan now, and in Thailand and Sri Lanka earlier), or below ground (minerals in Sierra Leone and Congo). Trade routes (in the Balkans and the Caucasus, for example) and pipelines (Chechnya) are other assets targeted by criminals, causing protracted conflicts;

— the presence of organised criminal gangs in these conditions of civil strife and high instability has usually led to protracted humanitarian crises, causing additional untold sufferings (famine, refugees and HIV/AIDS);

— corruption has also fed humanitarian crises in a predictable way. Criminals choose their entry/exit access points on the basis of detailed information regarding ports, airports, ministries, military checkpoints, or police barracks that can be bought - a fact not sufficiently appreciated by peace-keeping officials.

In many conflict situations, foreign criminals help local warlords plunder regions they control and use their power to trade in weapons, drugs and local primary resources. Such warmongers (call them insurgents, commanders, guerrillas, contras or whatever other term is in the thesaurus) deliberately block progress towards conflict resolution, and strive for the perpetuation of the anarchy and lawlessness under which their illegitimate business activities thrive.

Warlords and their (international) mafia acolytes grossly violate human rights and humanitarian law. Given that they operate under the guise of political motivations and their activities include both common and war crimes, "Foreign criminals/Local warlords Inc." represents a (new) criminal partnership hard to deal with. Not rarely, we find foreign political interests and geopolitical considerations caught-up in all this, creating gigantic political Gordian knots. Another example of rule of law violation is the trafficking of light arms by organised criminal groups used in the Balkan civil war, then re-exported to West Africa (Liberia and Ivory Cost).

There is evidence that these arms are now finding their way to Sudan and east Congo. Light arms trafficking has led to a dramatic increase in casualties during these conflicts and to criminal violence afterwards, both within states engulfed by conflict and in surrounding lands: a fact that needs to be seriously considered by law-makers in countries that have not yet ratified the UN Protocol against Firearms. Also tragic has been the distribution of drugs to child-soldiers in conflict situations, as a way of turning them into killing-machines. Only now (that they are children no more) is the UN Office on Drugs and Crime able to reach these young victims and help them cope with (what has become) a life time addiction.

Socio-economic development

Crime renders development unsustainable in two perverse ways. On the one hand, organised crime impedes economic growth. This becomes evident if the UNODC Index of Organised Crime is measured against the UNDP Human Development Index. The UNODC index includes several indicators: the extent of smuggling in a number of illicit commodities, public and business perceptions of the degree of organised crime and corruption, and the extent to which crimes such as homicide, robbery and corruption are closely connected to organised criminal activity. High levels of organised crime correlate with low levels of human development.

On the other hand, underdevelopment and institutional weaknesses provide the context for organised crime and corruption to thrive. Markets are bent out of shape, competition is undermined, investment decisions are distorted. Criminal organisations often operate through 'front companies', undercutting prices. They can do so by making their profits from illegal activities, effectively eliminating honest competitors. Economic and financial crime is also widespread, involving investors across the world. The most severe damage occurs to the banking systems of developing countries; the international financial system is hurt as well and loses credibility. This phenomenon is often dismissed in the world's major financial centres. Such a benign (at times, malign) neglect of the origins of the blood money is not a good example of integrity on the part of those who have established the rules of world financial probity.

Crime is also profoundly anti-social. While the Robin Hood-type mythical gloss is that robbing the rich is a form of wealth redistribution, in effect criminals mostly steal from the poor to fund lavish life-styles. Furthermore, the shadow economy fed by illicit profits means less revenue for education, health, pensions, and other necessities. In more exposed countries, crime constitutes a serious impediment to municipal government. Taking advantage of weak administration, organised crime controls city governments; it manages urban resources, determining the right to housing or other services. In addition, it influences, through the corruption and co-option of officials, decisions on land management and public investment, diverting funds from public good to personal interests and illicit financial gain.

When appropriate regulation and enforcement are not forthcoming, entire sectors of the urban economy are supervised by local gangs or warlords. The example of transport systems in many African cities is a case in point. Criminal groups even target development agencies: indeed a better understanding (and a reassessment of operating procedures) is urgently required by the Agencies engaged in emergency and development assistance, to protect themselves from criminal (or corrupt) activity.

Rule of law

Organised crime violates .human rights, subjecting

individuals and communities to high levels of violence, fear and increased exposure to disease. Look at the HIV/AIDS epidemic among injecting drug users, in prisons and in the sex industry in Eastern Europe, the Russian Federation and Central Asia. After the break-up of the former Soviet Union, various social institutions ceased functioning in the newly independent states (CIS), particularly in the drug control and the health care sectors. As a consequence, there was a huge influx and increased availability of drugs, supplied by foreign and local syndicates.

This development has led to a dramatic rise in the number of drug users. For example, in the Russian Federation, the number of injecting drug users (IDUs) is estimated at about 2 million. As a result, the incidence rates for HIV infection have increased dramatically. Today, it is estimated that there are approximately one million people living with HIV/AIDS in the Russian Federation, a significant proportion - estimated in 2002 at well over 50 percent - having acquired the disease by using contaminated needles. The situation in Central Asia is even more worrisome. Here there has been a particularly rapid increase in drug abuse given these countries' exposure to drug trafficking from Afghanistan.

Statistically, the correlation could not be more robust. The average proportion of HIV/AIDS cases related to injecting drug use in 2003 for the region as a whole is estimated to be in the order of 75 percent. In China the equivalent measure is 79 per cent; in Russia and Ukraine it could be as high as 90 per cent.

Indeed crime deprives individuals of their humanity and societies of their future, violates human rights and perpetuates humanitarian crises. Today crime is unprecedented, both in magnitude and in manifestation.

- — Take corruption, a most malignant criminal offense. By subtracting an estimated 1 trillion US dollars/year from legitimate business, corruption is one of the biggest enemies of development. It destroys public wealth, it undermines trust in governments and it makes life of the poor more difficult by causing the curtailment of basic services.
- — Take drug trafficking. Pain is first felt by farmers in the Andes and in Asia, then by addicts in favellas and shanty towns. Drug trafficking turns the misery of millions of people at the opposite ends of the drug chain (respectively supply and demand) into lavish life-styles for the criminal intermediaries who cash in over $200 billion/year.
- — Now take trafficking in humans, the modern form of slavery. One million people a year are trapped, chained and exploited in a bondage that screams for vengeance — in this life and in the next.
- — Finally, take terrorism. These days the list of casualties due to terrorism reads like a gruesome war bulletin: innocent lives lost for the crazy goals of a few madmen.

Legitimate Organisations and Organised Crime

There are at times little distinction between "legitimate" organisations and organised crime. For instance, corrupt businesses or non-democratic governments often bear strong resemblance to organised crime. Indeed, some have theorized that states are created from organised crime. Organised crime distinguishes itself from other non-governmental organisations, through its ability to provide its own protection. A legitimate business relies on a government to enforce its contracts, while organised crime must rely only upon itself. When such institutions gain legitimacy they become governments.

Non-traditional Organised Crime

In addition to what is considered traditional organised crime involving direct crimes of fraud swindles, scams, racketeering and other RICO predicate acts motivated for the accumulation of monetary gain, there is also non-traditional organised crime which is engaged in for political or ideological gain or acceptance. Such crime groups include terrorist organisations such as Al Qaeda, Hamas, and Hezbollah.

The crime is something more than violence against people and property. Indeed peace cannot be guaranteed, development cannot be sustained and justice cannot reign:

- if a country's economy is based on illicit activities;
- if trade is contaminated by narcotics, arms and worse of all, people;
- if the wealth of a nation is stolen by corrupt leaders;
- if laws are decided from the chamber of a gun, rather than of deputies;
- if public officials pursue private interests;
- if, otherwise respectable, business people bribe their way to success;
- if the banking sector is used to launder illegal proceeds;
- if a country's youth is robbed of their identity, and even of their bodies;
- if terrorist violence is allowed to influence a country's political course.

Indeed crime deprives individuals of their humanity and societies of their future, violates human rights and perpetuates humanitarian crises.

Why has crime, and its impact, changed so much in recent times? Because crime has evolved, as cause and consequence of changes in the way modern societies function and interact. Weak or collapsed governments, mass poverty, income inequality, corrupt behavior and armed conflict have become a weapon and shield for criminals, traffickers and terrorists. They have turned contemporary public goods — for example, the internationalization of activity, market deregulation, privatization, hi-tech communications and rapid transportation systems — into public bads. By operating in a modern business conglomerate style, with growing speed and ease, criminal groups have become multinational and agile, with their own tariffs, terms of trade, management structures, financial arrangements and means of enforcement.

Has the international community remained passive in the face of these frightening developments? Not at all, although the measures undertaken have fallen short of what is required. In the same 2004 Peace Day message, the Holy Father made another important point: "The legal systems of the individual societies progressively grew up into norms which came to be known as jus gentium, the law of the nations.... This process has led to the formulation of universal principles which are prior to, and superior to the internal law of States, and which take into account the unity and the common vocation of the human family." What are the new components of the jus gentium advocated by John Paul II?

In the UN context, one segment of the jus gentium is the United Nations Convention on Trans-national Organised Crime, a new instrument of world governance and a new means to combat anti-social behaviours. This convention has just come into force. Significant also are its three supplementary instruments:

(i) the Protocol on Trafficking in Persons;

(ii) the Protocol on Smuggling of Migrants; and

(iii) the Protocol on Firearms. Interestingly, while the first two protocols have already entered into force, the third one (on firearms) is running into serious opposition and ratification is lagging behind.

The newest building-block in the world governance system is the United Nations Convention against Corruption, adopted by the General Assembly in October 2003, signed by over 100 countries and yet to come into force (possibly in 15-18 months). Also noteworthy are the twelve UN instruments against terrorism. These, combined with earlier legislation (for example, on the Elimination of Discrimination Against Women, and on the Rights of the Child) provide an increasingly comprehensive global response to injustice and insecurity. They constitute a legal framework and a stimulus for action.

2

Transnational Organised Crime

The World Inter-Ministerial Conference on Transnational Organised Crime was held in Naples in November 1994 under the auspices of the United Nations. Two years later, when the President of the United States, William Clinton, presented the revision of the National Security Strategy to Congress, he mentioned for the first time the fight against international organised crime as a matter of national security. Governments from many other countries throughout the world have included such disruptive phenomenon among the new actual or potential threats to domestic and international security. The most industrialized nations belonging to the G-7 group, the Council of Europe, as well as other regional organisations, have also given warnings with respect to the problems caused by transnational organised crime and have encouraged taking action against this menace.

European Union institutions, in particular, are increasingly worried with the phenomenon, now the objective of police cooperation between member states. As a further example of this common concern, the New Strategical Concept of North Atlantic Treaty Organisation, completed in 1999, remarks that Alliance security interests can be affected, among other risks, by organised crime. This perception about the challenges posed by organised crime, though sometimes exaggerated by state agencies and non governmental organisations, arose during the last decade due to the combined effect of both the observed evolution of such disturbing phenomenon and changes in the focus of international relations once the Cold War was over, following the collapse of communism.

IMPACT OF GLOBALIZATION

In just one decade, organised crime has gone from being considered a problem limited to certain countries or regions, the result of specific historical circumstances and scarcely affecting the political decision making, to become one of the basic factors when defining threats to the national security in general and democratic governance in particular .

Organised crime is no longer considered a delicate problem of criminality which has become spread and structured to a certain extent, but a phenomenon operating on a wide scale likely to harm the functioning of society and politics worldwide, although its effects vary depending on certain conditions. If this is to be meaningful, the concept of organised crime must free itself from the narrow visions embedded in the legalistic theses and those often similarly presented by the security agencies, so as to find out about the differences between groups of people who systematically commit crimes and what is specifically considered to be organised crime.

Although it is possible to observe functional relationships between criminals gangs and organised crime, and these become more acute when dealing with local performance of transnational organised crime, there are two basic differences between both notions. First of all, organised crime exists when the type of offenses perpetrated have particularly serious social repercussions. This may be due to the violence involved in their execution, the financial losses produced or other features implying anxiety or indignation among the general public. However, a second characteristic must be added before organised crime can be considered to exist: it is able to protect itself against the state and other external agents which constitute a potential danger to its continuity and the expansion of its activities. Such protection is achieved basically in two ways: on the one hand, intimidation through the actual use of violence or the threat of using it; on the other, corruption which blocks action by state institution or civil society entities.

Within this lax definition, the range of activities organised criminals may carry out is extensive and these vary in accordance with the internal and external variables faced by each group. They can include the combination of one or more markets and a relatively limited or large number of countries, although recently a strong tendency could be detected towards the concentration of business in a lesser number of groups dedicated however to a greater number of illegal fields. Their repertoire of activities certainly include professional and financial crimes, but organised crime as a whole is far more articulated and incorporates strong control instances. However, at certain points both criminal models tend to amalgamate . Organised crime may even resort to terrorism as a part of its violent methods at certain times or during particular stages.

A wide ranging inventory of organised criminal activities include the supply of illegal goods and services, such as the production and trafficking of drugs, trading in weapons, children, organs, illegal immigrants or nuclear material, gambling, usury, forgery, hired killings and prostitution; the sale of stolen property, especially luxury cars, animals and works of art; helping out legitimate companies in illegal matters such as breaking environmental or labor laws; the use of legal networks for illicit activities including the management of transport companies for drug trafficking or construction investment to money laundering; finally, systematic predatory action such as piracy, extortion and kidnapping.

Among the large groups typically considered to belong to the category of organised crime and to be involved in one or other of these illicit activities are those pertaining to quite a long list of organisations dedicated almost exclusively to drug trafficking on a wide scale in Europe, Latin America, South Asia; the Italian Mafia in a global expansion program originated decades ago; the Japanese Yakuza; the Chinese Triads; and, finally, the magma of organised crime coming from Russia and other Eastern European countries.

The evolution of international relations together with the transnationalization of organised crime has endowed this phenomenon with a new role as a growing threat to democratic regimes. Although there is no unanimity with respect the extent of organised crime as a threat, its importance being reduced to a potential risk by some authors, recent research has given weight to the challenges it poses for national security. On the one hand, the collapse of the Soviet Union and the acute financial and political crisis in current Russia, have led to a fundamental redeployment of the ideas governing the concept of national security. Thus, the organisations which played a major role during the Cold War and the set of institutions which were central actors in the confrontation between military industrial complexes suddenly found themselves deprived of the theoretical justification supplied by opposing superpowers and nuclear deterrence.

In this new scenario where the supreme threat disappeared, these agencies, which have been externally forced to redefine themselves, the reasons for their existence and their high expenditures in an environment with strict financial controls, require a new kind of justification. Thus, following the way set by the Soviet Union, which went from monolithic Communism to being broken up and becoming a prey to organised crime, the Soviet block fell behind as far as security concern and the mafiyas, which gained control of a large amount of resources in the republics which emerged from the break up of totalitarianism, became a clear menace as were its homonyms in other parts of the world.

Generally speaking, this shift in focus is part of a redefinition of the concept of security, which is more akin now to the one existing in the period between the two world wars than to the prevailing one during the Cold War, which was based on the confrontation between antagonistic blocks, geopolitical calculations and the realistic dimension of international relations. Nonetheless, apart from the arguments developed within the security agencies and armed forces, it is evident that recent trends in organised crime have led to the effective increase of its harmful consequences on national security in general, as well as on the normal functioning of democratic institutions and processes in particular.

Several factors facilitated this emerging situation and produced a new model of organised crime predominantly transnational in its character. This type of organised crime has three basic differences with respect to previous manifestations of the phenomenon: it tends to operate at a regional or global level, mobilizing extensive cross-border connections and, above all, has the ability to challenge both national and international authorities. Processes parallel to those which made possible the growth in economic globalization enabled also criminal organisations, once confined to restricted environments or countries, to perform at a broader scale.

The rapidity and the possibilities provided today by innovative technologies applied to transportation, together with a political commitment to global free trade, have increased the flow of licit as well as illicit goods. This situation has been aggravated as far as the most lucrative business of organised crime, that is drug trafficking, is concerned, since producing and consumption countries are in different continents, although distances tend to be reduced or even disappear with the increased use of synthetic drugs. In a symbiotic type of relationship, criminal organisations have combined the exploitation of business opportunities and routes opened up in the international market with the historically accumulated knowledge of contraband, which had always been very resistant to the action of the state . Thus, a very lucrative mix of old and new illicit activities were generated where specialization and widening of markets did not seem to be contradictory tendencies.

In this regard, it is not a mere coincidence that the activities and even the abuses carried out by large multinational firms, rather uncontrolled at the international level due to the lack of antidumping agreements and the increasingly more intense search for competitiveness, lay down the usual precedents for the introduction of organised crime. Research carried out in the United States and Western Europe show that there is a link up with the activities of the legitimate firms and that important segments of the legal economy have been penetrated by organised crime. The growth in world trade has been accompanied, or even favored, by a revolution in the financial networks.

Remarkable technological progress in communications, as well as efforts of the banking institutions to develop new options to avoid paying state taxes and to satisfy the growing demands of the transnational companies, together with the huge amount of money in circulation within the system and the ease with which it can be transferred at high speed, have greatly favored a basic stage in any illegal business: money laundering, that is the control of money, obscuring its illegitimate origin and its ownership, then legalizing profits.

The general lack of supervision on international financial activities, albeit recent efforts to introduce a certain degree of control, in addition to the complexity of such operations, make it extremely difficult to enforce regulations. Should any country undertake to reinstate the control on the flow of capital, this would not have the desired effect but, on the contrary, could lead to a rapid relocation of capital, loss of earnings for the powerful banking sector and greater complexity as regards the financial instruments.

Moreover, for many countries which receive these illegal funds they compose a substantial part of their economies, and a radical approach to the issue would eventually inflict strong economic and social hardship. Actually, these activities are carried out on a large scale in many countries, which are chosen according to factors such as banking secrecy and facilities to operate with tax havens, corruption levels, police training, the power of financial institutions and the currency exchange controls.

In addition, technological progress made in communication systems and the transfer of information have had other effects on the evolution of organised crime. On the one hand, it has allowed the flexibilization of organisational structures and has enabled them to function in networks which tend to maximize profits and elude the state security forces. On the other hand, it allows the reduction of accumulated paperwork and so eliminates much incriminating evidence which could facilitate repressive police action.

However, as an underlying trend, there has been a change in the nature of threats to national security, which previously were related with great accumulation of power,.

resources and territory, and are now associated with the generation and control of information. Regarding this point, new vulnerabilities appear in the security defenses of the states as the criminal organisations, with their enormous financial potential, can access information which they may eventually use to improve and expand their business.

The globalization of information through mass media, which allows the immediate presentation to the whole world of well-being enjoyed in developed countries, the parallel appearance of a multiplicity of regional conflicts, and the progress made in transportation, have led to an important increase in immigration flows and the gradual creation of ethnic networks throughout the globe. Despite the vast majority of immigrants being respectful to the laws of the host countries, criminal organisations have taken advantage of this ethnic dispersal so as to develop their own transnational networks within which they are in permanent contact through advanced communications systems. Although the main criminal groups still have a strong national identity and haven headquarters from where they co-ordinate their activities, the precarious living conditions of many immigrants facilitates their expansion into new markets.

Ethnic links, with their systems of loyalty, solidarity and sanctions often superimposed on the legislation of the countries where immigrants live, indirectly facilitates the implantation of organised crime. Police intervention among these groups is hindered by language and cultural traits, which are strengthened by kinship ties leading to group solidarity and suspicion of national authorities . This situation is further worsened by inappropriate action taken by administration agencies which do not make the distinction between members of criminal organisations and people located in a wider social segment, who generally tend to be those who suffer the damage of discriminatory practices. Regarding this point, the existence of frontiers which have become increasingly porous has produced a partial shift in police action, from border control to the surveillance of specific social groups, eventually criminalizing certain ethnic communities. A determining factor in this change has been the inconsiderate and alarmist treatment of both immigration and organised crime given by certain mass media.

Parallel to this process, multicultural urban areas are growing fast, functioning as nuclei of the world economic system. To a certain extent, these plural cities can be regarded as the heirs of those classical port towns which were central to the first global networks of organised crime. Such cities provide a combination of elements, which include power centers, highly developed financial and banking systems, significant economic inequalities, a cosmopolitan population which guarantees anonymity, the relaxation of social control and ethnic diversity, all of which can intentionally or unintentionally facilitate the penetration and maintenance of transnational criminal networks.

Organised crime is also familiar with the rapid spread of technological progress in other domains than those already mentioned. In fact, owing to its enormous economic potential, large criminal groups have faster and more efficient access to technological resources than the average person experienced in the field. It is common knowledge, for instance, their ability to acquire and deploy any kind of new device, which they also continually experiment with. This progress is especially relevant with respect to drugs, as has been shown by the spread of new synthetic narcotic substances, in the field of weapons and in the forgery of all types of goods.

Moreover, their access to new control and communications technology is achieved more quickly than the security forces responsible for pursuing such criminal organisations, the becoming less vulnerable to state repression. But progress in transport and communications technologies has also given rise to the multiplication of social contacts and the immediate transmission of any kind of novelty, this paving the way for experimentation with new drugs and very often for uncontrolled abuse.

The excess of wealth and an environment where massive consumption takes place in the context of industrialized countries have created new recreational and leisure opportunities accompanied by an increase in illicit goods and services. The fact that a part of these sought after goods and services is legally prohibited has aided the growth of some specialized branches of organised crime and the expansion of old groups into new, lucrative business.

Finally, organised crime is also involved in the great international political conflicts which have multiplied during recent years. In fact, global strategy of the large criminal organisations has been profoundly influenced by geopolitical events. While under normal conditions organised crime prefers stability, it tends to prosper when there is political and economic unrest. Communications and transportation enables them to transfer to zones in conflict or unstable areas, where there is an obvious loosening of controls, large amounts of capital which covers the flight of legal funds at times when hard cash is necessary and where returns on investment are usually high due to the risks assumed.

The end of the Cold War has meant a diminishing in world tension and, therefore, in conflict areas a relaxation of any type of indirect or even direct control by Western authorities responsible to less polarized audiences. Some events in recent years have been particularly relevant for transnational criminal groups, such as the Yugoslavian civil war, German reunification, economic reform in the

Chinese Popular Republic, the emergence of both new trading blocks and new industrialized countries.

The disappearance of the Soviet Bloc has been a crucial event encouraging organised crime expansion. Helped by the lack of internal controls once the communist regimes had fallen, the transnational criminal groups were quick to make contacts in Eastern European countries. This has had extraordinary and very harmful consequences for the future development of these states as well as for the consolidation of pluralistic regimes. The triumph of capitalism, a weak or unexisting civil society, and a peculiar political culture in many of these countries has led to the troubled establishment of free market mechanisms without the accompanying control measures. This change has initially led to internal disorder, the demise of previous authority structures, reluctance on the part of the population to new official control, the revival of ethnic antagonisms, and a collapse in the judiciary and security agencies, often entailing their subordination to or cooperation with organised crime.

The vacuum of power and a previous history of organised crime, which has supplied the human resources and the required social networks, together with the progressive fall in the living standards have provided excellent conditions for recreating, establishing and expanding large criminal groups. At the present time, the overlapping of illegal and legal activities in most of these recently inaugurated market economies is intrinsic to the new situation.

Of all these activities, the greatest threat to regional and global security is perhaps trafficking in radioactive materials, which might fall into the hands of terrorist organisations or uncontrollable states, although evidence of such traffic is still scarce and in some cases has been manipulated by the intelligence services and the media. Nevertheless, some other geopolitical events which were believed to facilitate the expansion of organised crime, for example the disappearance of border controls between the Western European countries which signed the Schengen Agreement, seem to have had a very relative and doubtful effect in this matter.

In fact, border controls were already very lax during previous stages of the regional integration process and the smuggling organisations found alternative routes throughout history which had been used by the large groups of organised crime. On the whole, however, all the other factors considered in above pages unintentionally helped, during the last decade, to expand transnational organised crime on the eve of the 21st century. The phenomenon has evolved to much further reaching organisations than in previous times.

As a result, organised crime constitutes a growing threat to national security and international stability, can disrupt social institutions and economic development, has the ability to undermine democratic processes, and victimizes entire populations. Thus, a traditional problem of public order or internal security has become a challenge which could not only endanger the viability of societies, the independence of governments, the integrity of financial institutions or the functioning of democracies, but also the peaceful relations between states.

Political Impact of Transnational Organised Crime

The new nature of organised crime enables us to distinguish certain facts which imply substantial challenges to the governance of democratic regimes. However, it should be noted that transnational organised crime is not monolithic, but rather a diversified, complex and multidimensional phenomenon where collaboration between groups is more frequent than confrontation . It has different manifestations in specific countries and has been perceived differently throughout time and space. It does not function uniformly nor does it have a constant degree of impact on individuals, state agencies and non governmental entities throughout the world. The first political impact of organised crime has to do with sovereignty, an old concept which continues to dominate the sphere of relations between states.

States are separated by frontiers, which not only divide up territory but also mark out different legal systems, levels of economic development and political cultures. Pitted against this are the criminal organisations which, due to their illegal and transnational nature, ignore the sovereignty of states and have no respect for borders as far as their illegal business is concerned. Their plans for expansion are not concerned with the idea of national jurisdiction but on the flow of trustworthy people and goods which provide earnings. If they do think of state frontiers, this is always in terms of either specific criminal law systems with differing levels of risk and specific markets with opportunities for illegal earnings, or the blurring of the trails of illicit activities through the international division of work.

Despite the process of economic globalization, the establishment of emerging supranational structures, and the current political argument in favor of the free movement of goods, capital and people have all intentionally eroded an essential aspect of sovereignty, state control on the flow of goods and services through its frontiers continues to maintain sufficient levels of security for the general population. However, organised crime has created parallel indiscriminate routes in order to violate frontiers and this means a deficit or lack of control as regards the flow of goods and services into the country, which could grow in the future and endanger critical issues ranging from public health to democratic stability.

These illegal routes, previously established and very well protected from the irruption of the state, can even be used to supply subversive groups and organised crime with sophisticated and even nuclear weapons or introduce food without the required quality control as well as other potentially dangerous products into the country. Given that the capacity of governments to decide which individuals or merchandises cross national borders is a substantial and necessary condition for guaranteeing governability and sovereignty, the constant far reaching activity of organised crime which trespasses national frontiers with impunity supposes a serious challenge to the sovereignty of states. As a conclusion, organised crime manages to elude the principle of territorial control which is inseparable from the state and considerably corrodes the idea of national sovereignty.

Organised crime can also interfere in the political culture of a given country, that is to say, in the set of values and attitudes related with the understanding of political activity by the individuals and collectivities that make up society. In this sense, organised crime essentially affects the social and physical environments of democratic societies, distorting the lines which separate what is legal from what is illegal, generating alternative loyalties to the state and provoking changes in public opinion with negative effects on the functioning of the system. In their beginnings, criminal organisations have the single aim of surviving possible intervention by the state and its security forces as it pursues its activities.

Its success in illegal business, its rapid business growth and its accumulated wealth have led to new political, social and economic demands, which are specifically the aspirations of the criminal leaders to become part of the social elite from which they often feel they have been intentionally excluded. Thus, they try to legitimize their wealth in the eyes of the citizens in general and the ruling classes in particular erasing the origin of their fortunes. For this reason, they try to lead openly spendthrift lives and to relate with the elite of politics, the mass media, show business, and members of the administration of justice and the financial world.

Their financial power is of great help to them in this task aimed at creating social legitimacy. As regards their subordinates, who often include qualified as well as nonqualified workers, members of the public security forces, politicians, professionals and, frequently, a large private security organisation, the attachment fueled by salaries usually leads to the creation of a bond based on admiration which allows the occupation and use of a considerable number of social, rural and urban spaces, thus increasing the possibilities of impunity for illegal activities.

Apart from the individuals and groups which are economically dependent on the hard core of the criminal organisation and are generally provided with more rapid, though also more dangerous, upward social mobility channels than the normal ones, the leaders of these groups also use their financial resources for purposes of social investment. Examples can be the construction of housing for modest members of society, public donations which help their reputations, dazzling public shows and the offer of public goods to communities where the work of the state is defective or even non existent. Such activities provide the leaders of criminal groups with a relatively simple way to launder their earnings and, above all, a way to substitute in practice the tasks of the state and, consequently, producing a transfer of loyalty to the criminal leaders, a legitimization of the illicit acquisition of wealth, as well as the validation of new fields of impunity and protection.

The generation of alternative loyalties is more shameless and widespread in the former communist countries, where the emerging social and economic structures have been unable to generate alternative ties between society and state up to the present time. The incapacity to solve problems related with the basic needs of the population is evident and the justice system is still weakly linked with the new dimension of the market economy.

On the other hand, the transfer of legitimacy is easier among immigrant communities, where loyalty to the state is often strained by financial straits and strong social and emotional bonds with their countries of origin. These ethnic communities are ideal for recruiting members and creating loyalty to organised criminals in its most important markets, due to the growth of immigration in an increasingly interdependent world and to the opacity and the closed environment resulting from linguistic and cultural barriers. Moreover, this closed atmosphere frequently generates inappropriate responses by the state, which are often led by ignorance or even racism.

In turn, these rekindle the sense of being unprotected by the state. In this breeding ground, the large criminal groups manage to exploit the feelings of alienation from the state for their own benefit and at a minimum cost in terms of social resources, building up new loyalty bonds, which are ethnically based, and so stronger and more lasting. But this transfer of legitimacy does not only appears among relatively extensive but well defined groups.

Organised crime may eventually lead to a questioning of the most far reaching legality in force by confronting the population with a view of the normative code as inefficient and unable to control social behavior. While the official discourse talks of formally accepted juridical and moral regulations, which exalt work, sacrifice and democracy, in reality there is a widespread repudiation of these values by conducts which tends to maximize profit irrespective of its source and the social consequences. Thus, norms may be seen to be invalid and inefficient for normal social development, what is legal becomes illegitimate and what is illegal becomes reasonable and necessary.

Organised crime is, thus, strengthened not only by economic social structures but also by a deviant collective mentality and culture. As a result of all this, leaders of criminal organisations become more invulnerable to the forces of the state. Despite the fact that on most occasions they reproduce patterns similar to the dominant social ideologies, they manage to procure loyalty which is seen by citizens as an alternative to, and in systematic confrontation with, the state. This generates a reserve army for the criminal groups or at least inaction and the sympathy of many members of society discontented with the general functioning of the state. In certain cases, the admiration of the leaders of criminal organisations can turn to fascination because, once presented and the legitimizing network set up, they represent a good part of the main social values and the repeated yearnings of excluded groups and the middle classes.

Apart from the transfer of legitimization carried out by organised crime, this can also affect the national collective identities of the populations which make up the essential basis for the territorial division between states and inside each state. On the one hand, it can cause different types of territorial fractures within a country by encouraging conduct and attitudes which confront different groups within society. If a particular territory or social group has a significantly greater level of organised criminal activity than others within the country, the situation can worsen as feelings of rejection arise in certain segments of the less affected areas. On the other hand, organised crime takes advantage of the migrations which have been taking place over recent decades. Problems of xenophobia may then arise leading to extreme right wing violence and social confrontation. The generalization of accusations against culturally different small communities produce a break up of the social cohesion which is necessary for democracy.

Inversely, organised crime can also manipulate the feelings of entire populations, in many cases those populations which are relatively backward in economic terms and the victims of inequalities, to such an extent that they confront central governments or supranational institutions. When accusations and activities aimed against organised crime are confused with attacks on cultural and social traditions, many people belonging to certain homogeneous ethnic collectivities, or even whole countries, might feel tempted to resort to aggressive nationalistic feelings in response to what are considered to be meddlesome attacks on the population as a whole. In this regard, it is essential that care be taken with public policy towards criminals when dealing with the specific features of the populations among which organised crime lives, by not allowing official discourse on crime to focus on foreigners, nor specific ethnic or national groups be criminalized .

Organised crime can also have a decisive effect on the political institutions. Criminal groups could try to exert an appreciable influence on the decision making capacities of the three classical powers: the executive, the legislative and the judicial. This attempted infringement is the natural consequence of the very dynamics of the illegal organisations on a grand scale, which in certain cases is similar to other large, legitimate groups, and has two main aspects. On the one hand, it tends create its own systems for dealing out justice and, on the other hand, it tries to turn the machinery of the state in its favor. Both aspects have the same objectives: to reduce the cost of viability for the group over the long run and to increase income.

A fundamental source of problems for these organisations is competition which must be kept at controllable levels . Monopoly, as it happens in the legal economy but on a larger scale, is the optimum environment for maximizing profits and reducing risks. As history shows, there is nothing more harmful to the permanence and growth of these criminal groups than free competition, which leads to conflict as regards illegal territorial or sectorial interests. Apart from the monopoly on illegality, these organisations need an authority which can enforce the fulfillment of the agreements required by their illicit activities, without resorting, by their illegal nature, to the state, its legality and its legitimacy, in order to solve conflicts. For both reasons, monopolistic or oligopolistic control of criminal business and the necessity of an authority to resolve conflicts mean that parallel systems of justice are needed as an essential prerequisite for survival.

These parallel systems of justice do not require a single authority nor specific written regulations. But this does not reduce its coercive efficacy. Since imparting this justice is determined largely by the personalities and the relationships between the leaders, loyalty to the system is directed towards persons rather than the institutions and, along it, there is a tendency to personalize important parts of the legal culture. These illegal norms regulate the social and economic relations of organisation's members and require unquestioning loyalty to the group in general and the leaders in particular. They also make up the rules of coexistence with other rival organisations. In this regard, whatever decision is adopted among different criminal organisations in order to prevent the excessive growth in business costs, and these can range from mutual respect and pacific collaboration to open confrontation and terrorism, the governability of democratic societies is hampered.

The widespread use of violence, which is characteristic of these alternative norms of the private justice systems faced with a lack of other means to impose sanctions, even when used exclusively against members of their own organisation, can lead to instability and alarm in society reinforced by the inability of the government to put an end to the killings, which are often carried out cruelly in order to set an example. This can end in delegitimizing the institutional machinery, regarded as incompetent to solve a problem concerning public safety and the protection of the citizens. The existence of these parallel systems of justice for a group of the population questions the universality of legality and also means that a complex system for imparting justice has been set up alien to the state and whose rationale is precisely the monopoly on violence within the criminal organisations. This opens up the possibility of alternative social and juridical regulation through the creation of territorial or sectorial sanctuaries, where state sovereignty may be minimal and from where it is possible to constantly challenge the forces of the state with impunity.

This situation would invalidate the monopoly on the exercise of justice, eventually including the use of physical coercion, which in principle is in the hands of state authorities. When criminal organisations reach a considerable size, the most efficient means to enforce this alternative justice is through the establishment of private armies . These do not usually confine their activity to the members of the organisation itself in order to back up the system of justice and set an example for the population in general, by letting them know of the existence of an extralegal method of conflict resolution and thus prevent their interference through intimidation.

They are also often used against external members who put their illicit interests at stake, these may be members of other gangs, civil servants or concerned citizens. These private security groups can be used to strongly challenge the state's ability to impart justice and the psychological stability of the citizens, by using terrorist tactics. This leads to demands for action by a state which is overwhelmed by the power of the criminal groups, which, by their very nature, are difficult to break up or paralyze.

Although the private justice systems described above have well defined aims, such as restricting competition, maintaining transaction costs at a minimum level and respect for the hierarchy, generally speaking they have neither the ambition nor the ability to supplant the state legal systems in their totality. In fact, a large part of these internal resolutions do not require the use of violence but sufficient financial resources and there are constraints on the creation of a generalized judicial system.

On the one hand, the pacific coexistence of a legal system of justice and another illegal system gives organised crime the opportunity to externalize substantial business costs and to take maximum advantage from both worlds. On the other hand, the creation of a generalized system of justice for everyone would not be economically feasible for the development of the criminal organisation itself, and in most cases would be an unreachable objective despite the enormous amounts of money they often handle.

Consequently, the construction of strong, lasting bonds between the legal system of justice and the illicit normative code which allow pacific coexistence and mutual assistance is essential for the survival and growth of the criminal organisation. Complicity between both systems is necessary in order to allow the solution of conflicts between criminal groups and elements external to the organisation in favor of the former. This may also involve controversies within the organisation or between different groups and avoids the negative cost of the use of violence being in private hands, ensuring the support of state legitimacy and its coercive forces. Thus, several business costs related to illicit activities are intentionally transferred to the state with the awareness that this cession will not bring negative consequences in the foreseeable future owing to the control exercised over the deciding bodies.

The price of this cooperation or its availability is that of intimidation and corruption, which often involve important sectors of the judicial and police agencies. In the first place, intimidation requires that the threat of violence be credible and this is possible due to the existence of the aforementioned private security armies, which are often provided with the latest technology , earn much higher salaries than their state counterparts and have clear solid lines of command.

Secondly, the unequal financial capacities of both the state and organised criminal groups, and their area of action facilitates penetration or corruption. Whereas the state is obliged and endeavors to attend to all citizens equally, which, due to diversification, means high costs, the criminal groups act skillfully to protect and extend their own limited interests by breaking the principles of equality before the law fundamental to a state bound by law.

The growth of the interests of organised crime has meant that its earnings are more and more dependent on the general environment and, thus, resort to breaking the normal functioning of the legislation may become a general rule. At some specific point it may happen that these groups endogenize the complete system of justice provided by the state and this generates more benefit as it adds additional financing for them from the tax contributions of citizens while the organisation protects its own wealth. Apart from this corrupting effect, the nature and extent of the groups' activities can distort the functioning of the legal system due to saturation arising from increased illegal activity. When the effectiveness of the security forces and the judicial machinery are overwhelmed, this leads to a feeling of defenselessness faced with crimes which threaten their own security, and also it may delay the effective application of justice and prolong in excess the resolution of all the conflicts which arise in the process of the normal functioning of a democratic society.

Faced with the inefficacy to protect rights and liberties, some may choose even to recruit private armies to substitute the state's provision of security, thus, encouraging an escalation of violence and the resolution of conflicts outside the legal system leading to the paramilitarization of society and the break-up of the social fabric. Moreover, there is an increase in interpersonal conflicts due to the fact that impunity spreads to greater areas of community life in democratic societies. In addition to the negative influence on the aforementioned judicial machinery, organised crime can also corrupt the legislative and executive process in a variety of ways: diluting democratic ideals, subverting the popular will through illicit means and corroding the legitimacy of the democratic political system and those actors involved.

As it is a troublesome, underground organisation, with problems related with the control and legality of its wealth together with the very continuity of the business, the criminal groups are vitally interested in molding the political institutions so as to favor their security and their accumulated assets. The need to pervert the political system in order to place it at the service of the interests of organised crime and, more often, to turn it against the general well-being, adopts different forms. First, organised crime tries to corrupt the representatives elected by the people at both executive and legislative level by offering them substantial sums of money or the constitution of common financial interests. Secondly, it subvert popular will expressed in democratic elections by the threat of violence against those representatives opposed to their criminal activities or the use of information through the mass media allied to or controlled by these criminal groups.

As the earnings obtained from the efficient influence on the process of legal creation grows, organised crime resorts to more sophisticated and innovative techniques to influence the legislative power, and in many cases this fits in with the interests of other economic, business and social sectors. Thus, they create or control intermediary organisations, such as commercial associations, lobbies or committees for political action aimed at putting pressure on politics in pursuit of their own interests. Their ultimate resource for influencing the legislative process is the invalidating of the mechanisms for controlling political activity and the organisation of civil society.

In order to affect these processes, which are so necessary for the survival of democracy, they can use various methods. On one hand, they can gain control of substantial parts of the flow of information generated in democratic societies by acquiring media firms and by bribing or intimidating members of the press, which would lead to a strong bias in the creation of public opinion, an increased credibility with regard to the threat of violence and the molding of political debate in their favor .

At the same time, criminal groups can also use intimidation in order to eliminate social leaders who are not in their payroll, and thus prevent the formation of interests which are a substantial part of pluralistic democracy. As the attract of organised crime to influence the social system grows, the fields of the political process and spectrum where intimidation is credible also increases, and this corrodes important values necessary for democratic coexistence such as freedom of speech and the freedom to associate. Organised criminal groups can also resort to manipulating the electoral process by presenting their own candidates and provide them with huge financial resources together with information from their illicit business or, in regions where clientelism is endemic, they can supply the candidate with the constituency required for victory in exchange for his future help once elected. Their economic power, which sooner or later becomes political power, is so extensive that they can even subjugate certain political parties or create their own parties so as to gain greater control over the structure for taking decisions in political institutions.

At times when there is a reduced turn out for elections and when the election is decided on a small margin, even the control of a small political party or a reduced number of voters can be effective in the game of political alliances and have disastrous consequences on law abiding citizens. This protection eventually articulated by organised crime in a democratic context, under these specific circumstances, damages the citizens' opinion about the legitimacy of the electoral process, which is seen to be subjected to illegitimate private interests instead of being a fair election between competing parties. Thus, they contribute to deforming and discrediting democracy both as a process and as a regime, to the extent that political life seems to be governed more by money than by ideas and principles, and authentic representation is replaced by the purchase of candidates and electors.

In its advanced stages, organised crime can hamper the formation of public policies through intimidation and corruption in the hope of directly obtaining substantial benefits, but it can also damage political activity indirectly in several ways. As organised crime spreads so does the level of its illegal or semilegal economic resources at national level concealed from those who take the decisions at executive and legislative level. Consequently, the quality of the data gathered by official or non official sources is reduced and the analysis of many economic relationships required for public policies formulation and implementation is hampered. For example, it is more and more difficult to determine the amount of goods and services imported and exported and the flow of capital, and the level of unemployment tends to be overestimated as it includes among the unemployed those who are working for organised crime.

The use of biased figures leads to the formulation of policies where the means and the ends are impaired due to substantial ignorance of the economic reality of the country, or at least a good part of this reality. Policies drawn up on such fragile bases tend to be ineffective or counterproductive, and give rise to even greater problems, helping on occasions to increase the illegal economy. The regulation of economic activity moves on a shifting surface and contributes to the creation of greater inequalities leading to a distortion of the legitimacy of the state as regulator of the economy. Eventually these policies can provoke economic upsets and instability, and lead to new types of more informal regulation of economic relationships. Another matter is the fact that due to its way of acting and its legal situation, the persecution of organised crime requires abundant financial, material and human resources.

Generally these exceed the capacity of existing police forces to deal with the problem of a generalized increase in organised crime and its sophistication. In times of restrictions in public spending, allocations to security tend to harm the policies for social redistribution, and again the sources legitimizing the modern democratic regimes are questioned. In the emerging democracies of the former soviet block this can also produce nostalgia of communism in important segments of the population, as it was able to provide social citizenship, albeit at a reduced level. However, the main result of a rapid substantial increase of the budget for the security forces is usually a lack of organisational control and the creation of semiautonomous corps which, contrary to their objectives, tend to facilitate the penetration of organised crime, and in many cases the systematic subversion of civil liberties.

Complementary to this, competency for the reception of resources and their preponderant role in the mass media among the different security agencies tends to lead to errors and gaps in the intelligence work, which is of prime importance in the fight against organised crime. Finally, organised crime leads to problems of democratic governability as it provokes financial instability, distortions and inefficiency in the markets, making the production and distribution processes less impersonal and so leads to structural flaws in the economy, which have a negative effect on the citizens and on the stability of the political system. Some of these alterations spring from the illegal activity itself and imply an inefficient share out of income in comparison with the working of the legitimate market as the distributor of earnings. Other abnormalities are connected explicitly with how the earnings generated are used illicitly. There are multiple facets which demonstrate these inefficiencies.

Firstly, there is the coercion exercised on certain segments of the population or territory, which is the usual practice of criminal groups and becomes an efficient protection racket which replaces or overlaps with the protection provided by the state , distorting prices. The costs are internalized and increase the prices of the goods and services subject to these extralegal taxes. This also implies a challenge to the state, which is the only entity which can legitimately impose taxes. Moreover, it discourages the free participation of individuals in the market as businessmen and, if the coercion is directed against the financial system, it puts the channels of investment and the citizens' savings at risk. Secondly, illegal drug trafficking, a fundamental activity of some groups providing them with huge earnings, means an extra burden for the treasury due to the costs of drug addiction treatments, the costs of repressing traffic and consumers and the loss of productivity for the economy in general .

Thirdly, the loss of legitimization of the political regime and the expansion of violence connected with organised crime mean additional costs for business activity. The increased cost of resolving conflicts, whether this be legal or extralegal, and the cost of protecting the rights acquired become barriers for the entry and the permanence in the market of legitimate participants. In these circumstances, the possibilities for national and international investment are considerably reduced and conditions arise for the massive flight of productive capital.

Forthly, organised crime is capable of destroying the efficacy of the state as a third party able to enforce compliance with the contracts which are generated in an economy . In the absence of this state activity, which throughout time has been seen to be the most effective instrument due to economies of scale and the guarantee of impartiality as long as there is stability, those involved would have to find a new body or person able to carry out this task, which would make the contracting process more expensive. In this regard, the climate of certainty usually generated by the state and put at risk by the large criminal organisations could collapse, and this would lead to the encouragement of a short term perspective on economic investment, which concentrates especially on immediate returns and contributes minimally to rational economic planning and long term economic growth.

Thus, even in the presence of a well organised and predictable form of corruption, an important section of the economy would be subjected to high degrees of uncertainty . The withdrawal of the state as third party to contracts, validating pacts and exchanges between persons through coercion, gives organised crime new opportunities to occupy more social spaces and direct the economy and society in general towards more simple, personalized structures which are contrary to economic efficiency.

In fifth place, the large-scale illegality of organised crime itself usually leads to less productive investment for the general economic system. Business investment is made in order to launder capital and not for reasons of growth and long term returns. It is directed at markets which generate little or no added value and are often very dependent on external resources and investment.

As regards property, widely employed as a means to launder capital, strong, generous demand by organised crime contributes to the appreciation of housing price with the consequent cost for the families and the state, which complies with almost universal constitutional precepts as regards this point. Moreover, the participation of companies which are fronts for money laundering and not for generating profits, and being competitive in the marketplace, allow these companies to sell their goods or services under the cost price, which means that legal businesses are pushed out of the market unable to compete in these unfair circumstances.

Finally, the criminal organisations constitute a threat to one of the main sectors of the economy, the financial sector, as it promotes unscrupulous financial institutions and erodes legitimate institutions through complex schemes for laundering money, which can finally undermine the citizens' confidence in these financial entities. The combined effects of organised crime in the economic field are inflation, the ineffective distribution of income, the break up of the free market and state regulation of the economy, a substantial loss of productivity , a short term view of investment which is counterproductive as regards prolonged economic growth, and, occasionally, monetary overvaluation. Concerning the financial system in particular, the volatility of capital in the hands of criminal groups hinders correct action in economic policy and destabilizes the banking institutions and the financial markets in general, which can lead in turn to a profound economic crisis.

Finally, organised crime provokes economic imbalance and long periods of economic recession, seriously damaging international competitiveness in an environment which is becoming more and more globalized. In the end, in countries with economies which are highly dependent on the criminal productive system, even addicts of the system, to use a term from drug dependence, any attempt to eradicate this and return to efficiently-run markets, political system and society in general would provoke economic recession and the resulting social response.

Nevertheless their harmful effects on democracy, criminal organisations seldom have an explicit antidemocratic program. However, under some specific circumstances organised crime can pose a direct threat to liberal democracy. The more serious threat to the democratic institutions by organised crime is then its activity from outside the political system. The result of this might be the collusion or alliance of these groups with insurgent terrorist or guerrilla groups .

Although there are substantial differences between the two types of organisations, they may reach agreements on tactics in order that their interests may prevail against those of the state. These alliances, which can end up accumulating substantial destabilizing potential, mean an increased impunity and much more destructive capacity for the subversive organisations. In this area, the state would have to confront a substantial challenge of an insurgent nature which would provide the chance to discredit democracy as a system able to solve problems of coexistence without the resort to violence. This threat could grow in the next millennium, when control of tons of nuclear material could be lost and a large part of this material could fall into the hands of smugglers owing to the political disorganisation in the counties which used to be within the orbit of the former soviet block. Such nuclear resources could be used to challenge democratic governments from other countries as well as from domestic or international subversive groups with extremist political, religious or nationalist doctrines.

Organised Crime and International Cooperation

The state response to transnational organised crime has not been uniform at international level nor has it been guided by the same principles, mainly because the type of challenge has neither been constant nor identical in all the countries. However, recently it has been observed some degree of convergence in the measures taken. This is the result, to a great extent, of previous successful national experiences and the activity of the multinational agencies, which tend to coordinate their responses and so prevent loopholes in legislation which allow the criminal groups to act more freely. But, apart from this diversity, fight against transnational organised crime is not a simple task. The intervention of the state machinery this phenomenon as a supposed challenge to the very functioning of the public administration presents a number of important problems.

Nevertheless, with the right amount of intelligence, legislation and respect for the law, experience has proved that these can be tackled with some degree of success. The most evident of these problems, which affects all aspects of public policy to deal with organised crime, is the disparity as regards the territory where both sides function, that is to say those involved in the systematic carrying out of crimes and those who pursue them. On the one hand, the security forces and state jurisdiction are confined by national borders and, in the best of cases, by international police and judicial collaboration, which is slow, precarious and limited. On the other hand, transnational organised crime functions at a regional or global level, where frontiers mark different market opportunities and also show safe havens where they and their funds are secure from the judicial action of other states.

Organised crime uses the porosity of frontiers resulting from globalization to the maximum, whereas this has little effect on the international functioning of the machinery for imparting justice, except for some well known exceptions. Therefore, government policies against organised crime must be carried out in two scenarios, the domestic environment and the relatively institutionalized co-operation with other states, with specific problems. But apart from this territorial duality, this policies has a fourfold dimension: social policy, legislation, judicial activity and policing. Consequently, state policy regarding organised crime can be considered to be cross-sectional and affects the three powers of the state.

With their components, which have multiple facets, these have to be borne in mind when handling the many variants of policy. Nevertheless, until the present time, in most cases social policy has not been applied as a way to fight organised crime, partly because it has proven that investment in these areas may eventually strengthen the criminal groups. These tend to seize the sums handed over and so contribute to establishing ties with business networks and tighten the parasitic relationship of protection with the social environment in which they are acting.

On the whole, legislative action taken against organised crime has tended to give new power and resources to security forces. Additionally, adaptations has been mostly designed to incorporate new bodies into the pursuit of crime, to create agencies specialized in this type of crime and to merge the work of the existing forces in order to procure greater collaboration. Judicial action has remained subordinated to legislative decisions and to the possibilities provided by the actions taken by the security forces. International co-operation in the judicial field has been left well behind in comparison with the progress made by the security forces, although these continue to be half-way and pose operational problems. Thus, the response of the state tends to resort, almost exclusively, on the security forces.

Efforts are being made to reduce the substantial difficulties regarding interstate action against organised crime as knowledge of these organisations expands, and more experience is accumulated from more and more countries fighting such type of crime. The first, basic problem is that in the fight against organised crime it is practically impossible to calibrate the effectiveness of the measures employed against such criminality.

The potential of the criminal groups and the performance of the security forces cannot be simplified to one indicator, such as the amount of confiscated drugs, the crime rate or the number of violent deaths, nor can it be reduced to the sum total of all these. The low level of violence carried out by these organisations may conceal extensive action which will have profound social and economic consequences. Large scale operations carried out by the security forces may be simply cosmetic, satisfying the political demand for action without affecting the hard core of organised crime and may even contribute to making it easier for one group to monopolize criminality.

The difficulty for measuring performance means that there is a high possibility that its corrosive effects may be manipulated, either by the mass media, due to the profits that such sensationalist presentations provide together with the haste which is typical of reporting, and by the security forces responsible for the fight against organised crime in its search for resources.

The extension of this activity leads to a situation in which the sensation of citizen insecurity is fostered and public spending in this area is increased and, consequently, other areas related with social welfare are abandoned. Consequently, distorted information about the phenomenon of organised crime, whose underground nature facilitates all types of inferences and unreal scenarios, may lead to wrong responses in public opinion, and large parts of society can then demand action based on imperfect knowledge.

Faced with this situation, the authorities may resort to options which limit civil liberties with the objective of increasing the effectiveness of the fight against organised crime and these are then applied to other situations which may arise but do not threaten the governability of the state but rather the status quo and the distribution of power. On the other hand, measures taken due to the pressure of public opinion rather than calm reflection may lead to easy solutions, such as blaming foreigners, and thus, to a certain extent join the migration policies with repression of organised crime.

This ineffective action affects specific social or territorial segments where no adequate difference is made between the population as a whole and its parasites, organised crime, and so the legitimacy of state action is weakened. In the absence of intelligence data required for such repression, state action combines ineffectiveness regarding the problem and a distortion of the relationship between the state and specific communities. Some of the problems occurring in the fight against organised crime are directly related to the bureaucratic dynamics of the security organisations while others are due to the different configuration of criminal groups and security agencies.

In principle, there are two main organisational differences between criminal groups and the security forces which enable the former to enjoy greater freedom of movement and greater difficulties to their control. Firstly, whereas police forces are organised on a strongly hierarchical bureaucratic base where internal transaction costs are high, in recent years criminal groups have been structured in networks, as recommended by business science textbooks and in the opposite direction to the classical composition seen in works of fiction.

This organisational model, which seems to be the most efficient structure for the era of globalization, has been adopted by the criminal groups at a much faster path than the security forces, where attempts at decentralization have met with profound internal resistance from bureaucracy. Thus, the security forces continue to be obstructed by internal dynamics and by the logic restrictions imposed by the rule of law. Additionally, as they are one of the essential pillars of the democratic state, the idea of change tends to be loathed by political leaders owing to the fear of failure in such a fundamental state institution. Obedience to the law is also the basis of the second difficulty in the fight against organised crime, which is the fact that action by the security agencies is mostly reactive to the activities of organised crime.

Proactive policies have been rarely used, are still very underdeveloped in most countries and often include ramifications such as encouraging the carrying out of crimes in order to secure sufficient evidence to cover cases which have been condemned by many civil rights groups. Therefore, action carried out by security forces is always a step behind the action of organised crime. While organised crime progresses towards new activities and markets and perfects others, the security agencies are overwhelmed by the task of gathering and analyzing information. As regards this point, apart from the restrictions of legality, the security forces are also confined by financial and budgetary constraints, which in most cases do not affect organised crime, which is quite free from such limitations. Other conflicts arising from the fight against organised crime are directly related to the security agencies' organisation.

There are many groups responsible for pursuing organised crime and these range from the traditional security forces to the intelligence agencies, and, more recently, the armed forces. This means that in most cases there is a complex division of work which hinders the optimum development of security activities. A misunderstood confrontation over the scant public resources for which these agencies compete, together with professional jealousy, add another dilemma to the fight against organised crime. This competitive situation, which exists among other public agencies, has been particularly harmful on most occasions and has become particularly serious in the case of security agencies where the gathering and analysis of information is fundamental to effective policing.

Such tasks tend to boost with any new information and the dispersion of intelligence data only multiplies the costs in human and physical capital by overlapping or doubling up of efforts, thus weakening police effectiveness. However, despite the harm caused by this division of efforts against organised crime, some authors also point out some positive aspects within this conflictive situation. The first of these advantages is the fact that distribution of effort and duplication of tasks to a certain extent immunize the state against the possible paralysis of the security forces as a consequence of infiltration and corruption. It may occur that one public agency is infiltrated by organised crime and thus, increases its power to intimidate, but this can be countered by the existence of other state structures unaffected by corruption, which can act in an emergency.

Inversely, the involvement of several state groups means a multiplication of the expenses required by organised crime to disrupt the security forces due to the fact that the efforts to corrupt and intimidate are split, the costs multiply due to the competition, which hampers their control of the state's security machinery. One final positive element related to the diversity of security forces may be the fact that competition among public services, when it occurs in one activity and in the framework of collaboration rather than confrontation, can improve productivity and competitiveness and so reduce the evils of bureaucracy which tends to affect public organisms in their activities.

These bureaucratic conflicts between public agencies which affect the different security organisations at state or any other territorial level, each one with their own competencies, often overlap with customs agents and the intelligence services, and these have been joined in recent years by military forces. Their intervention in combating organised crime, especially in the fight against illegal drugs, is especially indicative of the changed ranking of the perception of organised crime as a threat to national security. While during the Cold War organised crime was one more element in the confrontation of the two blocks , it has now become a threat in itself.

The participation of the armed forces in the fight against organised crime has been justified with the argument that the growing power, especially in capital, weaponry and technology, of the these illegal organisations has overwhelmed the operational capacity of the security forces and has also put the system of justice out of action, which has endangered the effective functioning of the state structure. On the one hand, the resources of the armed forces are more powerful and their participation in this new mission does not suppose additional expenditure for the treasure as the material and human resources already exist. On the other hand, it has been said that the legitimate use of military force does not have to be restricted to conventional conflicts between opposing armies but must be used when the state is in jeopardize and cannot respond with civil forces, such as the case of organised crime .

In addition, armed forces may also benefit from their activity against organised crime. For many military units and personnel the requirements of a conventional war are very similar to those of the fight against organised crime, especially as regards intelligence works. Therefore, the capacity of armed forces to confront real situations of war can be improved through participation in real action against organised crime. Justifications for this implication, however, have been generally vague and has been shown more from the point of view of its critics than from that of its supporters. As a consequence, the debate in this respect has been obscured by the importance of the armed forces participation in what has been considered a question of internal order by many people.

Nevertheless, it is not only the move towards militarization of the fight against organised crime what has been widely questioned by some critical authors but its practical implications. Although the resources of the armed forces are apparently more powerful and have been used skillfully for decades, in the field of organised crime there is no direct correlation between the measures applied and their effectiveness. Thus, this intervention may be more moral rather than noticeably effective . Military force is also counterbalanced by the tremendous capacity of organised crime for adapting to changing circumstances, and so the problem is simply transferred and no real solution is found. On the other hand, in this case, where intelligence is a basic tool, and the western secret services have generally been outstanding in the confrontation with the soviet block in their efforts to inform on the nature of the threat, the gathering of data is a long term matter involving years of intensive which eventually overlaps the work of other agencies.

Thus, it is reasonable to believe that it will take, without assistance from the internal security agencies, at least five years to reach the complete effectiveness of the military forces. Another point which has been questioned is the widespread idea that the participation of the armed forces in the repression of organised crime is free as it only requires the redeployment of certain resources and personnel. Practical experience shows that this demands increased allocations for the acquisition or reconditioning of appropriate resources and for training personnel in law enforcement tasks for which they have not been prepared. Even though the participation of the armed forces in some countries occurs at a micro-level, which in turn is where collaboration between the security forces and military counterparts usually obtains their better results, this opens the way to other problematic scenarios, among which are corruption of the armed force and the contamination of the relationship between the military and the civil.

The uncertain success of the military in this task, where the civil authorities have perceived their deficiency and have been forced to resort to the armed forces, could lead to the social support and the necessary awareness of the military to take on more sensitive undertakings. Finally, as regards the risks involved in the internal fight against organised crime, some of them come paradoxically from the legislation introduced to provide the security forces with more effectiveness. A large part of this progress in legislation, technology and human resources began in the United States and has then been transferred formally and informally to a large number of western countries, but without the parallel movement in the path of the United States' organisational schemes and its legal traditions. As regards this point, the employment of informers constitutes a risk of contamination of police action to such an extent that security forces and criminals may merge as far as their bureaucratic and economic interests are concerned. This situation becomes even more risky when undercover agents participate in the fight against organised crime .

Sometimes, in the short term, it is difficult to distinguish between the activities of organised crime and the repressive task of security forces during the performance of this type of investigation, and in the long term the futility of such action may lead to the paradox that the police forces become essential participants in the market for illegal goods and services. In any case, these interventions through informers and undercover agents can foster the organisation of criminality as it tends to eliminate certain criminal groups to the detriment of others, consolidating a monopoly by restricting the competition either because the groups more actively prosecuted by security forces are opposed to the informer's one or because the undercover agent manages to concentrate police action on a certain group thus freeing the others from the pressure of the security forces.

Although in the past it was crucial for breaking up criminal organisations, it has also been severely criticized in recent times. Firstly, reliability of much of the information provided by protected witnesses has been questioned as it is filtered through the personal and self-interested role of that person within the criminal organisation, influenced by the need to provide spectacular though fictitious data in order to enter the program, or by the desire of the security forces to present themselves to the public in the most favorable light. Secondly, the repeated use of this type of clemency considerably reduces the cost of belonging to a criminal organisation as it offers the chance to leave the organisation which is different from incarceration or death and, therefore, present another possibility to terminate a criminal career without the costs inherent to state repression.

International evidence shows that fight against organised crime within each state must be guided by three elements which could be distinguished through a correct intelligence action involving all agencies engaged in repression. On the one hand, the authorities must be aware that the main problems, and gains if correctly addressed by securitye agencies, are not in the confrontation with the underworld exclusively, which is numerically greater but marginal in terms of the economy and social impact and vulnerable in almost all aspects, but on the correct action taken against the criminal upperworld, more protected by the mechanisms of corruption and intimidation and responsible for the more dangerous threats to national security. The arrest of many low-level members or the indiscriminate control of the borders against drugs, for example, will have a minimum effect on organised crime as a whole.

Since 1950s in the United States and later in other countries, security forces have developed a focus which combines the preponderance of the organisation in repressive activity in opposition to the individuals' approach and action against the network which covers the prominent members of organised crime. Measures taken against the leaders of this criminal world and their main collaborators will tip the balance in favor of the state in the fight. However, this repression will be offset by the financial and social power of these individuals and groups. Protected by their influence on the media, and so liable to receive the favorable opinion of the public, safeguarded also by their contacts with the political and social elite, and their ability to keep their own activities and those of the justice system under extensive control, any successful prosecution taken against these prominent members could be a true measure of police efficacy .

However, this situation must be carried out in the strict context of law respect, because the claim of public pressure to find guilty persons may lead to indiscriminate incriminations and the transformation of the fight against organised crime into a way to solve ideological disputes among the political elite. As a consequece, this valuable fight could be functional, in the views of political elites, to introduce elements of authoritarianism into the system of government, which at the beginning would be justified under urgent and temporal basis appropriate for the special circumstances but in the long term may serve to other purposes. As regard to this point, it would be of great help to give preference to the measures against high political connections of organised crime and to incorporate economic crime as a specific form of organised crime. Economic crime with its highly qualified members and modern technology, as well as generate pernicious, huge alarm among public opinion, are the ideal appendix for larger criminal organisations.

Secondly, effective government policy requires that the political leaders have the capacity for sacrifice in order to differentiate between the short term or even longer beneficial effects that organised crime can generate and the generalized harm resulting from these criminal groups. The short-term improvement in the economic climate of a specific territory or social group at a particular moment as a result of having found a criminal niche in a world which is more and more interconnected at economic level can operate in opposition to the correct measures to be taken against organised crime in the early stages . Once these groups are completely established with close relationships to the political and economic elite, their extirpation is much more costly both in financial and democratic terms.

The electoral returns which can be generated by the social control held by specific criminal groups over concrete segments of the population, which are coveted in theory by all the political groups at times when ideological and electoral results are progressively being narrowed down, are a generous source for interweaving organised crime and the political elite.

The long term elimination of this connection can lead to the democratic system being completely deprived of all legitimacy. In the end, the citizens can perceive that the only way to be rid of the painful effects of organised crime includes the elimination of the political system as both are inextricably joined together. The correct punctual response, although it may be painful and misunderstood by specific segments of the population, is the best way to hinder the more harmful development of organised crime.

Finally, in order to obtain results in the fight against organised crime it is very recommendable to correctly identify it. Although agreements among various criminal groups seem to be becoming increasingly more frequent, the fact is that each one of these organisations has its specific peculiarities and weak points, which can only be found through intensive intelligence work. In the absence of this correct differentiation, both between countries and inside each country, to which the legislation and the specific actions of the security forces must be adapted, the efforts to put an end to such type of crime would be faced with contradictory responses which would simply transfer the activities of organised crime to other territories, groups or activities.

In any case, the problems mentioned are meaningless when transnational organised crime is able to effectively protect itself by corrupting and intimidating the police and justice machinery. As regards this matter, the main pillar in the fight against these criminal groups is the build up of security forces which are fully committed to democratic principles and the rule of law.

If contradictions in the internal front against organised crime are substantial, cooperation among states in the same goal has even more serious problems. The first and perhaps the most important of these has to do with a particular conception of the role of the state and international relations. The realist notion that has dominated this arena perceives the foreign environment as anarchic and conflictive and this is profoundly harmful to collaboration among states, even when this cooperation may eventually generate mutual benefits for all those involved.

A mistaken analysis of international relations produced by these conceptions related with the competitive character of states implies the idéa that organised crime can be a factor which erodes the position of other states, and so, inaction or the complicity of disinterest can be effectively faced with the antagonism of a third country, which constitutes the independent variable of the foreign policy of any state. In this ideological context of international relations, only the imposition of a more powerful state might generate interaction among states to confront organised crime and this does happen in many fields, or at least this is interpreted as so by some experts and political leaders in international relations, especially in the area of the production and trafficking of illegal drugs.

Nevertheless, the revision of this paradigm, together with the emergence of supranational polities, have opened up areas of collaboration by mutual agreement, both at bilateral and multilateral level since 1960s. This cooperation among states as regards organised crime is not a simple matter with clear, precise mechanisms but comes about through different agreements and independent or interdependent mechanisms. Among others, these instruments are the exchange of information through new and old international organisms with a greater or smaller degree of regional integration, co-ordination of combined responses through liaison officers, the participation of elements of the security forces in multilateral organisms and informal contacts among police officers. On the whole, all these activities leading to the coordination of a cooperative response to the problem of transnational organised crime occur at three levels: macro, meso, and micro. At the first level, are the commitments made by the governments to collaborate in police work and the multilateral structures set up to this end. The second level is confined to more or less formal agreements drawn up between the security forces of different countries and endorsed by the governments. The final level includes informal relationships between police agents from different states.

In addition, among the intellectual constructs which limit international cooperation are included in a Hobbesian conception of the state, which induces governments to worry about conserving what is considered to be an essential part of the state's authority. "Providing security for citizens has often been thought of as the kernel of the state's claim to authority; having effectively lost the role of being the sole guarantor of security from military threats". As the states are becoming more and more integrated in transnational organisations for external protection, such as NATO, "losing the role of sole guarantor of internal order could fatally undermine state legitimacy" .

3

Illicit Firearms Trafficking

Illegal firearms trafficking is the movement of firearms from the legal to illegal marketplace through an illicit method for an unlawful purpose, usually to obtain profit, power, prestige or to supply firearms to criminals". The diversion of firearms from the legal to the illegal market place includes international, interstate, intrastate trafficking, stolen firearms cases, illegal firearms transfers and straw purchases. The illegal trade of firearms usually occurs through three main channels. These include:

— *Clandestine military operations*: these are covert transfers of firearms by one government to a separatist or insurgent forces operating in another country;

— *Black market sales*: this is the criminalisation of other legal transactions, rather than black marketeering per se. What truly differentiates a black market from a 'legitimate' firearms deal is the covert methods of intermediating between supply and demand - firearms moving one way and money back the other. To hide their trail, purveyors of black market firearms will use concealment, mislabeling, fake documentation, and laundering of payment. Put simply, the essence of the black market transaction can be understood by thinking of "black" not as a colour, but the absence of light (transparency);

— *Grey market sales*: the grey market is more obscure than the black market. The grey market resembles the covert nature of the black market, but in reality it is very different. Unlike the black market, grey transactions usually are neither entirely legal not entirely illegal. The grey market represents not policy writ large, but policy in flux as exporting and importing governments experiment with new diplomatic links, cloaking possible policy changes in covert transactions. It is through the use of covert channels that officials on both sides can take greater risks, cultivating new relationships while minimising the danger and potential embarrassment.

Black markets were created by embargoes. They are the unintended by-product of embargoes prohibiting sales to particular countries, and since the Cold War, embargoes have been a standard instrument. Following each embargo placed on a country by the United Nations, new opportunities for black market sales arose. In other words, black markets were created in an attempt to circumvent embargoes on specific countries.

Nature of Illicit Trafficking

Given that access to firearms is one of the identified problems, understanding the supply of firearms is necessary in constructing an appropriate solution. Although more research is needed to track the movement of guns, firearms used in crime, injury or conflict, come from three principal sources:

— legal firearms which are misused

— legal firearms which are sold/stolen illegally (theft/ sales from legal owners to "criminals", theft/sales from military to civilians, the "gray market", etc.)

— illegally manufactured and traded firearms.

Understanding the interactions between formal (licit) and informal (illicit) markets is critical to understanding ways to reduce misuse and proliferation. While there are many factors which shape demand for firearms and while these cannot be ignored, mechanisms to address informal markets are not futile. While they share elements of distribution, illicit trafficking of firearms is unlike the illicit drug supply chain in important ways. The drug supply for the most part is illicit from production through distribution through consumption. In contrast, most firearms begin as legal products and may end up being used illegally through a variety of channels. Some of the important factors shaping this market include:

— Globalization: Interactions between national and international markets make effective controls all the more critical

— Interactions between licit and illicit markets

— A variety of means by which licit firearms move to illicit distribution networks and purposes including: theft, loss, straw purchases, illegal transactions by dealers, fraud and false information.

Diversion from legal sources, theft and illegal importation are among the principal sources identified. For example, South Africa is in the process of undertaking significant enhancements to domestic legislation in an effort to address this problem. Given the recognition that access to firearms is a factor in conflict and crime, there are a variety of measures that have been undertaken to address the problem. Addressing demand and the root causes of crime are undeniably important. Firearm regulations are based on the fact that there is a link between access and misuse, and that controlling accessibility helps reduce misuse.

As firearms tend to flow from unregulated to regulated areas and few countries have absolutely secure borders, international cooperation and coordination is essential. One of the major problems is "leakage" from licit sources to illicit purposes. Firearm theft contributes to illicit trafficking, by definition falling into the wrong hands. In the US and South Africa, over 15,000 firearms are reported stolen each year. In Canada, the number is roughly 3000. Another problem revolves around firearms which are bought legally and then sold illegally. Within Canada the old system created huge opportunities for "leakage" because imports were not recorded at time of import but at time of sale.

In between the border and the sale point many "disappeared". Traditionally, customs officials were required to record the value of firearm shipments rather than the quantity, type or serial numbers. Firearms described as hunting rifles have turned out to be military weapons. In other countries there are descriptions of a variety of means by which firearms are diverted, including complex and sophisticated cloning operations and forgery. Other incidents have been reported of "deactivated" firearms being exported with no controls only to turn up reactivated in other contexts.

Trafficked firearms are most often acquired by individuals with criminal intent and are often recovered in crimes associated with the illegal drug trade and organised crime. A large part of the problem is also associated with individual criminal "entrepreneurs". Illicit markets, by definition are difficult to assess because they are informal. The vast majority of the research undertaken is based on anecdotal sources. In order to identify illegally held firearms, one must be able to identify those which are held legally.

In other words, by tracking legal movements of firearms, one can identify those which are illegal. Firearms also flow across borders. In 1994 for example, foreign governments reported 6238 unlawfully acquired US original firearms to the Bureau of Alcohol Tobacco and

Firearms. Over half of them were discovered in Mexico. According to one study, at least half the handguns recovered in crime in Canada are illegally imported.

The importance of information to crime prevention and investigations is self-evident to those in the policing community. In many respects, policing is fundamentally an information processing activity and information about firearms has proved essential in a wide range of initiatives internationally. The US Bureau of Alcohol and Tobacco and Firearms (BATF) as well as Interpol use tracing information to determine where a gun was manufactured, where it was first sold at retail and who bought it. Investigations can be built on that information; whether the object is to uncover a particular low volume straw purchaser or to identify a large trafficking operation. The same principle applies to imports, exports and in transit movement.

By tracking the legal movement of firearms, we will be able to identify firearms which are being illegally imported, exported or transferred. Because of the ease with which firearms can be moved from one jurisdiction to another, we need international cooperation to address the problem of transnational trafficking in firearms. Tracking and tracing ability has also proved invaluable in criminal investigations. Major anti-smuggling initiatives have relied on firearms tracking to identify hot spots and aid in investigations. Canada has cooperated with other police agencies, notably the BATF, in a variety of inter-jurisdictional investigations.

As police agencies cooperate to combat transnational organised crime, consistent standards for information becomes increasingly important to assist in criminal investigations and reduce the illicit trade in firearms. We have found, at least in terms of handguns, that maintaining information about who owns what guns encourages legal owners to take their responsibilities seriously. We would anticipate that this same principle applies to manufacturers and dealers who are likely to be more careful about whom they distribute guns to if they know police can more easily trace guns to their source.

Information about the movement of guns from point of manufacture, through import, through wholesale and retail and resale is fundamental to stemming the illicit trade. Criminal investigations are based on information and registration is viewed as an important source of information to assist in police investigations. It is also core to the implementation of community policing which is underway in many different jurisdictions.

Transnational Issues

The greatest threat from the movement of weapons out of state control and into the hands of non-state actors, is that it results in a cycle of events that together results in an erosion of state authority. "States affected by firearms proliferation, are ... no longer "sovereign" structures". Transborder links between militants, organised crime and narcotics traffickers, takes away the legitimacy of borders, and reduces the decision making capacity of states. At the extreme end of this process are the "failed states". States fail when they are unable to provide basic functions for their citizens and when they can no longer exercise their traditional functions, such as guarding the territorial integrity of the state, and the exercising its' sovereign functions. The economy collapses, health care becomes inadequate, physical infrastructure deteriorates.

Crime and violence run rampant. These conditions foster opposition groups which often turn to armed rebellion. Weapons are commonly supplied through black market channels and are smuggled from hot zone to hot zone. Small arms, in particular firearms, leave a devastating legacy long after a conflict has officially ended.

They continue to be used for other forms of violence, such as crime and interference with the delivery of food and medicine to persons in need of reflief. There are many examples where the proliferation of firearms has contributed to state failure. One example is the Soviet Union where as a result of its collapse and an alleged corrupt Russian military, there has been a proliferation of weapons and military material. Firearms and other weaponry have been sold to national and transnational criminal organisations in and out of the former Soviet Union.

Firearms stolen or sold from Russian armouries have been used by criminal elements to eliminate rivals and intimidate business, government and law enforcement officials. In addition, in Lithuania, law enforcement authorities during the mid-1990s reported fifteen international organised criminal groups engaged in the illegal trade of weapons. Other examples of how the proliferation of firearms, and other small arms have contributed in the destruction of a society's infrastructure, government institutions, and political process include Somalia, Albania, and Sierra Leone in West Africa. In the case of Somalia, the withdrawal of US soldiers and the sheer quantity of firearms, especially American-made M-16 assault rifles, prevented a peace from being established, and eroded opportunities for future peace.

It has also been suggested that the proliferation of firearms has also impacted on neighbouring countries in the region. Lax border controls provided a conduit for both explosives and people to succeed in bombing US embassies in Nairobi, Kenya, and Dar es Salaam, Tanzania, in August, 1998. In 1997, the citizens of Albania overturned the government in response to being defrauded by pyramid schemes that resulted in a large majority of citizens loosing their life savings. It was reported that protestors raided and looted military bases, bunkers, arms depots and police stations. In the end about 80 per cent of Albania's total weapon stocks and over a million tons of ammunition were no longer in the control of military or police.

Through the assistance of the international community, and the United Nations, the Albanians have recreated a state, and have also begun a series of weapons collections programs in order to recover weapons still in the country. For almost a decade now, Sierra Leone in West Africa has been involved in civil and crossborder conflict with Liberia. Liberians have been reported to be assisting and supporting the Sierra Leone rebel group, the Revolutionary United Front, or RUF by providing them with weapons. In this specific case, the availability of firearms and light weaponry has enabled one of the poorest nations in the world to continue financing their weapons purchases in order to continue their participation in the war.

While these examples may seen far removed in terms of posing a threat to Australia's security, the fact that Australia is geographically isolated from most countries does not preclude it from experiencing some of the international consequences of state failure. "Failed states are important ... because of the demands that they foster. They bring increased refugees ... and they create insecurity in the states that surround the failing states, thus causing demands for other states to intervene". State failure has the potential to increase illegal immigration to Australia. According to the latest figures released by the Department of Immigration and Multicultural Affairs (DIMA), the greatest numbers of unauthorised air and boat arrivals to Australia in 1998-99 (in descending order) were from PRC, Iraq, Malaysia, South Korea, Turkey, Afghanistan, Algeria, Indonesia, Thailand and New Zealand.

Geographical location and the policies and practices of one's 'neighbours' have a direct impact on the firearms problem of some states. Research indicates that "borders" tend to be porous, and thus facilitate firearms smuggling. The foreign countries with which Australia shares its border would pose the greatest threat to national or regional security. At their closest point, Australia and Papua New Guinea (PNG) lie just 3. 5 km apart. At the northern-most tip of Australia, it takes exactly 15 minutes in a dinghy to cross the Torres Strait and to move from one country to the other.

The Torres Strait has been described as "one of the most exposed parts of Australia", but one which is "of growing importance from the law enforcement perspective, not only in relation to cross border crime, but also the regulation of our immigration, quarantine, fisheries and other high priority national interests". In a recent report presented at the Fifth Meeting of the Council for Security Cooperation in the Asia-Pacific region (CSCAP), it was reported that the illegal smuggling of firearms into PNG has become obvious along the common PNG borders with Australia, Indonesia, Solomon Islands, and the Federated States of Micronesia. The two main routes for the trafficking of firearms into PNG are the Torres Strait border with Australia, and the North Solomons border with the Solomon Islands.

Police records indicate that the major sources of firearms are from Australia and Asian countries, and this includes US made weapons. There is also some evidence to suggest that a small, but continuing level of trafficking of PNG cannabis to Australia and firearms and other commodities into PNG across the Torres Strait. It has been reported that there are four distinct markets for firearms in PNG:

— The Bougainville rebellion;

— OPM (Free Papua Movement) on the PNG-Indonesian border;

— Highland tribal fighting

— Rascal gangs in Port Moresby and other urban centres.

However, as a result of recent Australian Commonwealth Government initiatives, additional marine patrol resources and hours have been allocated to aerial surveillance. Also, specific consideration has also been given to proactive intelligence collection, coordination and dissemination; improved law enforcement armed response capabilities, and closer coordination and mutual support between government agencies represented in the Torres Strait. It has been suggested that the Asian economic crisis may have forced some business groups, political groups, and organised crime groups in countries such as Thailand, to turn to illicit trafficking in firearms for profit.

The problem is further exacerbated because Thailand shares its border with many countries, and some that are still involved in a civil war. As a result illicit firearms are easily trafficked into Thailand, rarely being detected by police. There have also been a number of reports in the print media stating that a number of Thai syndicates with 'corrupt military links' are using new sea routes out of Cambodia. "Intelligence sources say operations dominated by ethnic Chinese in Thailand are increasingly using contacts in southern China and Vietnam, as well as Cambodia, to buy and market weapons". The report also stated that the troubled Indonesian province of Aceh, at the northern end of Sumatra, is one of the developing markets for Thai smugglers and their Cambodian counterparts.

Furthermore, Thai and foreign intelligence personnel point to the use of the port of Rayong, in the Gulf of Thailand, as a centre of smuggling various types of contraband, including firearms, drugs, and fuel oil." According to one Western intelligence officer, Rayong has become the key to weapons transhipment mainly because its proximity to ports in southern Cambodia. Criminal gangs in southern China are one source of new weapons, and smugglers in southern Vietnam have also joined the arms trade".

Illicit trafficking in firearms affects Australia's national and regional security in a number of ways. Firstly, the uncontrolled proliferation and misuse of firearms contributes to the breakdown of civil society in many regions, including in the Asia Pacific. Australia, through its aid program, funds many projects, which address the humanitarian needs of conflict-affected communities. These needs include the demobilisation and reintegration of ex-combatants into productive civilian life, assistance with post-conflict reconstruction, reform and capacity-building of police, judicial and penal systems in conflictaffected areas and assistance to promote respect for international humanitarian law regarding the use of firearms. These projects have been located in Cambodia, the Philippines, Bougainville, Papua New Guinea, and more recently, in East Timor.

The illicit trafficking in firearms has the potential to impact on Australia's aid program, to destabilise regional countries and prompt a national response (eg. the situations in East Timor and Bougainville), to destabilise regional economies with a flow-on effect on Australia's economy, and possibly to impact on people and refugee flows in the region. Whether firearms are trafficked interstate or between countries in close proximity to each other, they still have the potential to impact on that country's stability, and it is widely acknowledged that instability can provide new opportunities for crimes such as drug trafficking, money-laundering, immigration racketeering, extortion and corruption. According to police and other sources, the existing black market in Australia is not an organised underworld.

It is mostly divided into criminal gangs, whose main focus are crimes other than dealing in firearms, or small networks of individuals who buy or sell by word of mouth. Nonetheless, firearms traffickers play a significant role in supplying firearms to persons with a criminal intent. Research suggests that the presence, or lack of, state law determines whether a location serves as a source area or a market area in the illegal world of trafficking. A source area usually serves as a place where individuals obtain firearms, especially handguns, more easily due to less stringent state laws. By comparison, in a market area, firearms often are not readily accessible. As a result, illegally trafficked firearms remain a commodity; sought by those engaged in criminal activities. "A symbiotic relationship between a market and source ares exists based on the principles of supply and demand".

For firearms traffickers, one of the main methods of illegal acquisition of firearms is through thefts from firearms dealers, military facilities and firearms owners. Since the implementation of the Nationwide Agreement on Firearms by each Australian state and territory, one would assume that this has impacted on the availability and access to firearms for both legal and illegal purposes in a number of ways. Firstly, the tightened storage requirements for firearms kept in residential homes, has resulted in restricted access to firearms generally and at the same time making it more difficult for home invaders or burglars to obtain easy access to these firearms. Secondly, the number of firearms dealers has also declined since the introduction of the new firearms legislation.

Reducing the number of firearms dealers in Australia, also results in a reduction in the number of potential dealers that could be targeted by professional thieves in their attempt to obtain firearms for resale on the black market. Another method of illegal acquisition of firearms for traffickers in firearms is through the reactivation of de-activated firearms. De-activation refers to the process involving the removal of parts or portions of parts from a firearm, and the addition of pins and welds so that the firearm can no longer chamber or fire ammunition. After the firearm has been de-activated, it is no longer operational. A report published in the United Kingdom indicates that "disturbing numbers of reactivated automatic weapons were recovered from police drug-related operations and shooting incidents".

The bulk of the weapons had originated from legal importations of surplus military automatic arms by dealers possessing the necessary documentation and authority. The weapons, often of East European origin, were deactivated and inspected by two officials, and then passed on for sale to the general public. When recovered by law enforcement, the firearms had been reactivated and their automatic fire capacity had been restored. This inquiry - codenamed Operation Shadow - revealed that a gang was involved in selling deactivated guns to criminals who had found that handguns were more difficult to obtain because of the legislation which led to their surrender following the Dunblane massacre. The National Crime Squad in the UK, believes that "there is a need for a review of the law which allows collectors to own decommissioned (deactivated) weapons; comments echoed by the judge who jailed four of the gang members".

Law Enforcement

In response to the need for a specialised law enforcement unit to investigate those involved in the illicit trafficking of firearms, the New South Police Service established the Firearms Trafficking Program (FTP), known officially as "Organised Crime (Firearms Trafficking), Crime Agencies". According to their charter, the FTP will focus on the tracing of recovered firearms and the identification, investigation and prosecution of those involved in the illicit trafficking in firearms. Recent media reports indicate that the FTP has seized more than 300 illegal firearms and uncovered a highly organised criminal syndicate with interstate connections distributing weapons in country NSW. According to the report "the syndicate is involved in the illicit trafficking of high powered handguns and gun parts".

Police suspended the licences of the two dealers involved who were allegedly supplying the black market trade of mainly large calibre pistols and parts. However, it is important to note that these are isolated examples that have come to light, in comparison to the overwhelming majority of law abiding firearms dealers in Australia. This point is further highlighted by the following example. Using data from the Bureau of Alcohol, Tobacco, and Firearms (ATF), a US study found that a small number of firearms dealers were the source of thousands of crime guns, that is, firearms used to commit crimes.

The study found that 140 or about one-tenth of one per cent of all federally licensed gun dealers accounted for nearly 20 per cent of all ATF crime traces. Seven out of eight crime firearms bought from this tiny slice of gun dealers changed hands before they were used in a crime. This proves that criminals get their guns almost exclusively through the unregulated secondary market where guns bought by someone with a clean record are quickly trafficked to criminals who cannot pass necessary background checks. ... one in three guns traced back to these same high crime gun dealers were recovered in a crime within one year of the gun being sold and half were traced to crimes within two years of the original sale - strong evidence that many of the guns that end up in the hands of criminals are trafficked, in the view of the federal law enforcement.

MISUSE OF FIREARMS

Firearms do not, in themselves, "cause" crime, easy access increases the lethality of violent encounters, the number of victims and the ability of children to become killers. Freedom from fear is a fundamental human right and violence is one of the major threats to the enjoyment of universal human rights and human security worldwide. The linkages between licit and illicit, national and international supplies of firearms are well documented. In order to reduce illicit flows of firearms and their misuse, it is imperative to track licit movements. The principles which apply in the context of domestic regulation also apply at the international level. Only by tracking licit flows can one identify and control what is illicit. A diverse range of international Non-Governmental Organisations support the proposed draft protocol as an essential part of an integrated approach to reducing the illicit trafficking and misuse of firearms.

UN's study estimated that roughly 200,000 people are killed with firearms each year in murder, suicide and accidents. This is roughly comparable to the rate with which people are killed with small arms in conflict and represents a global threat to health and security. Firearms also figure prominently in crime and create a huge economic burden. In Canada, the economic costs of firearms death and injury (including murder, suicide and unintentional injuries) have been estimated at 6 billion dollars per year. In the US the number of deaths and attendant costs are much higher. The economic costs of violence, including costs of policing as well as the value of life lost, have been estimated to consume 14% of GDP in Latin America.

In Brazil, 10% of GDP is consumed by violence but in Colombia the figure rises to 25%. In South Africa, violence has been named a serious threat to human rights.

Problems with firearms vary by region and country in terms of the types of firearms which are misused, the supply and the pattern of misuse. Even within countries there are significant differences according to region, gender, age and other factors which, in turn, affect the shape of the appropriate solutions. Measures aimed at reducing illicit trafficking in firearms are not a panacea.

Interventions which address the root causes of violence, conflict and injury include social development and value building. Once crime, injury or conflict occurs, there is recognition of the need to intervene with policing, enforcement, and "treatment". Regulations on firearms are intended to reduce the opportunity for violence or conflict and to reduce the severity of violent encounters by controlling the supply of firearms. While it is possible to kill with other means, firearms are particularly efficient and are more likely to cause death, severe injuries and multiple victims. In addition, firearms enable children who might otherwise lack the strength to kill more readily.

Future Directions

A number of countries are involved in negotiations with Vienna for a protocol on Illicit manufacturing of and trafficking in firearms, as part of the work on the Ad Hoc Committee on the Elaboration of a Convention against Transnational Organised Crime. Australia is involved in these negotiations, which are examining a wide range of international regimes to assist in the detection, prevention and investigation of illicit firearms trafficking activity. The regimes include internationally agreed measures for permanently marking firearms, licensing and recording all import/export movements, and seizure of illicit firearms. In addition, the sub-committee of the South-Pacific Forum (the South Pacific Chiefs of Police Conference) is developing a common regional approach to weapon control, with specific focus on the illicit manufacture of, and trafficking in firearms, ammunition, explosives and other related materials.

Last, but not least, one must not forget the important collaborative work undertaken by the Council for Security Cooperation in the Asia-Pacific (CSCAP), a 2Track (unofficial) 'think tank' supporting the ASEAN Regional Forum. Participants in the CSCAP Working Group are given the opportunity to discuss various issues relating to the illicit trafficking in firearms and transnational crime. Such meetings encourage regional cooperation, mainly through the dissemination of ideas and resulting discussions, accepting of the need to build on existing arrangements in the region wherever possible, rather than construct new processes and structures.

As is the case in the US with firearms traces, acquiring such knowledge would allow law enforcement in Australia to pinpoint whether particular firearms dealers were responsible for supplying firearms to criminals. It would also allow the linkage of crimes committed with specific firearms. In the United States, firearms traces are undertaken using the Integrated Ballistics Identification System (IBIS). IBIS is a computerised image-analysis system that acquires, stores, and analyses images of a large number of fired bullets, bullet fragments and spent cartridges. What is quite impressive about this computer system is its efficiency. An examiner can easily enter and correlate eight or more projectiles and casings per day.

In contrast, the same task could take up to a week to do utilising the comparison microscope. IBIS also allows firearms examiners to link crimes that were previously unlinkable, and furthers investigations by alerting examiners that the same firearm was used in two (or more) crimes. IBIS has produced numerable positive outcomes in the US demonstrating its merits, however, Australia jurisdictions would need to evaluate the feasibility of purchasing such systems to assist in the tracing of firearms to their origins.

It is also important to mention the establishment (although not yet operational) of a national firearms licensing and registration network. Such a network, when operational would allow law enforcement to determine whether a firearm used in the commission of a crime was registered in any state or territory in Australia, whether it was or was not reported stolen, and if registered, whether the person found to be in possession of the firearm is the same person that the firearm was registered to. This is currently in pilot phase with access to a trial number of users. The Australian Government is sensitive to issues relating the illegal traffic in firearms.

In order to regulate firearms at the international level, it is necessary to regulate them at both a regional and national level. The Australian Government has been instrumental in introducing initiatives such as the implementation of uniform firearms legislation, and more recently, tougher penalties for trading in prohibited imports/exports. However, there will always be individuals who will attempt to circumvent legislation for illicit purposes.

Resolution adopted by the General Assembly

[without reference to a Main Committee(A/55/383/Add.2)]

55/255. Protocol against the Illicit Manufacturing of and Trafficking in Firearms, Their Parts and Components and Ammunition, supplementing the United Nations Convention against Transnational Organised Crime

The General Assembly,

Recalling its resolution 53/111 of 9 December 1998, in which it decided to establish an open-ended intergovernmental ad hoc committee for the purpose of elaborating a comprehensive international convention against transnational organised crime and of discussing the elaboration, as appropriate, of international instruments addressing trafficking in women and children, combating the illicit manufacturing of and trafficking in firearms, their parts and components and ammunition, and illegal trafficking in and transporting of migrants, including by sea,

Recalling also its resolution 54/126 of 17 December 1999, in which it requested the Ad Hoc Committee on the Elaboration of a Convention against Transnational Organised Crime to continue its work, in accordance with resolutions 53/111 and 53/114 of 9 December 1998, and to intensify that work in order to complete it in 2000,

Recalling further its resolution 55/25 of 15 November 2000, by which it adopted the United Nations Convention against Transnational Organised Crime, the Protocol to Prevent, Suppress and Punish Trafficking in Persons, Especially Women and Children, supplementing the United Nations Convention against Transnational Organised Crime, and the Protocol against the Smuggling of Migrants by Land, Sea and Air, supplementing the United Nations Convention against Transnational Organised Crime,

Reaffirming the inherent right to individual or collective self-defence recognized in Article 51 of the Charter of the United Nations, which implies that States also have the right to acquire arms with which to defend themselves, as well as the right of self-determination of all peoples, in particular peoples under colonial or other forms of alien domination or foreign occupation, and the importance of the effective realization of that right,

1. *Takes note* of the report of the Ad Hoc Committee on the Elaboration of a Convention against Transnational

Organised Crime on its twelfth session, and commends the Ad Hoc Committee for its work;

2. *Adopts* the Protocol against the Illicit Manufacturing of and Trafficking in Firearms, Their Parts and Components and Ammunition, supplementing the United Nations Convention against Transnational Organised Crime, annexed to the present resolution, and opens it for signature at United Nations Headquarters in New York;

3. *Urges* all States and regional economic organisations to sign and ratify the United Nations Convention against Transnational Organised Crime and the protocols thereto as soon as possible in order to ensure the speedy entry into force of the Convention and the protocols thereto.

101st plenary meeting

31 May 2001

Annex

Protocol against the Illicit Manufacturing of and Trafficking in Firearms, Their Parts and Components and Ammunition, supplementing the United Nations Convention against Transnational Organised Crime

Preamble

The States Parties to this Protocol,

Aware of the urgent need to prevent, combat and eradicate the illicit manufacturing of and trafficking in firearms, their parts and components and ammunition, owing to the harmful effects of those activities on the security of each State, region and the world as a whole, endangering the well-being of peoples, their social and economic development and their right to live in peace,

Convinced, therefore, of the necessity for all States to take all appropriate measures to this end, including international cooperation and other measures at the regional and global levels,

Recalling General Assembly resolution 53/111 of 9 December 1998, in which the Assembly decided to establish an open-ended intergovernmental ad hoc committee for the purpose of elaborating a comprehensive international convention against transnational organised crime and of discussing the elaboration of, inter alia, an international instrument combating the illicit manufacturing of and trafficking in firearms, their parts and components and ammunition,

Bearing in mind the principle of equal rights and self-determination of peoples, as enshrined in the Charter of the United Nations and the Declaration on Principles of International Law concerning Friendly Relations and Cooperation among States in accordance with the Charter of the United Nations,

Convinced that supplementing the United Nations Convention against Transnational Organised Crime with an international instrument against the illicit manufacturing of and trafficking in firearms, their parts and components and ammunition will be useful in preventing and combating those crimes, Have agreed as follows:

I. General provisions

Article 1

Relation with the United Nations Convention against Transnational Organised Crime

1. This Protocol supplements the United Nations Convention against Transnational Organised Crime. It shall be interpreted together with the Convention.

2. The provisions of the Convention shall apply, mutatis mutandis, to this Protocol unless otherwise provided herein.

3. The offences established in accordance with article 5 of this Protocol shall be regarded as offences established in accordance with the Convention.

Article 2

Statement of purpose

The purpose of this Protocol is to promote, facilitate and strengthen cooperation among States Parties in order to prevent, combat and eradicate the illicit manufacturing of and trafficking in firearms, their parts and components and ammunition.

Article 3

Use of terms

For the purposes of this Protocol:

(a) "Firearm" shall mean any portable barrelled weapon that expels, is designed to expel or may be readily converted to expel a shot, bullet or projectile by the action of an explosive, excluding antique firearms or their replicas. Antique firearms and their replicas shall be defined in accordance with domestic law. In no case, however, shall antique firearms include firearms manufactured after 1899;

(b) "Parts and components" shall mean any element or replacement element specifically designed for a firearm and essential to its operation, including a barrel, frame or receiver, slide or cylinder, bolt or breech block, and any device designed or adapted to diminish the sound caused by firing a firearm;

(c) "Ammunition" shall mean the complete round or its components, including cartridge cases, primers, propellant powder, bullets or projectiles, that are used in a firearm, provided that those components are themselves subject to authorization in the respective State Party;

(d) "Illicit manufacturing" shall mean the manufacturing or assembly of firearms, their parts and components or ammunition:

(i) From parts and components illicitly trafficked;

(ii) Without a licence or authorization from a competent authority of the State Party where the manufacture or assembly takes place; or

(iii) Without marking the firearms at the time of manufacture, in accordance with article 8 of this Protocol;

Licensing or authorization of the manufacture of parts and components shall be in accordance with domestic law;

(e) "Illicit trafficking" shall mean the import, export, acquisition, sale, delivery, movement or transfer of firearms, their parts and components and ammunition from or across the territory of one State Party to that of another State Party if any one of the States Parties concerned does not authorize it in accordance with the terms of this Protocol or if the firearms are not marked in accordance with article 8 of this Protocol;

(f) "Tracing" shall mean the systematic tracking of firearms and, where possible, their parts and components and ammunition from manufacturer to purchaser for the purpose of assisting the competent authorities of States Parties in detecting, investigating and analysing illicit manufacturing and illicit trafficking.

Article 4

Scope of application

1. This Protocol shall apply, except as otherwise stated

herein, to the prevention of illicit manufacturing of and trafficking in firearms, their parts and components and ammunition and to the investigation and prosecution of offences established in accordance with article 5 of this Protocol where those offences are transnational in nature and involve an organised criminal group.

2. This Protocol shall not apply to state-to-state transactions or to state transfers in cases where the application of the Protocol would prejudice the right of a State Party to take action in the interest of national security consistent with the Charter of the United Nations.

Article 5

Criminalization

1. Each State Party shall adopt such legislative and other measures as may be necessary to establish as criminal offences the following conduct, when committed intentionally:

   (a) Illicit manufacturing of firearms, their parts and components and ammunition;

   (b) Illicit trafficking in firearms, their parts and components and ammunition;

   (c) Falsifying or illicitly obliterating, removing or altering the marking(s) on firearms required by article 8 of this Protocol.

2. Each State Party shall also adopt such legislative and other measures as may be necessary to establish as criminal offences the following conduct:

   (a) Subject to the basic concepts of its legal system, attempting to commit or participating as an accomplice in an offence established in accordance with paragraph 1 of this article; and

(b) Organising, directing, aiding, abetting, facilitating or counselling the commission of an offence established in accordance with paragraph 1 of this article.

Article 6

Confiscation, seizure and disposal

1. Without prejudice to article 12 of the Convention, States Parties shall adopt, to the greatest extent possible within their domestic legal systems, such measures as may be necessary to enable confiscation of firearms, their parts and components and ammunition that have been illicitly manufactured or trafficked.
2. States Parties shall adopt, within their domestic legal systems, such measures as may be necessary to prevent illicitly manufactured and trafficked firearms, parts and components and ammunition from falling into the hands of unauthorized persons by seizing and destroying such firearms, their parts and components and ammunition unless other disposal has been officially authorized, provided that the firearms have been marked and the methods of disposal of those firearms and ammunition have been recorded.

II. Prevention

Article 7

Record-keeping

Each State Party shall ensure the maintenance, for not less than ten years, of information in relation to firearms and, where appropriate and feasible, their parts and components and ammunition that is necessary to trace and identify those firearms and, where appropriate and feasible, their parts and components and ammunition which are illicitly manufactured or trafficked and to prevent and detect such activities. Such information shall include:

(a) The appropriate markings required by article 8 of this Protocol;

(b) In cases involving international transactions in firearms, their parts and components and ammunition, the issuance and expiration dates of the appropriate licences or authorizations, the country of export, the country of import, the transit countries, where appropriate, and the final recipient and the description and quantity of the articles.

Article 8

Marking of firearms

1. For the purpose of identifying and tracing each firearm, States Parties shall:

(a) At the time of manufacture of each firearm, either require unique marking providing the name of the manufacturer, the country or place of manufacture and the serial number, or maintain any alternative unique user-friendly marking with simple geometric symbols in combination with a numeric and/or alphanumeric code, permitting ready identification by all States of the country of manufacture;

(b) Require appropriate simple marking on each imported firearm, permitting identification of the country of import and, where possible, the year of import and marking, if the firearm does not bear such a marking. The requirements of this subparagraph need not be applied to temporary imports of firearms for verifiable lawful purposes;

(c) Ensure, at the time of transfer of a firearm from government stocks to permanent civilian use, the appropriate unique marking permitting identification by all States Parties of the transferring country.

2. States Parties shall encourage the firearms manufacturing industry to develop measures against the removal or alteration of markings.

Article 9

Deactivation of firearms

A State Party that does not recognize a deactivated firearm as a firearm in accordance with its domestic law shall take the necessary measures, including the establishment of specific offences if appropriate, to prevent the illicit reactivation of deactivated firearms, consistent with the following general principles of deactivation:

(a) All essential parts of a deactivated firearm are to be rendered permanently inoperable and incapable of removal, replacement or modification in a manner that would permit the firearm to be reactivated in any way;

(b) Arrangements are to be made for deactivation measures to be verified, where appropriate, by a competent authority to ensure that the modifications made to a firearm render it permanently inoperable;

(c) Verification by a competent authority is to include a certificate or record attesting to the deactivation of the firearm or a clearly visible mark to that effect stamped on the firearm.

Article 10

General requirements for export, import and transit licensing or authorization systems

1. Each State Party shall establish or maintain an effective system of export and import licensing or authorization, as well as of measures on international transit, for the

transfer of firearms, their parts and components and ammunition.

2. Before issuing export licences or authorizations for shipments of firearms, their parts and components and ammunition, each State Party shall verify:

   (a) That the importing States have issued import licences or authorizations; and

   (b) That, without prejudice to bilateral or multilateral agreements or arrangements favouring landlocked States, the transit States have, at a minimum, given notice in writing, prior to shipment, that they have no objection to the transit.

3. The export and import licence or authorization and accompanying documentation together shall contain information that, at a minimum, shall include the place and the date of issuance, the date of expiration, the country of export, the country of import, the final recipient, a description and the quantity of the firearms, their parts and components and ammunition and, whenever there is transit, the countries of transit. The information contained in the import licence must be provided in advance to the transit States.

4. The importing State Party shall, upon request, inform the exporting State Party of the receipt of the dispatched shipment of firearms, their parts and components or ammunition.

5. Each State Party shall, within available means, take such measures as may be necessary to ensure that licensing or authorization procedures are secure and that the authenticity of licensing or authorization documents can be verified or validated.

6. States Parties may adopt simplified procedures for the temporary import and export and the transit of firearms, their parts and components and ammunition

for verifiable lawful purposes such as hunting, sport shooting, evaluation, exhibitions or repairs.

Article 11

Security and preventive measures

In an effort to detect, prevent and eliminate the theft, loss or diversion of, as well as the illicit manufacturing of and trafficking in, firearms, their parts and components and ammunition, each State Party shall take appropriate measures:

(a) To require the security of firearms, their parts and components and ammunition at the time of manufacture, import, export and transit through its territory; and

(b) To increase the effectiveness of import, export and transit controls, including, where appropriate, border controls, and of police and customs transborder cooperation.

Article 12

Information

1. Without prejudice to articles 27 and 28 of the Convention, States Parties shall exchange among themselves, consistent with their respective domestic legal and administrative systems, relevant case-specific information on matters such as authorized producers, dealers, importers, exporters and, whenever possible, carriers of firearms, their parts and components and ammunition.

2. Without prejudice to articles 27 and 28 of the Convention, States Parties shall exchange among themselves, consistent with their respective domestic legal and administrative systems, relevant information on matters such as:

(a) Organised criminal groups known to take part or suspected of taking part in the illicit manufacturing of or trafficking in firearms, their parts and components and ammunition;

(b) The means of concealment used in the illicit manufacturing of or trafficking in firearms, their parts and components and ammunition and ways of detecting them;

(c) Methods and means, points of dispatch and destination and routes customarily used by organised criminal groups engaged in illicit trafficking in firearms, their parts and components and ammunition; and

(d) Legislative experiences and practices and measures to prevent, combat and eradicate the illicit manufacturing of and trafficking in firearms, their parts and components and ammunition.

3. States Parties shall provide to or share with each other, as appropriate, relevant scientific and technological information useful to law enforcement authorities in order to enhance each other's abilities to prevent, detect and investigate the illicit manufacturing of and trafficking in firearms, their parts and components and ammunition and to prosecute the persons involved in those illicit activities.

4. States Parties shall cooperate in the tracing of firearms, their parts and components and ammunition that may have been illicitly manufactured or trafficked. Such cooperation shall include the provision of prompt responses to requests for assistance in tracing such firearms, their parts and components and ammunition, within available means.

5. Subject to the basic concepts of its legal system or any international agreements, each State Party shall

guarantee the confidentiality of and comply with any restrictions on the use of information that it receives from another State Party pursuant to this article, including proprietary information pertaining to commercial transactions, if requested to do so by the State Party providing the information. If such confidentiality cannot be maintained, the State Party that provided the information shall be notified prior to its disclosure.

Article 13

Cooperation

1. States Parties shall cooperate at the bilateral, regional and international levels to prevent, combat and eradicate the illicit manufacturing of and trafficking in firearms, their parts and components and ammunition.

2. Without prejudice to article 18, paragraph 13, of the Convention, each State Party shall identify a national body or a single point of contact to act as liaison between it and other States Parties on matters relating to this Protocol.

3. States Parties shall seek the support and cooperation of manufacturers, dealers, importers, exporters, brokers and commercial carriers of firearms, their parts and components and ammunition to prevent and detect the illicit activities referred to in paragraph 1 of this article.

Article 14

Training and technical assistance

States Parties shall cooperate with each other and with relevant international organisations, as appropriate, so that States Parties may receive, upon request, the training and technical assistance necessary to enhance their ability to prevent, combat and eradicate the illicit manufacturing of and trafficking in firearms, their parts and components and ammunition, including technical, financial and material assistance in those matters identified in articles 29 and 30 of the Convention.

Article 15

Brokers and brokering

1. With a view to preventing and combating illicit manufacturing of and trafficking in firearms, their parts and components and ammunition, States Parties that have not yet done so shall consider establishing a system for regulating the activities of those who engage in brokering. Such a system could include one or more measures such as:

   (a) Requiring registration of brokers operating within their territory;

   (b) Requiring licensing or authorization of brokering; or

   (c) Requiring disclosure on import and export licences or authorizations, or accompanying documents, of the names and locations of brokers involved in the transaction.

2. States Parties that have established a system of authorization regarding brokering as set forth in paragraph 1 of this article are encouraged to include information on brokers and brokering in their exchanges of information under article 12 of this Protocol and to retain records regarding brokers and brokering in accordance with article 7 of this Protocol.

III. Final provisions

Article 16

Settlement of disputes

1. States Parties shall endeavour to settle disputes

concerning the interpretation or application of this Protocol through negotiation.

2. Any dispute between two or more States Parties concerning the interpretation or application of this Protocol that cannot be settled through negotiation within a reasonable time shall, at the request of one of those States Parties, be submitted to arbitration. If, six months after the date of the request for arbitration, those States Parties are unable to agree on the organisation of the arbitration, any one of those States Parties may refer the dispute to the International Court of Justice by request in accordance with the Statute of the Court.

3. Each State Party may, at the time of signature, ratification, acceptance or approval of or accession to this Protocol, declare that it does not consider itself bound by paragraph 2 of this article. The other States Parties shall not be bound by paragraph 2 of this article with respect to any State Party that has made such a reservation.

4. Any State Party that has made a reservation in accordance with paragraph 3 of this article may at any time withdraw that reservation by notification to the Secretary-General of the United Nations.

Article 17

Signature, ratification, acceptance, approval and accession

1. This Protocol shall be open to all States for signature at United Nations Headquarters in New York from the thirtieth day after its adoption by the General Assembly until 12 December 2002.

2. This Protocol shall also be open for signature by regional economic integration organisations provided that at least one member State of such organisation

has signed this Protocol in accordance with paragraph 1 of this article.

3. This Protocol is subject to ratification, acceptance or approval. Instruments of ratification, acceptance or approval shall be deposited with the Secretary-General of the United Nations. A regional economic integration organisation may deposit its instrument of ratification, acceptance or approval if at least one of its member States has done likewise. In that instrument of ratification, acceptance or approval, such organisation shall declare the extent of its competence with respect to the matters governed by this Protocol. Such organisation shall also inform the depositary of any relevant modification in the extent of its competence.

4. This Protocol is open for accession by any State or any regional economic integration organisation of which at least one member State is a Party to this Protocol. Instruments of accession shall be deposited with the Secretary-General of the United Nations. At the time of its accession, a regional economic integration organisation shall declare the extent of its competence with respect to matters governed by this Protocol. Such organisation shall also inform the depositary of any relevant modification in the extent of its competence.

Article 18

Entry into force

1. This Protocol shall enter into force on the ninetieth day after the date of deposit of the fortieth instrument of ratification, acceptance, approval or accession, except that it shall not enter into force before the entry into force of the Convention. For the purpose of this paragraph, any instrument deposited by a regional economic integration organisation shall not be counted

as additional to those deposited by member States of such organisation.

2. For each State or regional economic integration organisation ratifying, accepting, approving or acceding to this Protocol after the deposit of the fortieth instrument of such action, this Protocol shall enter into force on the thirtieth day after the date of deposit by such State or organisation of the relevant instrument or on the date this Protocol enters into force pursuant to paragraph 1 of this article, whichever is the later.

Article 19

Amendment

1. After the expiry of five years from the entry into force of this Protocol, a State Party to the Protocol may propose an amendment and file it with the Secretary-General of the United Nations, who shall thereupon communicate the proposed amendment to the States Parties and to the Conference of the Parties to the Convention for the purpose of considering and deciding on the proposal. The States Parties to this Protocol meeting at the Conference of the Parties shall make every effort to achieve consensus on each amendment. If all efforts at consensus have been exhausted and no agreement has been reached, the amendment shall, as a last resort, require for its adoption a two-thirds majority vote of the States Parties to this Protocol present and voting at the meeting of the Conference of the Parties.

2. Regional economic integration organisations, in matters within their competence, shall exercise their right to vote under this article with a number of votes equal to the number of their member States that are Parties to this Protocol. Such organisations shall not

exercise their right to vote if their member States exercise theirs and vice versa.

3. An amendment adopted in accordance with paragraph 1 of this article is subject to ratification, acceptance or approval by States Parties.

4. An amendment adopted in accordance with paragraph 1 of this article shall enter into force in respect of a State Party ninety days after the date of the deposit with the Secretary-General of the United Nations of an instrument of ratification, acceptance or approval of such amendment.

5. When an amendment enters into force, it shall be binding on those States Parties which have expressed their consent to be bound by it. Other States Parties shall still be bound by the provisions of this Protocol and any earlier amendments that they have ratified, accepted or approved.

Article 20

Denunciation

1. A State Party may denounce this Protocol by written notification to the Secretary-General of the United Nations. Such denunciation shall become effective one year after the date of receipt of the notification by the Secretary-General.

2. A regional economic integration organisation shall cease to be a Party to this Protocol when all of its member States have denounced it.

Article 21

Depositary and languages

1. The Secretary-General of the United Nations is designated depositary of this Protocol.

2. The original of this Protocol, of which the Arabic, Chinese, English, French, Russian and Spanish texts are equally authentic, shall be deposited with the Secretary-General of the United Nations.

IN WITNESS WHEREOF, the undersigned plenipotentiaries, being duly authorized thereto by their respective Governments, have signed this Protocol.

4

People Smuggling

People smuggling and trafficking in human beings are now distinct, internationallyagreed criminal offences and have been defined by the international community through the UN as part of the effort to combat them. Trafficking of human beings is defined as:

> "the recruitment, transportation, transfer, harbouring or receipt of persons, by means of the threat, or use of force or other forms of coercion, of abduction, of fraud, of deception, of the abuse of power or of a position of vulnerability or of the giving or receiving of payments or benefits to achieve the consent of a person having control over another person, for the purpose of exploitation."

The UN Protocol to Prevent, Suppress and Punish Trafficking in Persons, Especially Women and Children.

The smuggling of people is defined as:

> "The procurement, in order to obtain, directly or indirectly a financial or other material benefit, of the illegal entry of a person into a state Party of which the person is not a national or a permanent resident."

The terms "asylum seekers" and "illega l migrants" often appear in the same context as people smuggling and human trafficking and are increasingly used interchangeably. Therefore, an understanding of these terms is also important. An asylum seeker is a person who meets the UN criteria for consideration of refugee status, and has begun the process of being accepted as such by the host country in order to obtain the protections and rights to which refugees are entitled.

An immigrant is most simply defined as someone who moves to another country and becomes resident. There are various legal channels of migration, for example obtaining various visas or residency permits. However, the term is frequently used in the context of illegal immigration, that is, someone who enters a country other than that of which they are a citizen, and yet has not taken the proper legal channels to become a permanent or temporary resident and is therefore not able to obtain any of the benefits to which an immigrant may otherwise be entitled An illegal immigrant also by definition normally has no lawful excuse for remaining in that jurisdiction, and is liable for deportation. Possibly also they are liable to be charged with criminal offences that relate to their illegal entry and/or stay.

The term "illegal migrant" is used to cover all of those who are in a country illegally and, commonly is used with clear prejudice. Illegal migrants are often viewed less-thangenerously by resident populations, and may include people who are subject of the various migration-related phenomena of which we speak. Some may be victims of trafficking, some may be smuggled, some may have falsely arranged to enter the country, or some may have overstayed or breached the conditions of their visa. The two most confused terms are human trafficking and people smuggling. It is important as these terms to be more commonly used, that they are used with clarity so as not to confuse these two very different phenomena.Identity of the Victim.

In human trafficking there is an identifiable human victim; a person subjected to exploitation of a kind that goes beyond what other illegal migrants might experience.

For example, an illegal migrant may be paid lower wages than a resident worker, while a victim of human trafficking is likely to be paid no wages at all for their labour. A key point is that this exploitation is part of the process of trafficking and does not come from outside sources. Various aspects of what constitutes a victim of human trafficking are explored below. It is enough here to note that there is a clear identifiable individual in human trafficking cases who can be termed a victim within the terms of the internationally agreed definition. The essence is that in trafficking, there is a clear human victim - it is a crime against the person.

In people smuggling there is no victim in the traditional sense beyond the State which immigration laws have been broken. In people smuggling, generally, a smuggler is paid a sum or promised a sum of money by the person wanting to move from one country to another. This smuggler provides a service by facilitating the smuggling. The person being moved is a client of the smuggler. There are a range of situations where for example a smuggler takes advantage of those being moved and extorts them for more money, or fails to deliver the service in a safe manner, but at the end of the day it is an illegal but essentially commercial relationship between the smuggler and the intending immigrant. In people smuggling there is only a State victim - it is a crime against public order.

Consent in Trafficking

The question of consent in trafficking is a tricky one at times. Essentially though, not all trafficking is done without consent. However all trafficking is undertaken without valid consent. A trafficked person will often consent to the movement, after all this is what they need to do to get to the place of employment promised.

However, it is after this movement that consent is nullified if they end up being exploited. It is important that the intention was not to be exploited, but to move somewhere else for work. No-one can consent to being enslaved or exploited in slave-like conditions. If someone ends up in a trafficked exploitative situation, then their initial consent is nullified by the deception. In short, the intending migrant is not complicit.

Almost without exception, people smuggling occurs with complete consent. This consent is often conditional, that the intending migrant will consent to the facilitation of the smuggler within the scope of the activity. So for example in agreeing to be smuggled across a border, the intending migrant consents to acts that are consistent with getting them across the border. In short, the intending migrant is complicit.

Movements of People

Both human trafficking and people smuggling involve movements of people. However, a key distinction between the two distinct crime types is the purpose of the movement. As with any criminal act, intent is a key element. Especially for law enforcement purposes it is important to be able to distinguish between intentions of those parties to a crime. For human traffickers, the purpose of moving people is the intended exploitation at destination. The intent ab initio on the part of the trafficker is to exploit the person and gain profit or advantage from their exploitation. This is an exploitative purpose. For people smugglers, the purpose of moving people is in furtherance of a contract with a migrant, to steal them across a national border. The intent ab initio is not to control the migrant, nor to extort or exploit, but to move the person. This is a facilitative purpose.

Destinations

We may also distinguish between trafficking and smuggling by differentiating between the intended destinations. Human trafficking can be international, i.e. occur across national borders or it can be domestic, for example rural to urban, north to south etc. Further, as we have pointed out the reason for the trafficking is for exploitation. It does not suit this purpose for a trafficked person to be left to their own devices once they have been moved. The trafficker must control the victim to the point of exploitation, for example, the actual brothel, mine, or factory. The destination in trafficking cases is the actual site of exploitation.

People smuggling can only occur internationally. The sole purpose is the illegal entry of an intending migrant into a State in which that person has no lawful right of abode. It is further the case in people smuggling that often the task of the smuggler is simply the crossing of the border, for example, the landing on the coast of Australia. It is then up to the intending migrant to find their way to their eventual destination. The destination in smuggling cases is more simply just the would -be migrants' intended State of residence.

Recruitment and Procurement

In human trafficking a "recruiter" is generally the person who makes initial contact with the victim. This is the first-level trafficker. It is the job of this first-level trafficker to find people who fit a profile in demand, for example cute or injured children for begging, or pretty young girls for brothels. The first- level trafficker will often initiate contact with these people, with the intention of deceiving or coercing them to move for the purpose of exploitation. Victims of trafficking frequently consent to the initial movement, however this consent is later nullified by the victim's exploitation. The people smuggler often is an existing operator, and may in fact have little need to 'recruit'. They may 'advertise' their services, or tout for business, but this is far from the trafficker having to identify and lure victims. Quite often the smuggler will await those seeking to move to come to him, and they will gladly pay for his services.

The Chinese 'snakehead' is such a person - their business reputation is often built on successful movements and intending migrants being safely ensconced in their destination remitting funds to family and friends in China. The snakeheads become known locally and often have little need to deceive people to move, in fact it may undermine their business to deceive clients. A smuggler will often be sought to provide a border-crossing service, in a much more business-like arrangement.

Customer Relationship

The 'customer relationship' differs markedly from trafficking to smuggling. In human trafficking, the customer relationship exists between the recruiter sourcing the right type of individual for someone who wishes to exploit someone, for example a brothel owner or a plantation owner. In this 'transaction', the victim then takes on the role of a commodity, so mething to be brought and sold. The customer relationship exists between the traffickers and the eventual exploiters, and the victim is not a party to this relationship.

In people smuggling the customer relationship is very different. Here, it is the services of the smuggler that are being sought and bought. The smuggler's job is to secrete someone across a border, and the individual wishing to cross that border will pay for this. For all intents and purposes this intending migrant then becomes a customer of the smuggler. The customer relationship is between the smuggler and the intending migrant - person being moved is a party to this relationship.

At first glance the trafficker's victim and the smuggler's customer may present as one and the same; they both may seek to move from their place of origin to another destination in the hope of securing employment and consequently a better future for themselves and their families. This is often as deep an analysis is made of illegal migrants at point of detection - why so many trafficked victims end up being treated as illegal migrants and confused for smuggled people. Investigations must go into much more depth to distinguish between the two.

The customer of the people smuggler may be moving to escape persecution in some form and may be intending to claim asylum on reaching his/her destination. Or they may simply be an economic migrant, seeking employment or a better life elsewhere. As a rule, the smuggler is simply providing a paid service and cares little about the identity or characteristics of the person being smuggled. In smuggling, the identity of the customer is often not relevant to the purpose of the movement.

However, the victim of human trafficking possesses some key attributes which make him/her attractive to the trafficker according to the intended industry for which they are being recruited. For women and girls, this may range from simply being female, to having good looks or exotic features, to having quick fingers able to operate a sewing machine. For men, physical strength or simply age are often key factors. In both cases the victim is likely to have some vulnerability that will make him/her easy to entrap with visions of exciting city life and job opportunities. In trafficking, the identity of the victim is often directly relevant to the purpose of the movement.

Knowledge and Control

In human trafficking, the traffickers possess knowledge of the means and process of the movement. The trafficker also has quite absolute dominion over the victim. The individual, once being lured into going with the traffickers for example, have no decision- making power. The victim can neither negotiate the destination, the means, the process, the conditions or the timings. They also cannot negotiate what job they will do there. Importantly though a victim will often not know that they have no control until it is far too late. It is also the case that the trafficked victim is considered to be, and importantly related to as, being owned by the trafficker. It is characteristic of trafficking that a victim loses complete control over what eventuates. In people smuggling, the customer has both knowledge and control over the situation.

The destination will be a place largely decided by him/her and having reached a bargain with the smuggler the individual is then free to pull out at any time (although we note they are unlikely to receive a refund!). Dramatically unlike trafficking, the migrating individual generally exercises control over their situation upon arrival; where the individual goes and what opportunities he finds are often up to him.

Important to remember that it is not the intention of the genuine people smuggler to exercise dominion over the intending migrant. The only time the individual may place total control in the hands of the smuggler is during the actual process of border crossing. Additionally, control is also lost often when something goes dramatically wrong in the process, for example upon detection or upon disaster such as sinking of the boat. As a general rule, it is a characteristic of people smuggling that the smuggled person retains control over what eventuates.

Source of Profit

The source of profit in these acts is a significant point for differentiation. It should be remembered that both phenomena are crimes, and both involve the illegal making of money. It could be said in fact that both phenomena revolve around the making of money, and so it is noteworthy that the way of making money in each cases differs markedly. Human traffickers make profits at several points along the trafficking chain. The first level and subsequent traffickers may make money directly from the sale of the victims. This sale is either to a higher level trafficker, or to a site for exp loitation such as a brothel or factory.

With trafficking it is critical to note that the most profit is generated from the continuing exploitation of the victim. The profit realised through this continuing exploitation is the raison d'etre for the trafficking in the first instance, and reaps both the most significant and the longest lasting returns for the trafficker. For example fees paid by brothel customers are kept by brothel owners, and very rarely passed on to the victims. Further, medical treatment, such as abortions or surgeries, are costs often borne by the victim in the form of an increased debt. Factory owners do not pay human trafficking victims and again medical treatment is usually added onto the victims "debt" which might translate into more working hours, rather than actually being paid for by the owner.

The smuggler's profit is derived from the retail payments made by the customer for being transported across the borders. The amount of profit made is decided by the smuggler in negotia tion with the intending migrant. The smuggler, in setting a price, will take into account transportation costs, bribery costs, the cost of forged documents and of course their profit margin.

Role of Violence

These two very different crime types are again distinguished on this point; one is a violent crime, the other is a migration offence. For human traffickers violence is very much a part of the trafficking process as victims need to be subdued and forced into compliance. Thereafter, continuing vio lence becomes necessary to ensure continued compliance and to keep the victim controlled. This very serious violence, including deprivation of liberty, marks trafficking as one of the world's most serious crimes and human rights violations.

People smugglers have little if any need to use violence. They have already made their profit from being paid to facilitate the movement. Except perhaps where the intending migrant defaults on the debt or payment, there is no need for a smuggler to harm his 'cargo'. People smuggling is not classed a violent crime, and does not involve deprivation of liberty.

The Arrival

Trafficking and smuggling can also be distinguished by what occurs upon arrival in the destination country or area. Upon arrival at destination, the victim of a human trafficker will be sold or put to work in the industry she/he was brought to service. She will continue to be owned by someone in a controlling position and will be dominated by that person. At destination, the victim cannot control where they go or what they do - their behaviour and actions severely restricted by the traffickers. Further, trafficked victims will be deprived their liberty and often confined to the site of exploitation. Their travel documents, if they were needed, are almost always held by the traffickers. Upon arrival at destination, a trafficked victim is captive.

By significant contrast, the person who buys the services of the people smuggler is free upon arrival at the destination to do and go where he/she pleases. The smuggler may try to provide additional services for the immigrant, for example, a safe house, work etc, but after payment of the transportation costs the immigrant is generally under no obligation to the smuggler. The migrant may use further services of the smuggler, and would pay for those services, but may already have his own contacts helping him to secure housing and work. Some smuggled individuals may choose to claim asylum on arrival, although many just disappear into the population of the new host country. Upon arrival at destination, a smuggled migrant is generally free to choose their next course, constrained perhaps only by their illegal status.

Perceptions of the Illegal Immigrant

Once in the country without the correct documentation both the victim of human trafficking and the smuggled person become illegal immigrants. Despite this umbrella term, there are nevertheless significant differences in the way that they are perceived and treated. Smuggled illegal immigrants are unlikely to receive a sympathetic response from either the police or immigration officials, unless they claim asylum in which case there are specific procedures which need to be followed and according to the country, they may be housed in a detention center or housed in the community and allowed to work.

Smuggled immigrants are understood to be in breach of migration laws and can expect to be deported once their status has been determined. In the press and media, smuggled migrants may receive little or no sympathy. Smuggled migrants are rarely welcome in any country. As mentioned earlier, due to incomplete understanding of the nature of trafficking, most trafficking victims will at point of detection present as illegal migrants, and will mostly be assumed by authorities to be smuggled. Trafficked victims are from this point often treated exactly as a smuggled migrant - as an illegal entrant to be detained and deported once their status is confirmed.

The UN Trafficking Protocol deals with the criminal justice responses to trafficking. In addition, it sets out numerous recommendations for the treatment of victims. It is clear that on the international agenda, States are obligated to not treat trafficking victims as smuggled migrants. It is abundantly clear that States and enforcement authorities must take whatever means necessary to ensure that trafficked victims are not treated simply as illegal migrants, should not be detained and deported but treated as victims of crime. This is very often not the case due to the erroneous presumption of their guilt as illegal migrants. Few countries have implemented the internationally agreed recommendations and therefore the treatment that trafficking victims receive varies widely from state to state.

There is however evidence of a growing awareness that a victim of human trafficking should not be treated as if she were an illegal immigrant, but instead as an individual who has had a terrible experience. The translation of this perception into national policy varies. Countries including the US, UK, and Belgium have taken the lead in shoring up their mechanisms to more properly respond to trafficking victims. In the US, for example victims may be granted temporary right of abode, while in Belgium a victim is granted a "reflection period" to decide if she/her wishes to take action against the traffickers.

In 2001, the US Foreign Ministry estimated that profits from human smuggling amounted to USD 10 billion worldwide. According to a report by Interpol, it is estimated that between 300,000 and 450,000 people are trafficked to Western Europe each year. This figure could be as high as one million worldwide. The number of people smuggled into Switzerland is unknown. This is due, on the one hand, to the fact that the phenomenon is difficult to assess on account of its illegality.

On the other hand, various authorities are responsible for different areas of trafficking, which makes it difficult to gain a complete picture. The fact is, however, that each year thousands of people are caught trying to cross the border into Switzerland illegally and thousands are also convicted of assisting or abetting illegal entry into or residence in the country. It is to be assumed that there are also a large number of unreported cases. However, not all illegal migrants make use of the services offered by traffickers.

Illegal migration and human smuggling is a punishable offence in Switzerland according to the Residence and Settlement of Foreign Nationals Act (RSFN). According to Article 23, Paragraph 1 of the Act, it is an offence to forge or misuse identity documents, to enter or reside in Switzerland illegally or to facilitate a person's illegal entry or residence in the country even without personal gain. If convicted, the offence is punishable with imprisonment of up to six months and/or a maximum fine of CHF 10,000. Facilitating a person's illegal entry or residence for personal gain or if the perpetrator acts on behalf of an organisation that offers its smuggling services professionally, is also punishable according to Article 23, Paragraph 2 of the said Act. It is, in fact, this paragraph that deals with human smuggling. The offence is punishable with imprisonment of up to three years and a maximum fine of CHF 100,000.

Border Crossings and Convictions

As the statistics illustrate, illegal entry into Switzerland is subject to considerable fluctuation. The number of illegal migrants arrested at the border by the Swiss Border Guard Corps fluctuated between its highest levels of 8,500 and 15,800 in 1993 and 1998 respectively (a result of the war in Bosnia and Kosovo) and its lowest levels of around 5,000 in 1991 and 2001. In 2002, numbers rose sharply again to approx. 7,400. There was also a noticeable shift in activity from the southern to the western border of the country. In the last few years, not only have illegal migrants been arrested at the border, but also helpers (without intent on personal gain) and smugglers (with intent on personal gain) .

The statistics do not differentiate between these various categories. The statistics on convictions, on the other hand, include not only those persons arrested by the Border Guard Corps and handed over to the judicial authorities in the cantons, but also those arrested inside the country by the airport police or the cantonal police authorities. The statistics show that the number of convictions for illegal entry and illegal residence - between 7,000 and 9,000 annually - has been relatively stable over the last few years while the number of convictions for assisting illegal entry and residence has been more liable to fluctuation. What is apparent is the discrepancy between assistance without intent on personal gain and human smuggling .

Difficulties in Preventing Human Smuggling

Fighting and preventing human smuggling via legal means is difficult due to the relatively lenient sentences. The present sentence of three years' imprisonment and a fine qualifies human smuggling as a misdemeanour in Switzerland, which means that prosecution is the sole responsibility of the cantons, and that police and judiciary are not permitted to use certain investigation methods such as telephone tapping. Moreover, the penalty is light in European comparison. The EU has recently issued guidelines that suggest a maximum sentence for professional and organised human smuggling of eight years imprisonment.

Another difficulty is that illegal migration and human smuggling affect various areas such as border control, migration, asylum, police, judiciary and foreign relations. Jurisdiction is divided between several offices on a federal level and the cantons. One consequence of this is that, at present, there are no integrated statistics. Furthermore, turning away people promptly at the border and insufficient police resources mean that investigations are seldom conducted on the people behind human smuggling and the methods they use.

In Switzerland, the Federal Council has declared the fight against and prevention of human trafficking and smuggling as one of its objectives. Switzerland signed the additional protocols to the UN Convention on Transnational Organised Crime regarding human trafficking and smuggling in April 2002, thereby joining international effo rts to defeat these evils. In January 2003, the Swiss Coordination Unit against the Trafficking in Persons and Smuggling of Migrants (KSMM), which was commissioned by the Federal Department of Justice and Police, started work. The KSMM has a permanent office incorporated into the Federal Office of Police and has been operative since September 2003.

KSMM's task is to fight and prevent human trafficking and smuggling in Switzerland effectively with the aim of protecting the victims and prosecuting the perpetrators. The Coordination Unit creates the necessary structures by coordinating the work of the Confederation and the cantons in the field of prevention, law enforcement and victim protection. Its main work in the field of human trafficking includes the following areas:

— increasing the penalty for professional human smuggling to five years in the new legislation on foreign nationals. This would qualify the offence as a crime;

— improving the level of information on human smuggling in Switzerland;

— issuing an interdepartmental report entitled "Human Smuggling in Switzerland" with recommendations.

The KSMM's main responsibility is to coordinate between national and international agencies with the help of interdisciplinary expert groups. The operative work in human smuggling remains the responsibility of the respective federal and cantonal bodies who are also members of the Coordination Unit.

Changing Methods of People Smuggling

Criminal networks that smuggle human beings for financial gain increasingly control the flow of migrants across borders. Due to more restrictive immigration policies of the destination countries and improved technology to monitor border crossing points, willing illegal migrants rely increasingly on the help of organised people smugglers. People smuggling is not a homogenous criminal activity; the price of the trip, conditions of travel, and status upon arrival can vary significantly.

Trafficking is distinct from smuggling in so far as the traffic of human beings involves the exploitation of the migrant, often for purposes of forced labour and prostitution. People smuggling simply implies the procurement, for financial or material gain, of the illegal entry into a state of which that person is neither a citizen nor a permanent resident. 'People smuggling has become the preferred trade of a growing number of criminal networks worldwide which show an increased sophistication with regard to moving larger numbers of people at higher profits than ever.'

It is acknowledged that the smuggling of people is a continuously growing global phenomenon. It is not only a transnational crime, but also an enormous violation of human rights and a contemporary form of slavery. Currently, economic discomfort appears to be the main reason for illegal migration movement throughout the world. Nevertheless, many of the willing migrants undertake the hazardous travel to their destination country with criminal syndicates services specialised in people smuggling. These syndicates will arrange everything for the migrants, but at a high price. Very often the travelling conditions are inhumane, the migrants overcrowded in trucks or boats and fatal accidents occur quite frequently.

After their arrival in their destination country, the illegal status of the migrants puts them into the mercy of their smugglers, which often force them for years to work in the illegal labour market to pay off the debts incurred as a result of their transportation. If the migrants are not able to pay, often their relatives in their home countries are forced to pay the debts by the threat of the syndicates to torture or kill their family members abroad. People smuggling syndicates are still benefiting from weak legislation, huge profits and the relatively low risk of detection, prosecution and arrest compared to other activities of transnational organised crime. That creates the need for a structure, which enables police and other law enforcement agencies to co-operate on a global basis. Interpol fulfils that role and considerable efforts are being made to develop the services that it can offer.

Changing methods of the people smuggling networks as a response to legislative and law enforcement activities are necessary for their survival. Flexibility is thus one of the main characteristics of transportation and the choice of routes. This means that the routes used by people smugglers may sometimes be simple and direct, at other times circuitous. The time between departure and arrival may thus vary from some days to several months or even years. Smuggling is carried out either by land, air or sea. The following outlines some examples for frequently used for people smuggling. Migrants from the Asian region are mainly using the route via Kazakhstan, Kyrgyzstan, Uzbekistan, Tajikistan and Turkmenistan to Russia and from there via the Ukraine, Slovakia and the Czech Republic to western European countries or even further to the United States and Canada.

At the same time, the classical Balkan route from Asian countries via Iran and Turkey and from there via the Balkan states to western Europe is used for the smuggling of migrants as well as for the smuggling of all other kind of illegal of illegal goods like drugs, fire arms, etc. Especially during summer months, Spain has to face the arrival of thousands of illegal immigrants originating from the Sub-Saharan region on the African continent. These willing immigrants undertake the hazardous trip to travel from Morocco to southern Spain by using the narrow Strait of Gibraltar where only 21 km are separating Europe and Africa. Many people travelling in small, overcrowded boats, have already drowned in their desperate attempt try to reach Europe.

Australia is also facing a growing number of illegal immigrants mostly from the Middle East and southern Asia landing at its western coasts and especially on Christmas Island, which is located relatively close to the Indonesian archipelago. Most of the refugees originated from the Near East first enter Malaysia where they are taken to the south before making a short ferry crossing to the Indonesian island of Batam. From there it is not difficult to reach Jakarta and go on to the southern Indonesian islands of Bali, Flores, or Lombok where they embark for Australia. Smuggling migrants to the United States is mostly achieved by putting them on planes.

Ships with migrants on board are mainly bound for the west coast, but the use of this route has dropped considerably. Smuggling networks seem to focus more and more on Central and South America where they maintain the necessary links to Mexican people smugglers in order to move the illegal migrants via Mexico to North America.

SMUGGLED MIGRANTS

During the last years it has been established that people smugglers are making higher profits by smuggling increasing numbers of migrants at the same time. The arrival of the vessel 'East Sea', which ran aground on the coast of southern France in February 2001 caught great media attention. It had 894 illegal immigrants on board. This has now become a sad reality in the daily news. Vessels with some hundreds of migrants crammed on board are frequently reported. Hygiene is often impossible on board, as no toilet facilities exist. The vessels are mostly insufficiently equipped with drinking water and food. The treatment of the migrants by the crew and guards can be extremely violent and often sick people are thrown over board.

Africa is becoming more and more a transit area for Asian migrants, particularly for Chinese nationals. Much of this migration seems to be connected to South East Asian smuggling networks. A large number of Chinese nationals are travelling to the country with fraudulent documents or making questionable journeys to contact countries like Swaziland, Lesotho or Mozambique. From South and East Africa the willing immigrants often continue their journey to the United States by plane, but also to European countries.

Economic and Social Council

1995/10. Criminal justice action to combat the organised smuggling of illegal migrants across national boundaries

The Economic and Social Council,

Recalling that the General Assembly, in its resolution 48/102 of 20 December 1993, requested the Commission on Crime Prevention and Criminal Justice at its third session to consider giving special attention to the question of the smuggling of aliens, in order to encourage international cooperation to address that problem within the framework of its mandate,

Recalling also its resolution 1994/14 of 25 July 1994, adopted on the recommendation of the Commission on Crime Prevention and Criminal Justice at its third session, in which it, inter alia, condemned the practice of smuggling illegal migrants, recognized that such smuggling was a widespread criminal activity frequently involving highly organised international syndicates, acknowledged the substantial role played by organised transnational crime in such smuggling and called upon all States to take effective and expeditious measures, such as the enactment or amendment of domestic criminal law, providing appropriate penalties to combat all aspects of organised crime activities constituting such smuggling,

Alarmed by the significant increase in the activities of transnational criminal organisations that profit illicitly by smuggling illegal migrants and threatening the lives and human rights of migrants,

Concentrating its attention on crime prevention and criminal justice, in particular the activities of those who organise and facilitate the smuggling of illegal migrants,

Recognizing that organised international criminal groups are becoming increasingly active and successful in smuggling individuals across national boundaries,

Recognizing also that by trafficking in illegal migrants such criminal groups often make enormous profits that are frequently used to finance numerous other criminal activities, thus bringing great harm to the States concerned,

Concerned that such activities endanger the lives of the individual migrants involved and entail severe costs for the international community, including the costs of rescue, medical care, food, housing and transportation,

Acknowledging that socio-economic factors influence the problem of illegal migrant smuggling and also contribute to the complexity of current international migration,

Aware that smugglers, particularly in the State of destination of the illegal migrants being smuggled, often force migrants into forms of debt bondage or servitude, commonly involving criminal activities, in order to pay for their passage,

Convinced of the need for all States to provide humane treatment and to protect fully the human rights of migrants,

Recognizing that such illegal migrant smuggling has high social and economic costs, often contributing to official corruption, and burdens law enforcement agencies in all States where illegal migrants transit or are found,

Recalling the undertaking of States parties to the Supplementary Convention on the Abolition of Slavery, the Slave Trade, and Institutions and Practices Similar to Slavery, 1/ done at Geneva on 7 September 1956, to take all practicable and necessary legislative and other measures to bring about progressively and as soon as possible the complete abolition or abandonment of the practice of debt bondage,

Reaffirming respect for the sovereignty and territorial integrity of all States, including their right to control immigration flows,

Concerned that the smuggling of illegal migrants undermines public confidence in policies and procedures for lawful immigration and for ensuring the protection of genuine refugees,

Noting that the smuggling of illegal migrants can involve criminal activities in many States, including the State where the smuggling scheme was planned, the State of nationality of the migrants, the State where the means of transport was prepared, the flag State of any vessels or aircraft that transport the migrants, States through which the migrants transit to their destination or in order to be repatriated, and the State of destination,

Commending those States that have enacted effective domestic legislation permitting seizure and forfeiture of all property, both real and personal, that is knowingly used in organised criminal activities aimed at smuggling illegal migrants, as well as all property, both real and personal, that constitutes, or is derived from, the proceeds of the smuggling, illegal transport, or labour of illegal migrants,

Gravely concerned that a significant number of States have not yet enacted domestic criminal legislation to combat all aspects of the smuggling of illegal migrants,

1. Condemns once again the practice of smuggling illegal migrants in violation of international standards and national law, and without regard to the safety, well-being and human rights of the migrants;

2. Recognizes that the smuggling of illegal migrants continues to be a widespread international criminal activity frequently involving highly organised international syndicates that traffic in human cargo, without regard for the dangerous and inhumane conditions to which illegal migrants are subjected, and in flagrant violation of domestic laws and international standards;

3. Acknowledges the substantial and harmful role played by organised transnational crime in activities related to the smuggling of illegal migrants in many parts of the world;
4. Urges States to share information, to coordinate law enforcement activities between national authorities in cooperation with the competent international bodies and carriers engaged in international transport, and otherwise to cooperate, if their law permits, in order to trace and arrest those who organise the smuggling of illegal migrants and to prevent the illegal transport by smugglers of third-country nationals through their territory;
5. Calls upon Member States and relevant specialized agencies and international organisations to take into account socio-economic factors and to cooperate at the bilateral and multilateral levels in addressing all aspects of the problem of organised smuggling of illegal migrants, including by promoting technical assistance so as to assist countries, at their request, in developing and implementing policies to prevent and criminalize clandestine traffic in illegal migrants and to punish those who engage in organising such activity;
6. Reaffirms the need to observe fully international and national law in dealing with the smuggling of illegal migrants, including the provision of humane treatment and strict observance of all human rights of migrants;
7. Reiterates that international efforts to prevent the smuggling of illegal migrants should not inhibit legal migration or freedom of travel, or undercut the protection provided by international law to refugees;
8. Encourages States to take prompt and effective preventive measures, such as increasing vigilance at coastal ports, airports and land borders, as well as

enhancing the professional skills of relevant personnel, to frustrate the objectives and activities of those who organise the smuggling of illegal migrants, thus protecting would-be migrants from exploitation and loss of life;

9. Calls upon all States that have not yet done so to take effective and expeditious measures such as the enactment or amendment if necessary of domestic criminal law, with a range of enforcement measures, providing appropriate penalties to combat all aspects of organised criminal activities constituting the smuggling and transport of illegal migrants, such as the production or distribution of false travel documents, money-laundering, extortion and misuse of international commercial aviation and maritime transport in violation of international standards;

10. Welcomes the report of the Secretary-General 2/ and the note by the Secretariat 3/ on measures taken by Member States and relevant specialized agencies and intergovernmental organisations to combat the smuggling of illegal migrants, which were prepared pursuant to General Assembly resolution 48/102;

11. Requests the Secretary-General to remind Member States that have not yet done so of the importance of responding to the notes verbales sent to all Member States on 10 February and 9 June 1994 concerning the criminal legislation that they have enacted and other measures that they have taken to combat the smuggling of illegal migrants, and to submit to the Commission on Crime Prevention and Criminal Justice at its fifth session an updated report on measures to combat such smuggling, containing a compilation and an analysis of the responses of Member States;

12. Decides that the ever-growing problem of organised smuggling of illegal migrants across national borders

requires the continuing scrutiny of the international community in general and should be considered by the Commission on Crime Prevention and Criminal Justice at its fifth session in the context of the broader problem of organised transnational crime.

5

Illicit Trafficking of Women

Trafficking in women is a longstanding issue globally. Trafficking in humans may share common characteristics with alien smuggling and illegal immigration, but it has its own distinctive features and dynamics involving particularly grievous human rights abuses. As a first step, it is important to be clear on the definition of trafficking in women, as the characterization of the issue will determine the strategies to combat the problem and protect the victims.

The President's Interagency Council on Women, chaired by the Secretary of State, leads the coordination of US domestic and international policy on the trafficking in women issue. The President's Interagency Council on Women has formulated a definition on trafficking in women and children: Trafficking is all acts involved in the recruitment, abduction, transport, harboring, transfer, sale or receipt of persons; within national or across international borders; through force, coercion, fraud or deception; to place persons in situations of slavery or slavery-like conditions, forced labor or services, such as forced prostitution or sexual services, domestic servitude, bonded sweatshop labor or other debt bondage.

In essence, trafficking in women is the use of force and deception to transfer women into situations of extreme exploitation. Examples of this may include Latvian women threatened and forced to dance nude in Chicago; Thai women brought to the US for the sex industry, but then forced to be virtual sex slaves; ethnically Korean-Chinese women held as indentured servants in the Commonwealth of the Northern Mariana Islands; and hearing-impaired and mute Mexicans brought to the US, enslaved, beaten, and forced to peddle trinkets in New York City. Given the wide range of trafficking cases that occur in the US, debates on the definition often focus on whether or not the women were witting or unwitting about the type of work.

It makes no legal difference, however, whether or not the victim initially knew or agreed to perform the labor voluntarily. A person cannot consent to enslavement or forced labor of any kind. The Thirteenth Amendment outlawing slavery prohibits an individual from selling himself or herself into bondage, and Western legal tradition prohibits contracts consenting in advance to assaults and other criminal wrongs. If a person desires to stop performing the work, and then is forced to remain and perform the job against his or her will, then the work is involuntary regardless of the victim's purported consent. The use of force-be it physical or psychological-to hold someone against his or her will has also been debated when discussing the definition.

Some defense attorneys for the traffickers have sought to argue that if there was no physical confinement of the victims, there was no captivity. US law, nonetheless, recognizes that more subtle forms of restraint can be used to detain someone, and the victims' vulnerabilities are relevant. If defendants use force, threats of force, or threats of legal coercion to create a "climate of fear" to compel service, they are guilty of involuntary servitude. Additionally, the definition of force or coercion in the draft version of the International Protocol to Prevent, Suppress, and Punish Trafficking in Persons especially Women and Children encompasses both physical and psychological coercion.

Force or coercion includes obtaining or maintaining through act or threat the labor, services, or other activities of a person by physical, legal, psychological or mental coercion, or abuse of authority. Force or coercion also entails a person's reasonable belief that he has no viable alternative but to perform the work, service or activity, whether that is objectively correct or not. The definition also includes an extortionate extension of credit and debt bondage; threats of force, harm or violence to the victim or the victim's family; or unlawful restriction of movement and liberty, though this is not a necessary element.

In addition to force and coercion, another subject of frequent discussion is the degree of organised crime involvement in the trafficking industry in the US, and the definition of organised crime. Traditionally, organised crime is associated with selfperpetuating, hierarchical criminal organisations, such as the infamous Italian mafia families. None of the traffickers' names were found in the International Criminal Police Organisation's database indicating that these traffickers were not under investigation for trafficking or other illicit activities in other countries. This contrasts with Europe and Asia where there are more indications of large, hierarchical structures involved in trafficking women and children and numerous other illegal activities.

The size or structure of the criminal group, however, has no bearing on the violence, intimidation, and brutality that is commonly perpetrated on the trafficking victims, as many small trafficking rings are extremely vicious. Moreover, technology has made size irrelevant in terms of a crime group's ability to establish commercial or business-like structures. The traffickers have easily established businesses in the US and abroad to conceal their activities and illicit proceeds from law enforcement as well as to deceive the women. It is also important to recognize that only tentative conclusions regarding the level of organised crime involvement in the trafficking industry in the US can be reached at this point as the subject has received little attention from law enforcement.

US law enforcement officers readily admit they do not know to what degree large international organised crime syndicates are engaged in this industry. Asian and Russian organised crime groups are clearly present in the US and involved in alien smuggling and/or prostitution among other illicit activities. Some experts state that these large criminal syndicates are also involved in trafficking in women, and they will become even more immersed in trafficking to the US given the industry's extensive profits. In order to reach more definitive findings about the present and future role of organised crime in the trafficking industry, more resources need to be devoted towards bolstering research and data collection.

Trafficking in persons, especially women and children, this modern-day form of slavery, is prevalent across the globe and likely to increase in the United States. In this post-Cold War era, international borders and political entities mean less while economic issues mean more. Today, threats to society-such as international organised crime, terrorism, weapons of mass destruction and cyber attacks on our critical communications infrastructure-are both unconventional and destabilizing. As Attorney General Reno has said repeatedly, "all crime is international in its consequences." Traffickers in woman and children, much like terrorists and narcotics traffickers, operate boldly across sovereign borders. They have not only capitalized on technological and communications advancements, which have facilitated the flow of goods and people, but have also exploited the economic crises in Russia and Asia as well as regional conflicts, such as Kosovo.

Traffickers have taken advantage of the unequal status of women and girls in the source and transit countries, including harmful stereotypes of women as property, commodities, servants, and sexual objects. Traffickers have also taken advantage of the demand for cheap, unprotected labor, and the promotion of sex tourism in some countries. To the traffickers, people are highly profitable, low risk, expendable, reusable, and resellable commodities. Whereas alien smuggling usually involves short-term monetary profit, trafficking usually involves long-term exploitation for economic gain. Organised crime groups profit from both the trafficking fees and the trafficked person's labor.

In some cases, the traffickers may profit even further by using the trafficked persons as "manpower" for other criminal purposes, such as selling drugs. The trafficking industry worldwide also is closely intertwined with other related criminal activities, such as extortion, racketeering, money laundering, bribery of public officials, drug use, and gambling. For example, INS raids on brothels run by traffickers in Toronto have netted heroin and counterfeit currency. And the Wah Ching, an Asian organised crime group engaged in smuggling and trafficking Asian women, is also involved in gambling, robbery, murder, drug trafficking, and loan sharking. The Wah Ching also has connections to Asian organised crime groups in Boston, New York City, Los Angeles, Seattle, Dallas, Vancouver, and Toronto.

Trafficking also usually involves conspiracy, document forgery, visa, mail, and wire fraud. Even in the United States, some traffickers have been known to supply the women with fraudulent state identification and social security cards. This involvement in a multitude of criminal activities and ties among various criminal associations only serves to increase the burden on local and federal law enforcement agencies. Trafficking into the sex industry also has serious societal consequences as it contributes to the spread of HIV and AIDS.

Some trafficked women are required to engage in unprotected sex. Particularly disturbing is a case uncovered by INS where at least one trafficker was purchasing HIV-positive females because he found them to be cheap labor and since he believed they had nothing to live for. Moreover, the corruption commonly associated with the trafficking industry in many source, transit, and destination countries serves to undermine law enforcement and the rule of law. Many non-governmental organisations stress that the trafficking industry could not exist and thrive without corruption. The ripple effects of trafficking are enormous, as it is a political, economic, crime, health, migration, and most importantly, a human rights issue.

Overall, the global nexus of trafficking has fundamental policy implications. Isolated country efforts to combat trafficking will mean little without a larger coordinated international effort. The transnational character of trafficking means that the countries of origin, transit, and destination must work together collaboratively.

Trafficking in persons, particularly women and children, is significant on nearly every continent. Gauging the level of trafficking with precision, however, is difficult since it is an underground industry. Estimates of the trafficking problem in the United States vary, given differing definitions of what constitutes trafficking and research based on limited case studies. At present, no one US or international agency is compiling accurate statistics. Nonetheless, government and nongovernmental experts in the field estimate that out of the 700,000 to two million women and children who are trafficked globally each year, 45,000 to 50,000 of those women and children are trafficked to the United States.

Approximately 30,000 women and children are being trafficked annually from Southeast Asia, 10,000 from Latin America, 4,000 from the Newly Independent States and Eastern Europe, and 1,000 from other regions. There have been reports of trafficking instances in at least 20 different states, with most cases occurring in New York, California, and Florida. Some Florida law enforcement officials, for example, claim that the state is being inundated with trafficked women from Russia, Ukraine, and Central Europe. INS and Labor Department officials fear that the problem is not only bigger than they thought but also getting worse. For example, INS has discovered over 250 brothels in 26 different cities, which likely involved trafficking victims.

Evidence suggests that state and local law enforcement officials appear to have only scratched the surface of the problem. Trafficking cases are hard to uncover as the crime usually occurs "behind closed doors," and language and cultural barriers usually isolate the victims. The primary source countries for the United States appear to be Thailand, Vietnam, China, Mexico, Russia, Ukraine, and the Czech Republic. Women have also been trafficked to the US from the Philippines, Korea, Malaysia, Latvia, Hungary, Poland, Brazil, and Honduras among other countries. Women have been trafficked to the US primarily for the sex industry (prostitution, stripping, peep and touch shows, and massage parlors that offer a variety of sexual services), sweatshop labor, domestic servitude, and agricultural work.

Women have also been trafficked to provide maid services at motels and hotels, peddle trinkets on subways and buses, and beg. The average age of the trafficking victim in the United States is roughly 20 years old. Some of the Asian women may have been initially trafficked overseas at a much younger age, but then worked in cities such as Bangkok before being trafficked to the US. A review of several illustrative trafficking and slavery operations-involving sweatshop, agricultural, and other forms of labor-over the last eight years shows that these operations went unnoticed or were able to exist longer than trafficking operations involving the sex industry.

Labor trafficking operations generally lasted from 4½ to 6½ years whereas trafficking operations for prostitution lasted from a little over a year to approximately 2½ years before being discovered. Trafficking operations for other forms of the sex industry, such as exotic dancing and peep-and-touch shows, were in existence for anywhere from 10 months to 3 years. Once uncovered, trafficking and slavery cases usually take about a year and a half to investigate and prosecute, according to the Department of Justice's Involuntary Servitude Coordinator in the Civil Rights Division, Criminal Section.

Traffickers typically lure women to the United States with false promises of jobs as waitresses, nannies, models, factory workers, or exotic dancers. Capitalizing on rising unemployment, disintegrating social networks, and the low status of women in the source countries, the traffickers promise high wages and good working conditions in exciting US cities. Traffickers recruit women abroad through advertisements and employment, travel, model, or matchmaking agencies. Many women fall victim when they apply for work at seemingly reputable employment agencies which are unlicensed or unregulated.

Recruiters may also target beauty contest winners and entice them with "work offers." Additionally, traffickers send recruiters to villages and towns. In other instances, friends and acquaintances recruit women informally, through word of mouth. In almost all the cases, recruiters or agents front the money for provision of travel documents, transportation, and supposed jobs. Occasionally, bogus contracts are used to provide an image of legitimacy, lulling the woman into believing she is dealing with a reputable business. The Coalition Against Trafficking in Women (CATW) reports that the Internet is the latest place for promoting global trafficking of women and children as it is being used to lure women to foreign cities with false promises.

Once recruited, the women usually find themselves in situations with severely curtailed freedoms. The women's passports or travel documents are taken, their movements are restricted, and their wages are withheld until their smuggling debt is repaid. And because traffickers can also re-sell the women's debts to other traffickers or employers, victims are often caught in a cycle of perpetual debt bondage. Women are prevented from leaving by security guards, violence, threats, debt bondage, and/or retention of their documents. The traffickers may maintain control through isolation; in many cases, the women must live and work at the location.

The women may also be denied outside medical assistance when needed. Threats of physical abuse against themselves and/or their families are also common in order to force cooperation. Traffickers also play upon the women's fears of arrest and deportation. In additional cases, trafficking victims suffer extreme physical and mental abuse, including rape, imprisonment, forced abortions, and physical brutality.

Asian Criminal Enterprises

The Federal Bureau of Investigation (FBI) reports that Asian criminal enterprises involved in smuggling humans to the US fall into the following categories: 45 percent are Chinese, 29 percent Vietnamese, 7.3 percent Korean with Japanese, Filipino, Thai, Laotian, Cambodian and Polynesian comprising the rest. Asian organised crime organisations have played an intricate part in the smuggling of Asian females to the US and the running of the brothels whether it be as owner, extortionist, or protector. INS investigations have uncovered ties in some cities among the brothels, Asian street gangs, and Asian organised crime figures. Cities where Asian organised crime involvement with brothels has been noted are Los Angeles, San Francisco, Sacramento, Las Vegas, Nevada, and Dallas. INS has also seen Asian street gangs involved with brothels in New York, Philadelphia, and Chicago.

Asian organised crime in the US involved in trafficking in women tends to operate more like a loose confederation of organised criminal entrepreneurs or enterprises as opposed to one large criminal syndicate controlling the trafficking process from beginning to end. Criminal groups are business firms of various sizes depending on their maturity, according to FBI. There tends to be little formal hierarchical organisation among Asian organised crime groups. A loose joint venture may cut across ethnic and organisational lines and is often formed for a given opportunity. Trafficking in humans tends to be treated as a business. These criminal enterprises tend to be fairly organised, and will often subcontract out the work.

The trafficking-in-persons industry typically involves enforcers, transporters, recruiters, document forgers, brokers, brothel owners, and employment agencies. Brokers operate in the source country as well as in the United States. Thailand is one of the primary source countries for the United States. According to the American Embassy in Bangkok, at least four loosely organised groups smuggle and traffic Thai women for delivery to US brothels. They send roughly 20 to 30 women a month to the US and Canada, generally using altered or impostor Thai passports.

By other accounts, at least seven families in Thailand are engaged in smuggling and trafficking women into the United States for prostitution. Many of these women have been told they will be seamstresses and hostesses but arrive to find themselves forced into prostitution. This is often the case with Chinese victims trafficked from rural areas in the PRC. In other cases, Asian women are brought to the US with knowledge of their work as prostitutes, but find themselves in slave-like situations. Chinese triads and gangs in the US have been involved in alien smuggling and prostitution for years, and increasingly they are arranging for the direct recruiting and smuggling of sex workers from overseas.

NGO, the Global Survival Network (GSN) found that Chinese criminal groups have moved part of their operations to the Commonwealth of the Northern Mariana Islands (CNMI), where they operate significant money-lending operations which lend money to trafficking victims at exorbitant rates. GSN also found that Japanese organised crime groups operate in Saipan, where they control a large part of the sex tourism sector. Many Chinese women, who have been lured to CNMI to be waitresses, have been forced to work at nightclubs catering to sex tourists and work in sweatshops. Several of these Chinese women have claimed that they were threatened with death if they did not comply.

Brothels across the country generally receive protection from Asian street gangs, who may or may not live at the brothel location. Besides protecting the brothel from other criminal groups, gang members are there to watch over the women until their debt is paid off, according to the FBI. Gang members have also been used to kidnap girls and retrieve those who have escaped. According to one Californian non-governmental organisation, the Center for the Pacific-Asian Family, the Vietnamese and Chinese gangs are known to be the most organised and vicious of Asian gangs in California.

— In a New York trafficking case, the brothel owner was forced to pay protection money to the Flying Dragons-a Chinese street gang. The Flying Dragons are the enforcement sector of the Hipsing Triad, a Fukienese Triad. In order to maintain a low profile, the Hipsing Triad is registered under the Hipsing merchants association.

— The Wah Ching and Triads also employ Asian street gangs, such as the Black Dragons and Koolboyz, for protection at the brothels.

— In a 1998 internal trafficking case in California, a Fresno-based gang kidnapped Hmong girls, took them to other cities, and forced them into prostitution.

— A few years ago, some 65 Chinese citizens were held in a Maryland basement while arrangements could be made by their traffickers to sell them to Chinese gangs in New York for servitude in restaurants. The Chinese were also beaten and forced to call their families and ask for more money.

To evade detection from law enforcement, Asian traffickers shift their holding houses on a frequent basis; forbid the women from making prostitution out-calls; accept only Asian clients at the brothels; and use massage parlors, spas, sun tanning parlors, and beauty salons as fronts for the brothels. Many massage parlors in the United States are connected to large-scale smuggling and prostitution operations. Traffickers may purchase false massage licenses or certificates for the women, costing anywhere from $200 to $500, in order to appear legitimate in case a police officer enters the premises.

Though many prostitution houses operate independently, they appear to share information with one another regarding any possible law enforcement raids, and some have hideaways to conceal the women and girls from the police. Corruption also facilitates the industry. For example, there have been allegations made against New Orleans police department officials that they were

accepting bribes from local brothels, likely in exchange for tipping the brothels off to impending raids.

Russian Crime Groups

All levels of Russian organised crime, from individuals to smaller groups to larger syndicates, appear to be involved in trafficking women to the United States, though law enforcement entities disagree as to the degree of involvement of Russian organised crime. By some accounts, Russian individuals-likely with Russian organised crime connections- are importing women from Russia, Ukraine, the Baltic States, and Central Europe for the sex industry, namely for stripping, escort services, and prostitution. INS agents in New York claim there are many cases involving the trafficking of these women by freelance criminals for stripping or escort services. Frequently, the women's passports are taken by the trafficker and they are not free to leave until they have paid their debt of around $10,000.

INS believes these criminals have Russian organised crime connections overseas, but have not seen instances where the major Russian organised crime organisations are running the trafficking business to the United States. The Director of Operation Odessa, a Florida task force designed to combat Russian organised crime, believes that individual criminals, not necessarily organised crime, are trafficking Russian women to Florida. He claims that women are being trafficked to Miami, Orlando, Fort Lauderdale, Jackson, Palm Beach, and increasingly the Florida panhandle. In his opinion, Russian entrepreneurs, with ties to Russian organised crime, are importing women for Florida's sex industry. For example, one Russian, Sergey Skobeltsyn, with alleged ties to the Russian organised crime group Kazanskaya, bought two strip clubs, Pure Platinum and Solid Gold, for $8 million dollars in late 1996.

And Ludwig Fainberg, a Russian mafia figure with alleged ties to Colombian drug traffickers, was also heavily involved in running a strip club called Porkys, which likely involved trafficked women. FBI headquarters also has information that the following major Russian organised crime syndicates-the Izmailovskaya, Dagestantsy, Kazanskaya, and Solntsenskaya-are involved in the prostitution industry throughout the United States. Given the way these organised crime syndicates operate overseas and the brutality of these organisations, it is likely that this involvement in the US includes trafficking in women through the use of deception, threats, and violence. Russian women have also been trafficked to Florida, particularly the panhandle, for maid work.

FBI and INS agents in Florida claim that Russian and Central European women are answering ads in local papers for work in the US. Once in the US, these women provide maid service in motels and become virtual indentured servants, working long hours for little pay. The women are paid through a series of corporations so the women appear to be working only part-time and so the companies do not need to provide any benefits. FBI is unsure as to whether or not any larger Russian criminal syndicate is managing these companies. Another interesting trend identified by FBI agents in New York are situations where local Russian organised crime groups tried to "muscle in" and control a trafficking situation after they have noticed its profitability.

Bratva- the Brotherhood-a Russian crime group with ties to Russian crime boss Ivankov's successor organisation-used extortion, assault, and battery in July 1998 to control dance agencies and their drivers who were bringing Russian women in and delivering them to exotic nightclubs, bars, and escort services. FBI believes there are about 10 to 12 dance agencies specializing in Russian women, and hundreds of escort services in the New York and New Jersey area. Each dance agency is believed to employ some 60 to 200 women. Again, it is not readily apparent to FBI to what degree Russian organised crime is involved in controlling these 10 to 12 New York and New Jersey dance agencies. Some Diplomatic Security (DS) agents claim that many of these dance, modeling, employment, or service agencies are fronts for trafficking for larger Russian organised crime syndicates.

According to these DS agents, the agencies are used to hide the structural layers of the criminal organisation, which include deputies, associates, collectors, and drivers. They claim that Russian and Italian organised crime groups are collaborating in New York and New Jersey with Russian crime groups supplying the women for the multitude of nightclubs and peep shows that are managed by Italian mafia groups. In other instances, traffickers have capitalized on the reputation of Russian organised crime and used it as a means of control and intimidation. In a recent Chicago case, a Russian American frequently bragged about his Chechen organised crime ties and threatened Latvian women with harm to themselves and/or their families if they did not dance nude. He had originally intimidated one of the women into coming to the US, by telling her he would cut her face up if she refused and then escorting her to a mafia hangout for dinner so she would know that her face had been identified.

Threats, such as these, have been carried out in other instances. In one case, a Russian woman was brought over to be a maid but forced into prostitution to repay her smuggling debt more quickly. When this woman tried to leave, a Russian thug beat her so badly she had to go to the hospital where she was threatened by another Russian gangster not to talk to law enforcement officials. In another case, the authorities suspected mafia involvement in the gruesome murder of a Russian woman trafficked to

Maryland. The case was never solved, but some authorities think she was killed because she was holding back her earnings from her employers.

Profits in the trafficking industry provide a major source of income for the crime rings. In most of the major recent trafficking cases in the United States, the traffickers made anywhere from one to eight million in a period ranging from one to six years. Traffickers typically charge the women inflated prices for securing the alleged jobs, travel documentation, transportation, lodging, meals, and incidentals. To increase profits, the women are kept in poor, crowded conditions. It is also common for trafficked women to be charged to buy their passport back. The fee is usually around $900 for women from the Newly Independent States and Central Europe, though in one recent case in Chicago, Latvian women paid as much as $4,000 in cash.

Trafficked Asian women have been charged $1,500 to $3,000 for their passports. Women may also be charged for ID cards, driver's licenses, and driver's permits. Prices may vary, but typical fees are $700 for an ID card, $900 for a driver's license and $1,000 for an ID card with a driver's permit. It is illustrative to examine fees from one case involving an Asian trafficker that appears characteristic for other Asian traffickers. In this case, a Thai smuggler is paid between $13,000 to $15,000 for every successful entry a woman made into the US. The money covers the passport (typically sold for $1,500 to $3,000), airline ticket, and additional fees paid to the Thai recruiting agent and the "jockey" who assists in bringing the women into the United States.

Thai recruitment agents receive a commission of about $800 to $1,400 for each woman he or she recruited. The "jockey," or person who actually escorts a woman or girl from Thailand to the US, is usually paid about $1,000 per woman or girl he successfully admits to the US. Thus, the smuggler usually makes about $7,500 to $9,000 per woman. Traffickers have also come up with various means to transport the money back to Thailand and the agents. The "jockey" may be responsible for conveying the impostor passport and the $13,000 back to the Thai smuggler in Thailand. Alternatively, the money is wired through companies to Thai bank accounts.

Overall profits in the trade can be staggering, as several cases indicate. Thai traffickers, who incarcerated Thai women and men in a sweatshop in El Monte, California, are estimated to have made $8 million dollars over about six years.

— Thai traffickers, who enslaved Thai women in a New York brothel, made about $1.5 million over roughly a year and three months. In that case, the women were made to pay debts ranging from $30,000 to $50,000. The women were forced to charge $130 per client; the madam of the brothel would receive $30 and the smugglers would receive $100. Sometimes, a woman at the brothel might be sold outright to the madam for $15,000 or more depending on her beauty.

— One Thai trafficker estimates that he made about $215,000 over approximately two years. In this case as well, brothel owners would pay $7,500 to $15,000 for each woman, though her debt would be around $40,000. Less attractive women would be exchanged or sold off for less money.

— Chinese criminal syndicates, living in Malaysia, have also made $5,000 to $7,000 for each Malaysian woman delivered to the United States, according to the American Embassy in Kuala Lumpur. A kidnapped and trafficked Chinese woman in yet another case was compelled to pay a $20,000 debt through prostitution. Profits from trafficking women from Latin

America can be just as lucrative. A Mexican crime family, that forced deaf Mexicans to peddle trinkets made roughly $8 million, over four and a half years. In another trafficking case involving Mexicans, traffickers made some $2.5 million over two years by forcing Mexican women and girls into prostitution. The traffickers charged a client $22 for 15 minutes of sexual activity with a woman. Ten dollars of this amount went to the house and the remainder towards paying off her $2,000 to $3,000 debt. The traffickers then used the money to buy real estate and new trucks in Mexico. These assets were used to convince additional victims that they were successful businessmen who owned a legitimate landscaping company in the US

Challenges in Trafficking

The challenges associated with combating trafficking and protecting the victims are overwhelming but not unmanageable. The same government officials and nongovernmental experts who outlined their most pressing issues also provided some suggestions and recommendations for preventing trafficking, prosecuting the traffickers, and assisting the trafficking victims. The Non-Governmental Organisations (NGOs) feel that a multi-dimensional approach to addressing and eradicating trafficking must include not only legislative initiatives, crime prevention, and border control efforts, but also social welfare, job training, rights protection, and development initiatives in the source, transit, and destination countries and locales. Developing effective strategies must entail governments, governmental agencies, NGOs, advocacy groups, service providers, survivors, and affected communities all working together on the issue.

Prevention of Trafficking

Prevention of trafficking must incorporate economic

alternatives in the source countries, public awareness campaigns, and improved data collection on the issue. Trafficking prevention strategies must focus on the highrisk areas in the primary source countries. Prevention initiatives should develop or expand upon targeted micro-credit initiatives, small business development, and job and skills training. Moreover, grants should be awarded to non-governmental organisations to promote or accelerate the empowerment of women in political, economic, social, and educational roles at the local, regional, and national levels in the source countries. Prevention of trafficking should also include legal, social, and cultural reforms to eliminate gender discrimination.

In a recent survey completed by 3,000 people in 57 regions of the Russian Federation and in Georgia, Armenia, Azerbaijan, Ukraine, and Mongolia, young and old women listed poverty, economic depression, and unequal career opportunities as their top three issues of concern. High unemployment rates pose hardships on women. By some studies, between 70 and 80 percent of the unemployed workers in the Russian Federation, for example, are women. For those women who have jobs, they often must contend with sexual harassment in the workplace. It is this destitution and discrimination that make women especially vulnerable to traffickers' false promises of good jobs abroad.

In addition to addressing economic issues, NGOs call for programs to keep children, particularly girls, in elementary and secondary school as well as curricula which includes information about the dangers of trafficking. Some non-profit organisations claim that use of local drama clubs, student organisations, and church groups are not only cost effective but also a meaningful way to communicate with young people. Additionally, NGOs say public awareness campaigns must involve the use of the media, particularly television, radio, newspapers, and magazines. In the survey mentioned above, television was clearly ranked first as the best way to reach at-risk young women and their families. Of those respondents who had heard of trafficking, 7 out of 10 people had learned about trafficking from TV. When asked about computer access, only 15 percent of the vulnerable 10 to 19-year-old population said they owned computers; however, 93 percent expressed a strong desire to use e-mail and the Internet.

Some government experts who have studied the trafficking issue would like the Attorney General to establish guidelines for collecting data from federal, state, and local law enforcement agencies on human trafficking, particularly women and children, and the disposition of victims of these crimes. Data collected should be incorporated into existing and supplemental Department of Justice reports, including reports on criminal civil rights violations, organised crime, and exploitation of minors. The US is exploring additional ways to facilitate data-sharing, as appropriate, with law enforcement entities abroad, including developing further protocols.

There is a need for trafficking victims to receive medical, mental health, and legal services. Trafficking victims should have access to information about their rights and translation services. As mentioned earlier, appropriate shelters need to be constructed or designated for trafficking victims. Another solution is to further utilize existing shelters as well as health and legal clinics in immigrant communities. Such shelters and clinics should be vetted beforehand to ensure they are capable of meeting the needs of trafficked victims.

Moreover, staff at these shelters should receive specialized training. Government grants should also be awarded to those shelters and clinics with a proven track record of service, to enable them to provide victims with housing, medical, psychological, and legal services. In the area of legal services, the Legal Services Corporation Act might also be amended to permit LSC grantees to provide trafficking victims with legal services, similar to the exception that is made for illegal aliens who have subjected to domestic violence.

At present, the Department of Justice's Office for Victims of Crime and the victim-witness coordinators from the US Attorney's offices have the primary responsibility for ensuring the safety and protection of victims. The Office for Victims of Crime, Federal Crime Victims Division funds state compensation and state victim assistance programs. The Crime Victims Fund, established by the Victims Crime Act of 1984 and distributed to the states, is available to trafficking victims in terms of services but not in terms of direct funding. No state is permitted to give direct compensation to an undocumented worker only services.

Some government experts on the issue of trafficking would like trafficking victims in the US to be eligible for victim's services, compensation, and assistance under the Crime Victims Fund. Alternatively, a separate account, called the Trafficking Victims Protection Fund, might be established to provide the shelter and services for the trafficking victims. Criminal fines, penalties, and forfeited assets from the traffickers, which are not dispersed directly by the court to the trafficking victims, would go into this account.

Additionally, some policymakers engaged on the issue would like funding from the Violence Against Women Act to be available to trafficking victims as well as for the operation of hotlines, training programs for professionals, and preparation of anti-trafficking informational materials. Currently, funding from the Violence Against Women Act is for victims of domestic violence, stalking, and sexual assault.

Lastly, some NGOs call for better reintegration initiatives. In those cases where the trafficking victims will be returning home, advocates say an NGO representative should meet those victims at the border and/or airport. Wellthought out repatriation and reintegration programs should be in place to assist the trafficking victims make the transition and protect them from any retaliation by the traffickers.

6

Drug Trafficking

Illicit drugs is a term that designates many types of mind altering substances. The most commonly known illicit drugs are cannabis, cocaine, and heroin. Besides these more or less 'natural drugs' , made on the basis of the plants cannabis, coca, and opium, there is an increasing number of synthetic drugs on the market, the most known types being amphetamine, ecstasy (MDMA), and LSD. Roughly speaking one could say between 5% and 15% of the population of 12 years and over has ever tried drugs.

Cannabis, in the form of marihuana and hash, is the most used illicit drug in Europe. The available data tend to indicate that current cannabis use among the general population in European countries varies from 0.5% to 5%. When looked at younger age categories, it appears that the prevalence of cannabis use is higher; the proportion of, for example, 18 year old school students who admit ever having tried cannabis, ranges from approximately 10% to 35%. Despite the methodological limitations of the available data, it is safe to say there are, today, several millions of current cannabis users in Europe. Comparative longitudinal research reveals that the degree in which cannabis is used is not as much influenced by the national drug policy applied by a country, but that international social and cultural factors seem to be playing a more big important role in this regard.

In other words, drug use follows international trends, influenced by popular culture, youth culture and so forth, instead of being the result of the actual drug policy and law enforcement measures. In most western countries drug use increased in the late 1960s and early 1970s, followed by a decrease in the late 1970s and throughout the 1980s. In the 1990s drugs are experiencing a second phase of popularity; all-over the western world drug use is on the rise. Heroin, a derivative from opium poppies, is a drug often associated with compulsive or addictive patterns of use, for which reason it is considered the main problem drug. Although the substance is also occasionally used, very few is known about this category of users.

Most of the existing knowledge about heroin use is based on users from special populations, such as people in treatment. This means that even more than is the case with regard to the number of cannabis users, the figures are surrounded with a large degree of uncertainty. A very tentative estimate of the number of heroin addicts in the 15 countries of the European Union suggests that the number of heroin addicts is somewhere between 500,000 and one million. Per country this would mean that the number of people that is estimated to be 'addicted' to heroin at any one time, is under 0.5% of the general population.

Supply Side of Drugs

Even more than is the case with regard to drug use, knowledge about drug trafficking is surrounded by many uncertainties. The main indicators about the nature and the extent of this commerce, are drug seizures. However, their everlasting limitation is that one never knows whether they reflect the real trends in drug trafficking, or whether they are merely a reflection of law enforcement activities. Internationally, around 10% of the drugs in circulation are intercepted, a figure that is also applied by Interpol. However, this figure, already in use since many decades, has no scientific basis whatsoever.

Cannabis in Europe is usually available in the forms hash and marihuana. Although marihuana is gaining in popularity, hash is still predominant in Europe. A substantial part of hash on the European market originates from Morocco. Traditionally, the mountainous Rif area in northern Morocco has been a production region for cannabis, mainly destined for local consumption. Since a nearby European cannabis market become accessible, the acreage under cultivation in Northern Morocco has grown considerably. In 1993 it was estimated that between 64,000 and 74,000 hectares of cannabis were under cultivation in Northern Morocco. This would imply the acreage increased tenfold in the period of ten years.

Today, Morocco is considered as the world's main cannabis exporter. The potential of Moroccan hash production is estimated to be around 2,000 metric tonnes a year. In 1993 200 tonnes of Moroccan hash were seized, of which 112 in Europe. Besides Morocco, the European cannabis market is also supplied by other countries. Today, cannabis is cultivated on every continent of the world and the European cannabis market is supplied by different sources, such as from Asia, where hash exported from Afghanistan and Pakistan, and marihuana from Thailand and Laos. Important American producers like Colombia, Mexico, and Jamaica, not only serve the North American market, but also export to Europe.

In recent years marihuana production has increased in several African countries, especially in Western and Southern Africa, of which a part is exported to Europe. An parallel development is that an increasing part of the markets in the Western world are being supplied by local marihuana production, either indoors or outdoors. This can not only be observed in Canada and the USA, but also in Europe. The Netherlands are the European forerunner in this process; it is estimated that more than half of the total cannabis consumption is fròm domestic production. This international development of 'import substitution' - although it is not officially promoted as such by the authorities- has taken such proportions that in some western countries cannabis has become one of the main agricultural crops, a position that was until recently reserved to Southern producers. Spain and the Netherlands are Europe's main countries of entry for cannabis.

Since Morocco is Europe's main supplier, it comes as no surprise Spain is the main port of entry for hash. Boats, cars, and especially lorries are used to cross the Street of Gibraltar. The main means of transport by which hash is distributed throughout Europe are cars and lorries. The Diaspora of 1.5 million Moroccans living in Europe certainly facilitates the trade. The Netherlands are another important point of entry for cannabis, predominantly arriving by ships. Several reasons can be mentioned why the Netherlands -and Dutch criminal organisations- have attained an important international position in the cannabis trade. One reason can be found in the tolerant policy towards cannabis, in particular since its retailing has become permitted in the so-called coffeeshops since the 1970s, leading to a situation in which the trade in cannabis was also getting a lower law enforcement priority.

A second reason can be found in a certain tradition of smuggling, going back to the butter and cattle smugglers in the South of the Netherlands during the afterwar period. A third reason has to do with the Netherlands' geographical position and their dominant role in transport and distribution. Heroin is made on the basis of opium poppies that are mainly produced in two areas: the Golden Triangle (Burma, Laos, and Thailand) and in the Golden Crescent (Afghanistan, Iran, Pakistan). Two countries can be considered as world's main opium poppy growers: Myanmar (Burma) with an estimated annual 2,500 tons, and Afghanistan that produces between 1,000 and 1,500 tons of opium every year. North America is mainly supplied by the Golden Triangle, especially Myanmar.

The European market on the other hand is mainly supplied by the Golden Crescent. Around 70% of the heroin in Europe is made on the basis of Afghan opium. After having been transformed into morphine base, the drugs are transported to Turkish laboratories where they undergo a second transformation to become heroin. Turkey plays a central role in the heroin trade destined for Europe. Its central geographical position, on the crossroads of Europe, Asia, the Middle East, and the Mediterranean Sea, having both many land and sea connections, gives the country the potential to play an important role in any trade. Turkey not only has these possibilities, in practice it is really having many international contacts.

Historically, going back to the Ottoman empire, Turkey has its spheres of influence in eastern directions, which is facilitated by the linguistic relationships Turkey is having with several (former) CIS republics. Due to the Turkish Diaspora in Europe, comprising 2.3 million people, there exists an international network for the distribution of heroin to the European market. An estimated 80% of the heroin on the European market is being processed in Turkish laboratories. Moreover, the heroin trade from Turkey to the European market is dominated by Turks, even though the Turkish authorities try to make it appear as if especially Curds -the PKK in particular- are involved.

Since many years, the most common way by which heroin arrives from Turkey into Europe is by the Balkan route. Historically, the Balkan route is the main overland connection between Asia and Europe. Every year, this route is taken by around 1,5 million lorries, 250,000 coaches, and four million cars. The most common way to transport heroin is a relatively small quantity of 20 to 50 kilos hidden in a lorry. Considering the scale of the trade on the Balkan trade, combined with the fact that it takes some hours to a whole day to search a lorry, explains why it is virtually impossible to really counteract these activities. It is estimated that 75 per cent of the heroin smuggled into Europe is transported along the Balkan route.

On an annual basis around 6,000 kilos of heroin are being seized in the European Union. Although this amount may look impressive, one has to wonder if this really is the case. Taking into account an estimated number of heroin addicts of 500,000 to one million, one has to conclude only a -very- small part of the heroin on the market is intercepted. This can be supported by the fact that although seizures have almost constantly risen the latest years, the street prices have nothing but declined. Even major seizures of drugs have no impact whatsoever on the market prices.

Drug Trafficking

Because of the extremely high economic value and profit margins of drugs, they not only have become an interesting commerce for (organised) criminals, but also for (illegal) political movements needing money to finance their activities, such as guerrilla and independent movements. This has become even more apparent since the end of the Cold War, resulting in less opportunities to receive funding from one of the world powers. A category of drug traffickers that is not mentioned often are the traffickers who are more or less connected to governments, such as the secret services and the army,

working either independently of in cooperation with political movements involved in the drug trade. This latter observation can be illustrated by looking at the genesis of the two main opium production area's in the world, Burma and Afghanistan.

Alfred McCoy has described how, during the 1980s, Afghanistan became Europe's main opium supplier, because CIA covert operations transformed southern Asia from a self-contained opium zone into a major supplier of heroin for the world market: "CIA intervention provided the political protection and logistic linkages that joined Afghanistan's poppy fields to heroin markets in Europe and America". Although the Americans have left, Afghanistan, just like Burma before it, has remained a major heroin supplier for the world market.

With regard to the hash production in Morocco, the world's largest cannabis producer, it is known that people in 'high places' are involved in both the production and trade. The smooth and organised way in which the hash trade is taking place, makes it likely this situation is not only 'tolerated', but may even been co-ordinated by the authorities. It is known that every year the regional services of the Moroccan ministry of Agriculture provide highly confidential statistics showing the acreage under cultivation. Although the Moroccan authorities have agreed with the EU in developing substitute crops, and hash seizures in Morocco has nothing but increased, there is every indications the total hash production has increased as well. The total revenue of the hash trade in Morocco is estimated to represent twothird of the total exports and 10% of the country's income.

Since it is no longer a secret that the authorities are highly involved in the trade, including the royal family, one can wonder why the European countries have a relatively lenient attitude towards Morocco and King Hassan II in this regard. On political meetings the

European leaders regularly express their worries about drugs and the drug trade. One reason for these double standards can be found in the friendly diplomatic and personal relations Morocco and the King are having with some European countries and their leaders, France in particular. A more important reason why Morocco is not criticised too severely is that, un-der the current circumstances of the civil war in Algeria and rising Muslim fundamentalism in several Arab countries, Morocco is considered an important ally of Europe and barrier against a rise in Muslim fundamentalism.

A somewhat similar situation can be observed with regard to Turkish involvement in the international heroin trade. It is been extensively documented how different Turkish Mafia organisations are having a relatively free hand in the international heroin trade. Besides the more 'traditional' extended Mafia families, different political movement like the Grey Wolves, Dev Sol, and the PKK are also playing their part. Besides that, both the civil and the military secret services are involved in the heroin trade; two governmental agencies that are, in fact, competing with one another, sometimes resulting in assassinations. The involvement in, and protection by the Turkey's highest bureaucratic levels in the heroin trade were confirmed in November 1996, when a traffic accident occurred with four people sitting a the same car: an extreme right criminal on the run, a high ranked policeman, a beauty queen, and the only survivor, a parliamentarian of Prime Minister's Ciller political party.

The reason why Turkey, that is already having a customs union with the EU and is now applying for EU membership, is not criticised for their involvement in the heroin trade, are purely (geo)political. Due to its important strategic position, Turkey has been an important NATO partner since 1952. During the Gulf War, Turkey's strategic importance for military actions in the Middle East was confirmed. This also explains why, although the EU is hesitant about Turkey's membership, the USA is actually lobbying in the EU to have Turkey accepted as full EU member. Two geopolitical developments in the 1990s have changed the face of heroin trafficking in Europe: the war in former Yugoslavia, and the falling of the iron curtain. Until the war broke out, most heroin on the Balkan route was passing through (former) Yugoslavia.

The war resulted in a diversification of the trafficking routes, both in northern and in southern directions. For example, heroin was increasingly being transported from Greece to Italy, from where it could reach the markets. The Mediterranean Sea was also being used for the transport for heroin enabling to reach countries like France and Spain directly. In northern direction, new trafficking routes were also found, facilitated by the falling of the iron curtain that opened up possibilities to reach the EU on the eastern side. And, via the Black Sea heroin could be transported to Bulgaria and Romania, from where it could reach Slovakia, Poland and Germany. Another development connected to the falling of the iron curtain is that the territory of the Russian Federation is becoming a cross-road for illicit drug trafficking. The activities of organised criminal organisations groups and the removal of customs barriers between CIS member States have made it possible for traffickers to transport illicit shipments from the Golden Crescent through central Asia, the Russian Federation and Belarus without being checked.

Trends in Illicit Drug Markets

The evolution of the main illicit drug markets in recent years provides an uneven picture of positive and negative developments, depending on the drugs and the regions considered. Overall, the evolution of world heroin and cocaine markets shows some positive tendencies.

Heroin

Treatment data consistently shows that illicit heroin use has the most severe health consequences for drug abusers. In 2000-2001, UNODC estimated that about 15 million people abused opium and heroin in the world. Although this figure has not changed much since the late 1990s, gaps in the data prevent precise monitoring of changes in global demand for illicit opium and heroin from year to year. The impression of the relative stability of the global heroin market since the end of the 1990s can be supported by an assessment of the supply situation, for which there is more robust data. About 4,400 metric tons (mt) of illicit opium were produced in 1998. Four years later, in 2002, the production (approximately 4,500 mt) is more or less at the same level. Underneath the apparent stability of global production, however, major shifts are at work.

Statistics on agricultural land devoted to illicit opium poppy cultivation in the world show that the market is changing. While global opium production remained basically stable over a four-year period, illicit opium poppy cultivation declined by 25%. The answer to this apparent paradox can be found in a considerable shift of production from South-East to South West Asia. Progress made in Myanmar and the Lao PDR has resulted in a 40% reduction in the area under opium poppy cultivation in that region between 1998 and 2002. This downward trend continued in 2003. If the current rate of reduction in South-East Asia is sustained, the Golden Triangle could well become a minor source of illicit opium in the next few years. Meanwhile, a 16% increase was recorded in South West Asia from 1998 to 2002. The higher productivity of the irrigated opium fields in Afghanistan explains why the world.s opium output remained stable while the level of cultivation was going down. The result has been an increasing concentration of illicit opium production in a single country, Afghanistan.

Regional shifts have also reshaped the patterns of heroin abuse in the world. There are some improvements in West Europe, but the rapid growth of opium production in Afghanistan has fuelled the development of a large heroin market in the region and, further, in Central Asia, the Russian Federation and East Europe. Largely caused by the increase in intravenous heroin abuse, the HIV/AIDS epidemic has been expanding at an alarming rate.

The new heroin markets in East Europe, Russia and Central Asia are not yet as lucrative as the West European markets. The economic incentive they provide to traffickers is thus lower. They do, however, offer the potential to offset the reduction in profitability per transaction by expanding the consumer base. There are already more opiate abusers in those regions than in West Europe and the potential for further growth is large.

There is evidence to suggest that the effect of long-term demand reduction efforts can be catalyzed by rapid and shorter-term progress in the reduction of supply. Although stocks delayed and reduced the impact of the short-lived but considerable decline of opium production in Afghanistan in 2001, records show that heroin purity levels in Europe declined that year and that the trend continued in the first two quarters of 2002. One positive consequence was a decline in the number of drug related deaths in a number of West European countries. Similarly, there are indications that in the countries of Central Asia the growth of abuse declined markedly in 2002 as a consequence of reduced supply.

Australia provided another illustration. Following the dismantling of a number of trafficking groups supplying the Australian market, the availability of heroin in that country dropped significantly in 2001. As a result, declines in the number of drug related crimes and drug related deaths, as well as increases in the number of heroin addicts seeking treatment, were recorded. In 2003, however, there have been reports of the supply slack in Australia being partly taken up by heroin originating in, or being trafficked via, the Democratic People.s Republic of Korea (North Korea).

Cocaine

Cocaine is abused by about 14 million people in the world and comes second to heroin in terms of treatment demand. There are some signs of progress in controlling cocaine supply and demand. Of the three countries which supply the world.s illicit cocaine, Bolivia has now become an almost marginal source (less than one-tenth of world cocaine production), and Peru has achieved a reduction of about 60 % in coca cultivation since 1995. Although both countries are encountering difficulties in consolidating the decline and eliminating the remaining illicit cultivation on their territory, overall they have not produced more than one-fifth of world illicit cocaine during the past few years.

The main challenge is Colombia, where the production of cocaine from domestic cultivation increased roughly by a factor of five between 1993 and 1999. By then, the country had become the source of almost three-quarters of the world.s illicit cocaine. The good news is that, reversing an eight-year trend, and for the second year in a row, Colombia achieved a very significant reduction of coca bush cultivation on its territory in 2002. Cumulatively, this amounts to a 37% decline between 2000 and 2002. Combining the three source countries translates into an overall reduction of 22% of the area under coca between 1999 and 2002. If this trend persists there could be a major change in the dynamics of world cocaine supply.

In the United States of America (USA), the world.s largest cocaine market, student surveys show that the number of cocaine users has tended to stabilize in recent years. Annual prevalence figures for 2002 in that country were reported to be 15% lower than in 1998, and some 60% lower than in 1985. Nonetheless, there is some cause for concern on the demand side in other regions. Cocaine abuse is increasing in South America and cocaine traffickers have been finding new market outlets in Europe.

As in the case of heroin, there are indications of a shifting market. Although the bulk of cocaine trafficking is still in the Americas, there has been an increase in cocaine trafficking towards West Europe. The share of West Europe in global cocaine seizures more than doubled between 1998 and 2001, rising from 8% to 17% during that period. Information on consumption tells the same story. The majority of West European countries reported an increase in cocaine abuse for the year 2001.

Cannabis

Cannabis continues to be the most widely produced, trafficked and consumed illicit drug worldwide. Given the global spread of cannabis production and the virtual absence of monitoring systems, no reliable production estimates for cannabis are available. Rising levels of cannabis seizures and abuse suggest, however, that production is also increasing. About two-thirds of the 86 countries which reported cannabis consumption trends to UNODC last year, indicated an increase of cannabis abuse in 2001. Overall seizures of cannabis rose by some 40% between 1998 and 2001. A distinction should be made between cannabis resin and herb products. Seizure data over the period 1998-2001 suggest a relative stability in the trafficking patterns of cannabis resin, which continues to be primarily seized in West Europe (around three-quarters of all seizures). It was therefore cannabis herb seizures that accounted for the increase noted above.

More than 60% of all cannabis herb seizures in 2001 were reported from the Americas. However, the strongest increase was in Africa, probably reflecting a combination of large-scale cultivation of cannabis and increased enforcement efforts in recent years. More than a quarter of all cannabis herb seizures are now reported from countries in Africa, compared to little more than 10% in 1998-99. Finally, seizures of cannabis plants . an indicator of the efforts made by governments to eradicate cannabis fields seem to be declining, possibly an indication of lesser priority given to cannabis eradication by some governments.

There are, however, some positive trends. In the USA, for instance, cannabis abuse (annual prevalence) fell in 2002 among high-school students and was almost 10% lower than in 1997 and some 30% lower than in the late 1970s. In Australia, cannabis abuse among the general population declined by 23% over the 1998-2001 period.

Amphetamine-type stimulants

Amphetamine-type-stimulants (ATS) are synthetic drugs that include the chemically related amphetamine, methamphetamine and ecstasy. Unlike the traditional plant-based drugs, the production of ATS starts with readily available chemicals, in easily concealed laboratories. This makes an assessment of the location, extent and evolution of the production of such illicit drugs extremely difficult. In order to obtain a clearer picture of this complex situation, UNODC is presently undertaking a global survey on ATS. Seizures of laboratories and end-products, as well as reports on consumption, indicate that the expansion of the ATS market is continuing. More laboratories were detected and dismantled worldwide over the last few years than ever before, particularly in the United States. But the market is also changing, partly in response to drug control agencies. efforts to tackle the problem, and partly as a result of the dynamics of abuse patterns.

Trafficking in methamphetamine accounts for the bulk of trafficking in ATS and has been clearly shifting towards East and South-East Asia in recent years. Seizures in 2001 declined, however, possibly a consequence of better controls of ephedrine (one of the main precursors) and first successes in reducing methamphetamine production in the People.s Republic of China. The Democratic People.s Republic of Korea (North Korea) seems to be emerging as a significant source/transshipment area for methamphetamine going to Japan, which is the region.s most lucrative ATS market.

In 2000, close to 90% of all countries reporting to UNODC on trends in the abuse of methamphetamine reported an increase. By 2001 this proportion fell to 52%. Japan reported a stabilization in methamphetamine abuse in 2001, following years of increase. Thailand, in contrast, affected by large- scale methamphetamine imports from neighbouring Myanmar, seized the largest quantity of methamphetamine worldwide in 2001 and reported a further increase in ATS abuse for 2001.

Europe, notably the Netherlands, Poland and Belgium, continues to be the main centre of clandestine amphetamine production. Seizures of amphetamine in West Europe peaked around 1998 and have shown a downward trend since, but production and trafficking continued to increase in East Europe. This could signal an underlying shift of amphetamine production to East Europe, and possibly a less buoyant demand in West Europe. While half of all West European countries reported an increase in amphetamine abuse in 2000, this proportion fell somewhat, to 33%, in 2001.

Trafficking in ecstasy increased strongly throughout the 1990s. In 2001, however, ecstasy seizures declined, mainly in North America and West Europe. Europe (particularly the Netherlands and Belgium) is still the main centre of global ecstasy production. However, its relative importance seems to be declining as ecstasy production is appearing in other parts of the world. In the mid-1990s, West European countries reported around 80% of all ecstasy seizures. This proportion fell to around 50% in 2000 and 2001.

Trafficking in ecstasy has increased particularly in the Americas in recent years, though it is now found in other regions as well, notably in South-East Asia, Southern Africa and the Near and Middle East. Ecstasy abuse, after a period of decline, has again shown signs of increase in West Europe. In the USA it declined, for the first time in years, in 2002. In other regions, particularly the Caribbean and parts of South America, Oceania, South-East Asia, the Near East, and southern Africa, it seems to be accelerating.

Production, Trafficking and Consumption

Opium / Heroin

After the steep decline recorded in 2001, world illicit opium and heroin production recovered in 2002, despite a reduction of cultivation by 23% in Myanmar and 18% in Laos. This increase was due to the resumption of large-scale opium poppy cultivation in Afghanistan. Global illicit opium poppy cultivation climbed back to about 180,000 hectares in 2002 (against 144,000 ha in 2001 and 222,000 ha in 2000). The resulting opium production was estimated at about 4,500 metric tons (against 1,600 mt in 2001 and 4,700 mt in 2000).

In 2002, the relative distribution of illicit opium production among the main source countries was: Afghanistan (76%), Myanmar (18%), Laos (2%) and Colombia (1%). The remaining 3% came from other countries (Mexico, Pakistan, Thailand, Vietnam, etc.) where marginal production is reported.

Cocaine

For the second year in a row, illicit coca cultivation declined in Colombia. The 30% reduction recorded between November 2001 (145,000 ha) and December 2002 (102,000 ha) translated into an 18% decline in world illicit coca cultivation (from 211,000 ha in 2001, to 173,000 ha at the end of 2002). Peru.s illicit coca cultivation remained relatively stable during the year (52,500 ha in 2002). In Bolivia, where cultivation had recorded a continuous decline between 1996 (48,100 ha) and 2000 (14,600 ha), cultivation increased for the second year in a row (by 23% to 24,400 ha in 2002). The relative distribution of potential cocaine production among the three countries in 2002 was estimated as follows: Colombia 72%, Peru 20% and Bolivia 8%.

Cannabis and ATS

The lack of adequate data does not enable UNODC to precisely monitor trends in cannabis and synthetic drug production from year to year. However, indirect indicators suggest that global production of cannabis and amphetamine-type stimulants continued to increase in recent years, although regional variations could be observed.

Trafficking

Overall trafficking, as reflected in the number of seizure cases reported, continued growing in 2001, though at a slower pace than in the 1990s.

Cannabis

The largest quantities seized worldwide were of cannabis herb, followed by cannabis resin. Seized quantities of cannabis remained stable in 2001. The largest cannabis herb seizures in 2001 were reported from Mexico; the largest cannabis resin seizures were made by Spain.

Cocaine

The third largest quantities of drugs seized worldwide were of cocaine. They remained more or less stable in 2001. The largest cocaine seizures were reported from the USA, followed by Colombia.

Opiates

Overall, seizures of opiates declined by 23% in 2001. The decline is attributed to the considerable decline of opium production in Afghanistan that year. Most opiate seizures (opium, morphine and heroin) continued to be made by the Islamic Republic of Iran. The largest seizures of heroin, however, were reported from the People.s Republic of China in 2001.

Amphetamine-type stimulants (excl. Ecstasy)

Following years of massive growth, seizures of amphetamine-type stimulants (excluding ecstasy) fell in 2001 by 36%. This decline was mainly due to lower methamphetamine seizures reported by China, which in recent years accounted for the bulk of such seizures. Nonetheless, global ATS seizures (excluding ecstasy) were still four times as high as in 1995 and eight times as high as in 1990. The largest ATS seizures in 2001 were reported from Thailand.

Ecstasy

Ecstasy seizures fell by around 10% in 2001. Declines were recorded in a number of major markets, including the USA, Canada, Netherlands, France and Italy. The largest ecstasy seizures were reported from the Netherlands, followed by the United States.

Consumption

UNODC estimates that about 200 million people consume illicit drugs. The main problem drugs in the world, as reflected in demand for treatment, remained the opiates, followed by cocaine. In much of East and South-East Asia, ATS are the main problem drugs. In Africa, treatment demand continues to be concentrated on cannabis.

Opium / Heroin

Heroin abuse declined in East Asia, Oceania and West Europe in 2001, but continued to increase in the countries located on the Afghan heroin trafficking route towards Russia and Europe.

Cocaine

Cocaine abuse continued to increase in West Europe and in South America, while it was stable in North America and fell among US high-school students in 2001.

Amphetamine-type stimulants

The methamphetamine epidemic appears to be continuing in South East Asia, while abuse has stabilized in Japan. Amphetamine abuse stabilized in West Europe, but continued to increase in East and North Europe.

Ecstasy

Most countries reporting on Ecstasy saw increasing levels of abuse.

Cannabis

Cannabis abuse increased in Africa, South America, Europe and South West Asia. Declines were recorded in Oceania and South East Asia.

7

Organised Crime and Terrorism

Terrorism and transnational crime are now central threats to our national and international security. Yet more needs to be understood about the links between these two phenomena. Many illustrations of the crime and terrorism link in Western Europe and the United States have appeared in the mass media. Illustrations of the links between organised crime and terrorism are the following:

1) Terrorists engage in organised crime activity to support themselves financially

2) Organised crime groups and terrorists often operate on network structures and these structures sometimes intersect, terrorists can hide themselves among transnational criminal organisations

3) Both organised crime group and terrorists operate in areas with little governmental controls, weak enforcement of laws and open borders

4) Both organised criminals and terrorists corrupt local officials to achieve their objectives

5) Organised crime groups and terrorists often use similar means to communicate-exploiting modern technology

6) Organised crime and terrorists launder their money, often using the same methods and often the same operators to move their funds

Each of the points above will be illustrated with examples from the Pacific Region. The particular areas where these links will occur are in areas with weak controls and little effective political authority:

— Russian Far East

— Southern Phillipines

— Sri Lanka

— Golden Triangle

— Parts of Indonesia

The increasing share of the world economy attributable to illicit activity provides the financial resources for transnational crime groups to operate and hire expertise. The source of the illicit capital in the Pacific region are such illicit commodities as drugs, human beings smuggled and trafficked, small arms and valuable natural resources such as timber. A particular feature of organised crime in the Pacific region is piracy, some of it linked to the maritime transport of high technology. This is proving increasingly profitable for the organised crime groups. Counterfeiting of goods, dollars and CDs and other electronic equipment is a major financial problem for organised crime. This is not exclusively an organised crime problem as North Koreans are involved in the massive counterfeiting of dollars. The nexus of drug crime and terrorism widely recognized in Colombia (FARC) and in the Balkans (KLA) is highly prevalent in Asia.

The most notable examples of this are in Afghanistan (Taliban and Al Qaeda) and Sri Lanka (Tamil Tigers) but the linkages also exist in the Northern region of the Pacific Rim among the North Koreans, the Russians and other organised crime groups operating in the region. Many of these groups are involved in more aspects of the drug trade than just cultivation but help transport and even distribute drugs closer to the main markets. The blending of the legitimate and the illegitimate characterizes the financing of their operations.

The resources of the terrorists or the profits of transnational crime groups are combined with legitimate funds making it hard to detect where the criminal ends and the legitimate funds begins. For example, in the Bank of New York Case, millions of funds emanating from criminal activity were combined with legitimate accounts of corresponding banks in Russia. Al Qaeda uses charities to move money. Some of the charities funds are directed towards social welfare activities in the community whereas a tithe or more is used to support terrorists.

Transnational crime groups often operate on a network structure. The network structure is not unique to this group but characterizes many other terrorist groups and many of the new transnational organised crime groups. Unlike the top-down- hierarchical structure of a mafia-type organisation, newer organised crime groups such as Russian-speaking groups and terrorist groups such as the Al Qaeda function as networks. It gives organisational flexibility, reduces the possib ility of penetration and provides greater efficiency. These structures make it more difficult to identify leaders.

The newer criminal groups and leading terrorist organisations resemble more modern legitimate business structures than the older corporations like Ford and the steel industry. Organised crime group networks are often of the same nationality, though they form alliances with other crime groups to conduct their activities. In contrast, the networks of groups such as Al Qaeda are themselves transnational. They can unite individuals from the Middle East with those in the Far East. Likewise, the organised crime groups from the Russian Far East work with North and South Koreans, Japanese, Chinese and Vietnamese among others. The networks are not affiliated with any particular state. They are non-state actors striking at the citizens of a state, states or different states.

Organised crime groups and terrorists function where the controls of the central state are least, where there are porous borders and weak law enforcement. In areas with weak controls, transnational crime groups operate. Others provide the home base for terrorist groups. In some, a cooperative or/even symbiotic relationship exists between the crime group and the terrorist group operating within the region. The Russian Far East has become a central locale for the operation of organised crime and terrorists because it is far from the central controls of Moscow and the governmental and law enforcement structures are heavily infiltrated by organised crime.The same absence of controls characterizes the area adjoining the Golden Triangle.

The terrorist groups of Myanmar can support themselves by the drug trade and can operate with impunity near Southern China, Laos and to a lesser extent Northern Thailand. The Southern part of the Philippines remains outside of central state control. Likewise, the Fukian province in China from which so much human trafficking originates is an area outside the control of the Chinese central government where complicit officials allow the crime groups to operate. Indonesia, in the post-Suharto period, has lost the central controls of the previous period. The lack of state control, the weak and ineffective law enforcement and the multi- national nature of the society makes it possible for terrorist groups to operate in parts of the country. Furthermore, while significant transnational crime groups are not yet institutionalized, there are increasingly visible organised violent groups.

Organised crime and terrorist groups are dependent on officials who can be corrupted or look the other way. The bossism of the local political bosses in the Philippines, the corruption of cadres in the Chinese Communist Party, the pervasive corruption of the Soviet political system and the now infamous corruption of the Suharto government have provided a fertile ground for these crime groups to operate. In the Philippines, prostitution, smuggling and protection rackets of crime groups have been tolerated by the authorities, often because they take their local cut.In Thailand, the police derive a significant amount of their income from the pervasive prostitution. Pay-offs to the police are a central part of the operations of the crime bosses.This endemic corruption means that there has been no curb on the growth of organised crime.

In the Far East of Russia and in China, strong crime groups, with links to the surviving Communist power structure have stepped in to fill the power vacuum and now operate on a global scale. Members of the security apparatus, the FSB, in Russia and in Public Security Bureau of China are involved. In China, as in Russia, the collusion of government officials is central to the capacity of smugglers to operate. Crime groups also work with corrupt officials in other countries and cooperate with international crime groups as necessary. The trade in human beings from both countries owes much to the legacy of corrupted Party power structures.

Money Laundering

Money laundering is a central part of organised crime activity in the Pacific Rim as well as elsewhere in the world. The problems of investigating this activity are particularly severe because of the widespread use of underground banking systems in the region such as hawala in the communities of the Asian sub continent and the gold exchanges of the Chinese community. Russian organised crime in the region has developed enormous varieties in the ways that it launders money. The absence of regulation of it its banking system has provided fertile ground for money laundering. Furthermore, the absence of controls in Japan over the banking system and the collusion between the banks and organised crime have aggravated this problem. The possibility of moving illicit funds so easily in the region promotes the ability of transnational criminals and terrorists to operate. Furthermore, it allows the funds of both these groups to commingle with facility.

Transnational Organised Crime

Terrorism is considered a form of transnational organised crime, indeed, the most visible and openly aggressive form of such activities which include illicit trafficking in arms, drugs, and people; money laundering; hijacking; bribery and corruption; and pirating of intellectual properties. Distinctions that are made between the two global bads often focus on motivation-transnational organised crime is viewed as having as its primary purpose the pursuit of financial gain or profit while transnational terrorists act out of some kind of political/religious/ethnic motivation. But, then, what about narco-terrorism and ransommotivated hostage-taking which serve as sources of funding for a large number of terrorist organisations?

Consider the example of the FARC in Colombia which currently survives thanks to funding received from the drug cartels in exchange for protection. And what about the exchange of drugs for weapons that is a common enterprise on the so-called Balkan Route involving the Kosovo Liberation Army and the Kurdistan Workers Party and Italian criminal groups as well as the intercepts of elements necessary for nuclear weapons moving across the porous and highly corrupt borders between Russia and the former Soviet republics? "The once clear lines between the international drug trade, terrorism, and organised crime are blurring, crossing, and mutating as never before".

In many respects, transnational organised crime has become the lifeblood for terrorist groups and networks. "There is no region of the world without criminal organisations operating on its territory. Even the most remote islands of the world now host transnational organised crime because many of these places provide the safe havens and offshore banking systems that allow organised crime to thrive". And just like the so-called "modern" terrorist networks, these criminal organisations have begun to evolve from hierarchical structures with a small cadre of leaders at the top to more network-based groups whose functions and activities are more dispersed. They possess "leadership structures that are more difficult to identify and target with a decapitation attack". Moreover, they have moved to using violence more discriminately and more symbolically as well as have demonstrated an increasing interest in gaining specialized military weaponry and advanced intelligence gathering devices.

The evolution from the Medellin to Calli models for a drug cartel in Colombia is a case in point. Consider also the eight to ten thousand Russian criminal gangs ranging from 10 to 50 members that are networked and function transnationally and the 500 small Nigerian crime cells that operate across the globe. These networked transnational criminal organisations "employ specialists, farm out work, and are vertically rather than horizontally integrated". Transnational criminal and terrorist organisations come together in what some have called "criminal enclaves" and others "black spots". These are areas which are characterized by weak state structures and high levels of corruption providing a lawless and relatively sovereignty-free environment; they are generally in the vicinity of an international border or borders so that individuals can move easily across jurisdictions.

Generally these areas float under the radar of the international community while being uncontrollable or untouchable by the governments in whose territory they reside. One such black spot is the area around the Pakistani city of Peshawar. It is located on the "frontier" with Afghanistan and proximate to the federally administered tribal areas which are quite literally beyond the control of the Pakistani government. This is the region which has been repeatedly described as the hiding place for fleeing or regrouping Al Qaeda and Taliban operatives; the area is also a smuggling center where almost anything can be bought or sold on the black market.

Another such spot is the area around the Paraguayan city of Ciudad del Este where the borders of Argentina, Paraguay, and Brazil come together. This Tri-Border Area, as it is often called, is a place where "terrorism interlocks with organised crime... in a postmodern free city that is a haven to Middle Eastern terrorists, a hub for European and US drug trade, a center for compact disc, video, and software piracy, and a base for gunrunners diverting US weapons" to various arenas around the world.

There are more than 100 landing strips scattered around the Tri-Border Area-none of them regulated by any authority and all in constant use by small planes-and the presence of a similar number of formal and informal banks. Indeed, Ciudad provides a "safe haven" and meeting place for members of transnational criminal and terrorist organisations, a training ground, a refuge and hiding place, a base of operations, and a place for the development and strengthening of command and control operations. Thus, for example, Hezbollah is known to have based their operatives in the Tri-Border region while planning and carrying out the 1992 bombing of the Israeli embassy in Argentina and the 1994 bombing of a Buenos Aires Jewish community center.

In January 1999, the Uruguayan authorities arrested the Egyptian terrorist, El Said Hassan Ali Mohamed Mukhlis, a suspect in the 1997 killings at Luxor and with knowledge about the bombings of the US embassies in Kenya and Uganda, when he emerged from his hideout in Ciudad del Este. Some other known black spots in the world beside the two mentioned above are the Darien jungle on the border between Colombia and Panama, the Chiquibil Reserve cutting across Belize and Guatemala, the Akwesasne Mohawk Territory that crosses the border between the US and Canada, the Bekka Valley in Lebanon, the Pankisi Gorge between Georgia and Chechnya, and the Fergana Valley in Uzbekistan.

Globalization, the rise in free trade, the increasing movement of people, and the declining sanctity of borders provide the opportunity for more such enclaves. Consider, for example, how NAFTA, the Schengen Agreement among countries of the EU, MERCOSUR in the Southern Cone of Latin America have increased the ease with which not only people and trade cross borders but the ease with which transnational criminals and terrorists can penetrate both the trade and borders. Such capabilities may increase the creation of such sanctuaries.

In addition to the links between transnational terrorists and criminals are the links that transnational organised crime foster with politicians, police, and the military. In less developed countries and in transitional societies, this linkage may become quite lucrative for both the criminals and terrorists. Such a political-criminal nexus of power "exists in many Soviet successor states, Nigeria, Southern China, Japan, Colombia, Mexico, and Italy". If high-ranking military officers, for example, are corrupt, they may provide weapons or the elements needed to produce chemical, biological, radiological, or nuclear weapons to transnational criminal organisations that, for a price, will trade them to terrorist groups. This relationship seems of particular concern with regard to the links between Russia's transnational criminal organisations and its underpaid military personnel.

As an illustration, recall in late 2000 the discovery by Colombian police of a partially assembled Russian submarine in a warehouse in Bogota. The submarine was intended as a means of transportation for up to 10 metric tons of illicit drugs. Although links with terrorist organisations have not been proven, this incident raises the possibility of a terrorist organisation acquiring a single submarine for a potential terrorist attack. And then there are the attempted thefts of 4.5 kilograms of highly enriched uranium from the naval shipyard in Murmansk, Russia, reported in the press in late 1994 and General Alexander Lebed's letter to the US Congress in 1997 warning about missing Russian suitcase-size nuclear bombs. The issue here may be one of supply and demand.

Where are the components for such weapons accessible, which groups can hire or have the requisite skills to assemble such weapons, and who can pay what is required to offset the risks involved in acquiring these components? Russia and the former Soviet states are certainly one area where there is a volume of un-safeguarded fissile material available. The border controls along the Russian border with these other states remain unsatisfactory and corruption levels are quite high. Moreover, we observed above a number of so-called black spots in this area. These conditions make it possible for transnational terrorist and rebel groups in South Asia, particularly those like Al Qaeda that are intent on achieving high levels of destruction and martyrdom, to consider seeking such weapons.

But given the money that would probably be necessary for such a venture, a cost-benefit assessment might lead the organisations to decide it is better to talk about having the capability and act as if one did rather than to go about actually acquiring it. What seems more likely is the creation of a "dirty bomb" with the components that are more accessible and less expensive in combination with an improvised explosive device to increase the terror effect and the "theater" surrounding an incident. Here is where the black spots or criminal enclaves may become particularly useful in providing relatively protected places where such devices can be developed and where people with the skills needed may already reside. It is important to recall that as both transnational criminal and terrorist organisations have evolved into networks, they have become more subtle in their use of violence.

There is evidence that engaging in psychological disruption, information operations, and perception management has grown in importance. Networks provide flexibility, adaptability, deniability, multidimensionality, and the capacity to do things at a distance, often through surrogates. Satellite communications, the internet, and the Web have become indispensable for "keeping in touch," coordinating actions, and engaging in threats and disruptive activities. Although it is important to engage in destructive, violent activities periodically to insure one's credibility, such actions can be used to create an environment of terror and fear to be played upon through the management of information. Thus, having chemical, biological, or nuclear weapons may not be as important as leading others to believe one does. Governments typically perceive world reality through the lens of national borders.

Transnational criminal and terrorist entities are rarely limited by such jurisdictional boundaries and use them mainly to avoid the legal reach of a particular country.

Thus, national responses by themselves to such transnational organisations are usually ineffective in the absence of broader international cooperation. Moreover, these organisations often locate their bases in places like the black spots that are, in effect, sovereignty-free or in countries that are themselves adversaries and unlikely to cooperate. The networked and linked nature of these transnational criminal and terrorist organisations also causes problems for governments. "Squeezing the balloon" in hopes of eliminating these organisations in one place often leads them to pop up in another.

Consider the US war on drugs in Colombia that has led to the increased production of coca in the surrounding Andean countries. Or, the US government forcing Osama bin Laden and Al Qaeda out of the Sudan only to see them relocate in Afghanistan. The leadership of Hamas has the ability to change as one is killed by the Israeli Defense Forces since others are in Syria and in places like the Tri-Border Area. At issue is does it take a network to "fight" a network? Because governments tend to be organised hierarchically and into bureaucracies with different functions and foci, cooperation among agencies is made more difficult. Sharing of information becomes harder. In the US, the Department of Homeland Security was formed in order to break down these barriers. Should it be encouraged to function more as a network, developing new techniques for interagency and cross-jurisdictional cooperation and adopting the flexibility of a network so that individuals and units can move easily to support one another?

Louise Shelley and her TraCCC enterprise have begun to map the criminal organisations in Russia and the former Soviet states including Central and Eastern Europe. The US State Department has done the same for a large number of terrorist organisations. What do we know about the linkages among these various organisations; can we gain information by examining locations and activities? It would seem possible from something like the Monterey WMD Terrorism Database to link incidents to particular locations and organisations. In other words, could we create something like a Geographic Information System (GIS) database that maps organisations and their movements transnationally?

Such systems provide the possibility of doing overlays to show how incidents interact with location and organisation, to indicate where we know the component parts for WMD are located, and to engage in "what if" scenarios to examine what happens when certain types of components "disappear." Who might have access, what known smuggling routes are nearby, what organisations have been known to use such components, etc.? Structured comparative case studies could also prove useful in helping us learn about the "blurring of lines" between criminal and terrorist organisations. Such case studies compare cases that are similar and different on specific types of characteristics and ask similar questions of the cases in order to make the comparison more systematic.

For example, what about comparing several transnational organisations that move worldwide with some that function within a particular region; comparing several organisations that have engaged in a wide range of different types of criminal activities with those that tend to emphasize one type of activity; comparing some organisations that emphasize the use of violence over other types of behavior versus those that emphasize criminal behavior over the use of violence; or comparing organisations that have engaged in a CRBN incident with those that have not. The particular questions that are asked of the cases are developed to cover the various factors we have identified as being important theoretically. The information, though initially qualitative in nature, can often be transformed into nominal and ordinal quantitative data by categorizing the responses to the questions asked of the cases.

CYBERCRIME

The phenomena of transnational crime, terrorism and corruption are all too often viewed as separate phenomena. These phenomena have grown in tandem because the economic and political conditions that give rise to these phenomena are quite similar. The evolution of the transnational crime-ideologically based or economically based depends on specific environmental factors that have proliferated in many developing and transitional countries that have not successfully integrated into the global Economy. Terrorists and transnational criminals use many of the same strategies to promote their operations, chief among these being the use of information technology to plan and realize their activities. The rise of greater international mobility and the proliferation of information technology throughout the world have facilitated the growth of both transnational crime and terrorism.

The ease of communications in the contemporary era makes the location of groups and actors less significant than it was previously. The ability to exploit security holes in the system makes crime groups and terrorists operate out of unexpected locales rather than their home territories. Most transnational crime and terrorist groups are based in transitional and developing countries. The illicit businesses are now the largest and most profitable to be located in the developing world. For example, the drug trade now represents about 7% of world trade according to late 1990s estimates of the United Nations. Their vast profits and enormous assets make them powerful actors in their home countries and in their regions. Because they are so large relative to the legitimate businesses based in their region or in the countries through which they operate, they have a large influence on politics and business.

The vast profits of illegal businesses allow them to hire the best specialists domestically and internationally. Facilitating this trade, is an ever greater reliance on information technology to promote their activities secretly. For example, international drug traffickers are among the most widespread users of encrypted messages, coded messages by cell and satellite phones and use anonymizer features on computers. They also are able to hire technical specialists capable of using steganography and other means to make messages hard or impossible to decipher. This access to high level specialists allows illicit businesses and terrorist organisations to transcend borders and operate internationally without detection.

Often the crime and terrorist groups do not need to go outside their region to hire such technical specialists. Some of the leading specialists in the technical area are located in regions that house major transnational crime groups and terrorist organisations. The presence of many highly trained technical specialists in the countries of the former Soviet Union and in the Indian subcontinent means that transnational crime groups means that a vast array of specialists are available for hire. While some specialists will not work for criminal or terrorist organisations willingly, some will do it unaware of their employers whereas others will agree to provide assistance because well-paid legitimate employment is scarce in their region. The widespread problem of corruption in many developing countries allows the proliferation of transnational organised crime and terrorism.

The official corruption facilitating this activity may assume many different forms and is not just based on bribery. Top government officials provide falsified documents to smuggled criminals and terrorists, restrain law enforcement from acting against suspicious groups and provide them a safe space to operate. Because of this, criminals can use the high level technology available in the former Soviet Union and the Punjab region to facilitate not only their own crime and terrorist groups but those of other regions of the world which find save haven on their territory. In this way criminals exploit information technology to carry on their operations in a safe and secure manner.

The connections between transnational crime and terrorism are not unique to developed and developing countries. As investigations in the advent of September, 11th have shown, terrorists in developed countries use criminal activity to survive. Arrests in Spain revealed that terrorists were selling counterfeit airline tickets to survive and such groups in the United States were surviving by means of money laundering and other criminal offenses.

Influence of Information Technology

Terrorists, like transnational organised crime, exploit information technology to maximize the effectiveness of their operations. They use cellular and satellite telephones, the Internet, email and chat rooms. They code their messages through encryption and steganography (hiding messages within other messages). They exploit the anonymyzer features of the Internet to evade detection. The Internet is a tool for perpetration of their crimes. Whereas, organised criminals run gambling on the Internet, terrorists solicit funds through websites for charities that fund terrorist groups. International fund movements are facilitated by information technology. Instructions for money transfers through the financial centers of the legitimate global economy are made through the phone and Internet. Yet, the underground banking system of hawala (the banking of the Indian subcontinent) is even more dependent on rapid and secure transmissions of information by phone and web.

Drug traffickers use encrypted messages to direct their operations. Terrorists use the anonymizer feature of computers to coordinate their activities across countries. Websites facilitating all forms of transnational crime, for example dissemination of child pornography or recruitment sites for terrorist organisations, are often posted in developing countries without the law enforcement capacity to bring down these sites. Furthermore, law enforcement in these developed countries cannot hire or retain the personnel needed to combat the criminal activity of transnational crime groups. The low salaries and the corruption of law enforcement means that individuals with highly developed technical skills cannot find desirable employment in the state sector.

Computer experts in developing countries choose not to work for low law enforcement salaries, instead they work for the private sector and others will work consciously or unknowingly for criminal and terrorist groups. In some countries, even if the state paid adequate wages, the state law enforcement sector may not be a legitimate alternative to the criminal sector. The institutionalized corruption of much of law enforcement and its close links with the criminal sector in some regions of the world means that the criminals can pay for specialists within and outside the government. In the developed countries, there is a shortage of personnel with adequate IT skills. Many of those who work in the high technology sector in Europe and the United States are immigrants from less developed countries and are not able to serve law enforcement in the countries in which they reside.

Moreover, law enforcement has not been able to compete with the private sector in terms of the pay it offers or the promotional options which it provides to make it an employer of choice to talented IT specialists. Criminals have been very successful in exploiting the international inconsistencies in the system and the failure to regulate technology across jurisdictions. As the love virus from the Philippines illustrates, there are limits on sanctioning offenders whose crimes are extremely costly to society because individual countries have not enacted legislation. While the perpetrator of the love virus did not intentionally cause the harm to computer systems around the world, individuals who intend to cause serious harm exploit the environments in which there is little regulation of computers and little law enforcement capacity to act against this crime.

One website containing child pornography was posted on a website indicating that it was located in a Central Asian country. Over four million individuals downloaded images from the site before it was brought down. The reason being is that there were an absence of computer specialists in that country to take down the website. The lack of coordinated legislation has been exploited not only by criminals but by terrorists as well. The hijackers of the September, 11th planes were aware that their phones and cell phones might be tapped. Before post-September, 11th legislative changes, separate warrants were needed to tap each phones in the three jurisdictions of the Washington area-Virginia, Maryland and the District of Columbia.

The terrorists exploited this knowledge of the limits of law enforcement and used different phones in these different jurisdictions to prevent monitoring of their conversations. Just as the future terrorists exploited jurisdictional differences in the Washington metropolitan area to reduce risk, they also did the same internationally. Much of the plotting for the September, 11th attack was carried out in Germany that has the greatest limits on undercover activity.

With its protections on the right to privacy and its limitations on police powers, a legacy of the abuses of the

Nazi era, terrorists could use the advance telecommunications networks to their advantage without detection. Intelligence and analysis by the terrorist cells helped ensure the ultimate security of operations with access to the most sophisticated information technology. The merger of transnational organised crime with terrorism is seen on a regular basis. Terrorists use criminal activity to support their operations.

The growth of information technology facilitates terrorists' attempts to gain significant profits with relatively low risk. Terrorists can finance their operations without resorting to violent assaults or bank robberies that would raise the risk of detection. Criminal activity committed internationally via the Internet supports terrorist activity as they can tap into credit card bases and commit various forms of lucrative fraud. Ukrainian specialists at a TraCCC conference in 2000 reported that their country is the source of many financial crimes committed by computer and the Internet. But while Ukraine may be the source country for much of this criminality, it is not now clear that only Ukrainians are committing this crime.

There are many foreigners using the computer resources of Ukraine and they may be also contributing to this economic crime because they have identified this country as one with limited capacity to act against this crime. By means of corruption, they are able to obtain the right to reside and operate within the country. Countries with high capacity in information technology and low capacity to act against crime committed using computers and telecommunications become havens for transnational crime and terrorism. The concept of a safe haven acquires a different concept when the weapon is not a conventional one but a piece of information technology which allows plotting, financing and possibly even executing a serious crime.

Before the advent of widespread information technology, the pace of international communications and transactions was slower. Secure measures of communications required trusted carriers, funds could be moved only slowly and planning across borders was slow and laborious. In the age of information technology, messages can be transmitted instantly without leaving a trace, massive wire fund transfers can occur across multiple jurisdictions in an hour and international plotting can occur within chat rooms and protected communications within a computer system. There has been a movement of money to areas where regulation is less.

Even traditional systems of underground banking such as hawala or Chinese underground banking have been revolutionalized by the ability to provide almost instantaneous instructions on the delivery of funds. The criminal and terrorist exploitation of information technology has proceeded in tandem with its growth by the legitimate multinational community. In fact there is evidence that those who seek to promote illicit ends have been as fast if not faster to introduce this technology into their operations. The possibilities of introducing technology rapidly into transnational crime groups and terrorist organisations exists because the most modern organised crime groups and terrorist cells are organised as networks.

Unlike the traditional mafia structure or the traditional top down corporation that react slowly to innovation, these new transnational criminal actors enjoy enormous flexibility. They have high level technical specialists within their organisations or employ the top specialists. Both terrorists and transnational criminal organisations such as Colombian drug traffickers or Russian-speaking organised crime have used the full variety of information technology to achieve their desired results. This includes cell phones, satellite phones, computers, and virtual private networks. The latter are particularly valuable for undetected international operations.

Anonymity increases the difficulty of decoding encrypted messages. Both encryption and anonymizers are increasingly used by transnational crime groups. Once encrypted messages represented a very small share of the communications of transnational crime groups. But the use and the sophistication of the encryption have been increasingly exponentially. Therefore, increasingly messages are staying outside the capacity of law enforcement and the intelligence community to decipher. With the enhanced information gathering in the contemporary era, which law enforcement and intelligence cannot digest, those messages which are encrypted have even less chance of being incorporated into the analysis needed to address these groups.

Private safe, secure and rapid communications are key to the spread of organised and ideologically motivated transnational crime. The anonymity offered by computers in internet cafes and computer services allows criminal groups in many parts of the world to interact. Investigators found that terrorists in the United States used computers as Kinko's, a computer and copy store, to conduct their businesses. In other countries, millions have access to Internet through anonymous computers that sell their services by the hour. Without knowing the identity of those who use the computers and using constantly changing on-line addresses, messages are not traceable.

Instant messenger provide the possibility of on-going interactive communication without leaving a trace that investigators can follow. Information technology facilitates many aspects of the operation's of transnational crime groups and terrorists from their financing, to the documents that they need for their operations. The transnational illicit actors are able to produce fraudulent documents on the computer to provide them new identities, covers and to provide a paper trail which covers their operations. Human smugglers produce high-quality false identity papers for those who need new identities. These computer-produced documents may be of such high quality that their fraudulent nature is not discernable to even sophisticated law enforcement.

Computer systems help finance criminal and terrorist operations. The revolution in information technology has facilitated covert banking, more efficient underground banking, electronic fund transfers, and the use of debit and credit cards. Piracy and counterfeiting of goods, facilitated by information technology, is an important financial source for criminal groups. This is particularly true in the software area and other areas involving intellectual property. Criminals and terrorists can commit fraud on the Internet, can solicit banking information from gullible citizens, tap into insufficiently protected banks of credit card information or even tap into the online orders of some mail-order businesses. These are not hypotheticals but examples of the kind of financial activity used by these groups already detected by international law enforcers. The logistics of transnational crime groups and terrorists are aided by information technology.

The Internet aids the transport, tracking, monitoring and diversion of shipments. Part of the reason that drug traffickers can respond quickly to law enforcement crackdowns is that they monitor their shipments through elaborate computer systems. Identifying points of vulnerability, they are able to rapidly reroute their shipments to reduce the risk of intervention. Combing analysis with sophisticated computer programs, Colombian drug traffickers ensure that over sixty to seventy percent of drugs shipped enter the United States successfully. Less covert means can be used by terrorist organisations that use the worldwide web to recruit and fund raise.

Therefore, they can reach a broad audience in many regions of the world. Those who are the most likely recruits for terrorist organisations are youthful males who are also the individuals in their countries most likely to have access to computers and the Internet. Therefore, investment in information technology provides a very valuable marketing tool to reach the most receptive audience.

Domestic and International Problems

Many of the problems that impede transnational crime and terrorist investigations have already been cited. But examining them together reveals the fundamental challenges which exist in this age in which there are such discrepancies available to investigators and intelligence in the developed and developing and transitional worlds. Furthermore, the fact that the transnational groups have been among those to take most advantage of the globalized information system, highlights the very serious problems that exist in a world where laws are state-based and criminals and terrorists operate across many states simultaneously to carry out their activities. The presence of so much of the information technology system in private hands and the presence of control over this system lying in state hands provides very serious impediments to regulation and control.

The concept of public-private partnerships which exists in the United States is not an internationally recognized concept. It works haltingly in the United States and often proceeds only as an alternative to state intervention in the operations of Internet service providers (ISPs). Cooperation with law enforcement in pursuing purveyors of child pornography on the Internet is a preferential alternative for many ISPs rather than search warrants being issued to have access to their data bank.

Much tracking of crime committed over the Internet can be done by American law enforcement because so much Internet traffic is routed through the United States. But in traffic that does not pass through the U.S., the situation is more difficult.

Different legal codes and procedures impede cooperation on the international levels. Many countries lack needed laws to address computer crime and crimes committed by means of information technology. Compounding the problem is that the global information infrastructure is outside the jurisdiction of anyone country. Criminals and terrorists, as previously mentioned, exploit the weaknesses in laws and law enforcement capacity to execute their crimes. These are not casual decisions on how top operate effectively by computers but are instead based on calculations and careful training and analysis. The potential of the Internet is realized not only by the telecommunications industry but also by those who seek to foster their crimes and terrorist acts in effective ways.

Future Trends

Over the past years there has been a rise in the use of existing forms of carrying out covert operations by means of information technology. These include ever greater use of encryption, money transfer facilitated by computer system and increasing fraud over the internet. With the retention by top information technology specialists by transnational crime groups and terrorists, we can expect to see new and innovative uses of information technology by these groups. Of greatest concern to many governments and international financial systems is the possibility of serious intrusions into critical systems. These intrusions could include the introduction of viruses that would destroy critical data, the posting of harmful websites that cannot be brought down and even the full scale incapacitation of critical computer systems.

The disruption of international financial markets remains a serious concern. The present interdependence of the world's economic system means that a disruption in one region of the world will have ripple effects in other regions. The constant monitoring of stock, bond and commodity markets by financial analysts world wide means that an intrusion and/or disruption of these systems would not go unnoticed. It would send shock waves outside of the market which is the source of the problem. Money laundering is increasing with the amount of money outside regulated markets growing. This is a result of the growth of the illicit global economy that is supported by the profusion of offshore havens.

The proliferation of information technology increases the possibility of moving money covertly outside of any system of regulated banking. Therefore, the recent crackdowns on the banking sector and The Patriot Act, which has ripple effects in international financial markets, means that illicit and terrorist money may increasingly be pushed outside the regulatory system. Movement of money through tangible commodities, businesses and hawala like currency transfers may be ever more possible because of the monitoring and facilitation of computer systems.

One distinct concern is that there will be more successful mergers and/or cooperation between organised criminal and terrorists in the information technology area. Cooperation between organised criminals and terrorists exists in Latin America, Europe, Asia and other regions of the world. Information technology expertise may be commissioned by one type of transnational criminal group and then subsequently exploited by another either for mutual advantage or as a business proposition.

Already there is enhanced exploitation of areas with sophisticated information technology and corrupt officials and corrupted and incapable law enforcement. This means, for example, that members of terrorist organisations can pay corrupt officials to obtain residence permits in a region where there is a high level of IT capacity. Then they can use the Internet resources or even finance their IT outlets and market them as public facilities. Incompetent law enforcement will not think to look at public Internet outlets as havens for terrorists.

If they were to detect such a phenomena, they could be bribed to look the other way. In this way terrorists have secured a safe physical space but also a safe space in which to run their operations. Enhanced mobilization and recruitment for terrorism by the Internet is an existing concern. This mobilization can be of funds and people. By using steganography, disclosing secret messages within other messages or pictures, communications can be made secretly to a large number of people. Without the linguistic capacity or the intelligence capacity to intervene in these groups, technology can be used to ever greater advantage.

Legitimate civil liberties concerns in many countries may curtail or limit monitoring of information technology. Because most information technology is controlled by the private sector, it is their primary concern to protect their customers rather than to counter transnational crime or terrorism. As cooperative as information technology companies may be, once a risk is defined, their initial interests are to make a profit rather than to prevent a crime or a terrorist act. The constitutional protections existing in countries which now enjoy information technology dominance place a premium on the privacy and rights of citizens. Therefore, the possibilities for information gathering are limited.

Tools to Respond

A strong dichotomy exists between the way states and multinational organisations respond to transnational crime and terrorism generally, and the particular threat posed by cybercrime committed by these groups. Because information technology is primarily in the private sector, public private partnerships are needed to locate abuse of the Internet by transnational criminals. This may include network monitoring by private corporations to detect suspicious websites or usage patterns. The development of international teams of computer specialists incorporating information technology specialists from developing countries with advanced computer skills to work in cooperative ways to monitor transnational crime and terrorism.

International cooperation in a mutual process of information sharing is a key response to the problem. There is a need to develop and support international security research teams with specialists from both developed and developing countries. There are a need for partnership relationships in which both parts of the team believe that it is in their interests to respond to any manifestations of transnational crime and terrorism that are evident through investigations of cybercrime. This may include a system of rewards that provide multinational incentives rather than those which are based on the country in which the investigation may occur.

The rewards may be too low for the investigators and the chance of corruption may be too great. There is a need for citizen assistance in identifying problematic and suspicious websites. Citizen support has been particularly valuable in identifying child pornography websites in the United States and in sites that are lures by human traffickers in Russia. In both of these countries, citizen groups have warned of abuses in order that Internet service providers can bring down these websites. This may not be possible in many situations where the citizens have sympathy with the goals and objectives of the terrorists but it can be most effectively done in cases of sexual exploitation, financial fraud on the Internet and potentially in relation to money laundering schemes on the Internet. Penalties should be established for computer specialists who assist in international organised crime and terrorism.

Just as the legal system has moved against lawyers and accountants and money launderers who serve criminals and terrorists, there needs to be the ability to readily prosecute the computer facilitators. There needs to be the harmonization of laws that individuals cannot operate out of safe havens which allow individuals to commit computer crimes without any risk of arrest and prosecution. Investigations of the information technology component of the crime and the terrorist act must be an integral part of the overall investigation and not exclusively the domain of computer specialists. Coordination among citizens, private corporations, states and multinational organisations is central to addressing cybercrime that facilitates organised crime and terrorism.

8

Women and Organised Crime

Women certainly do not currently receive the level of protection they are entitled to expect from the criminal justice system against the many forms of exploitation and violence they suffer at the hands of transnational criminal organizations. Furthermore, the impact that criminal law, the criminal justice process and crime prevention strategies generally have on women's lives continue to deserve urgent and careful scrutiny. One can argue that only a few among contemporary forms of transnational crime actually involve gender-based violence and exploitation, but some of them definitely do. This is clearly the case of various organized criminal activities relating to trafficking in women and children for the purpose of various forms of exploitation.

There is clear evidence of women's and children's particular vulnerability to certain forms of transnational organized crime. There are also reports of increasing recruitment of women into criminal organizations. Under the United Nations current definition, violence against women means any act of gender-based violence that results in, or is likely to result in, physical, sexual or psychological harm or suffering to women, including threats of such acts, coercion or arbitrary deprivation of liberty, whether occurring in public or in private life. The primary focus of that definition is on traditional forms of violence at the domestic level.

However, it also includes other forms violence related to exploitation, forced prostitution and trafficking, all of them crimes which are often committed across borders and are likely to involve criminal organizations. From the point of view of international law doctrine of state responsibility, the principle of due diligence is gaining international recognition. In accordance with article 4 of the Declaration on the Elimination of Violence Against Women, States must exercise due diligence to prevent, investigate and, in accordance with national legislation, punish acts of violence against women, whether those acts are perpetrated by the State or by private persons.

Global media coverage and increased travel have resulted in a greater awareness of opportunities elsewhere and an increased movement of both legal and illegal migrants. Over the last decades it is claimed that in Europe, for example, smuggling and trafficking of humans has become a determining factor in migration trends. An unabated demand for migration, in the face of stricter entry controls and requirements, has provided criminal entrepreneurs with new opportunities for profits. There are high profits to be made. Today, organized criminality in migrants trafficking is reaching every region of the world and it is now recognized internationally as major enforcement, human security, and human rights issues.

Traffickers exploit the phenomenon of illegal migration and supply a variety of services to illegal migrants, such as smuggling, the provision of fraudulent travel documents, transportation, accommodation, job brokering, and even training in how to claim asylum or deceive border officials. The same criminal organizations are also quick to use deception and coercion to exploit illegal migrants themselves. Current international discussion speaks openly of slavery-like conditions of which the indentured status of trafficked persons is a prime example. According to the Special Rapporteur on violence against women, its causes and consequences, Ms Rhadika Coomarasamy:

> Each year, thousands of women throughout the world are trafficked; they are tricked, coerced, abducted, sold and, in many cases, forced to live and work under slavery-like conditions as prostitutes, domestic workers, sweatshops labourers or wives. Such trafficking occurs for diverse purposes but the movement of women within countries and across frontiers is usually a result of their unequal bargaining power and vulnerability to exploitation. Today, women are primarily trafficked from the South to the North and increasingly from South to South: from countries in which structural adjustment has bankrupted the State economy, deforestation has destroyed villages and forced families into urban areas and the feminization of poverty is most apparent, to countries where the gross national product and the standard of living for the average citizen are higher. Consequently, trafficking in women is fuelled by poverty, racism and sexism.

Although trafficking has been of international concern since the beginning of this century, little has been accomplished to effectively combat the flourishing trade in women. Admittedly trafficking in women presents complex enforcement issues due to its international character and the numerous actors involved. With few exceptions, countries of origin, transit countries and countries of destination, refuse to accept responsibility to protecting trafficked women. The primary concern of most States is the illegal status of the victim who, if discovered, is quickly targeted for deportation.

Of particular note is what has been termed the feminization of migration. Historically labour migration was predominately male and the typical migrant was male. This is changing. For example, Soviet women are everywhere Beirut bars, hotels in Hammamet, cabarets in Cairo and escort services across the globe. It is estimated that eighty percent of those people who lost their jobs in the former Soviet Union were women. Likewise it has been acknowledged that the Asian financial crisis had and continues to have, a disproportionate impact on women. Women were the first to be let go when companies were forced to cut down their staff, and in general terms more women live in poverty than men. Poverty, desperation and displacement are having a direct impact on the movement of these women.

However, while financial situations may be exacerbating the position of women, their marginalized status and powerlessness in some of the societies remain a critical issue. These factors - the increasing amounts of migration, the gender element, the involvement of organized crime, the brutality inherent in some of the indentured arrangements -all speak of the need for a global response to human trafficking. Combating trafficking in human beings requires a two-fold approach: a criminal justice response (to prevent the crime and deter the offenders) and a human rights response to protect the trafficked persons and their rights. However, even if law enforcement was considered to be the answer, experience indicates that law enforcement alone will not seal the borders or restrict the trafficking.

Moving beyond the war on illegal migrants rhetoric, the international community is emphasizing the need to understand the context: political, economic and social environments; the motivations of the illegal migrating populations and other non-illegal migrant groups; the identity of those who exploit and/or are serviced by the migrants. Punishment, prevention and protection (including human right protection) must all be remain the main pillars of an effective strategy to combat trafficking in human beings. In their zeal to punish traffickers and protect the integrity of their borders, states must take care not to inadvertently violate the principle of doing no harm to trafficked persons, for example, by increasing the risk of exposure to abuse by third parties. There is a clear need to ensure that the individuals falling victim to such criminal practices are protected

The 1999 Trafficking in Persons report by the Office of the High Commissioner for Human Rights states that the two fundamental principles in the area of trafficking are that:

1) human rights must be at the core of any credible anti-trafficking strategy; and,
2) such strategies must be developed and implemented from the perspective of those who most need their human rights protected and promoted.

The FWCW Platform for Action (The Beijing Platform for Action) formulated a strategic objective (D.3) aimed at eliminating trafficking in women and assisting victims of violence due to prostitution and trafficking. Governments of countries of origin, transit and destination, regional and international organizations, it was recognized, had to take appropriate measures to address the root factors, including external factors, that encourage trafficking in women and girls for prostitution and other forms of commercialized sex, forced marriages and forced labour in order to eliminate trafficking in women, including by strengthening existing legislation with a view to providing better protection of the rights of women and girls and to punishing the perpetrators, through both criminal and civil measures.

Recently a number of specific recommendations were also put forward as a result of the NGO Consultation with the United Nations and Intergovernmental Organizations on Trafficking in Persons, Prostitution and the Global Sex Industry. In every countries, criminal law and the criminal justice system in order to make them as effective as possible in preventing crime against women. They are also asked to consider how criminal justice systems can become more relevant to women s experience and aspirations and more effective in protecting their rights. However, the required legal and systemic reforms are both delicate and complex.

The question of how these changes can be effected raises a number of issues concerning the relative effectiveness of various strategies to address systemic biases, cultural and subcultural opposition to change, the system s own inertia, or the lack of necessary human and financial resources. In December 1997, the United Nations General Assembly adopted a resolution which urged Member States to develop and promote crime prevention strategies that reflect the realities of women s lives and address their distinct needs. The resolution also included a document entitled Model Strategies and Practical Measures on the Elimination of Violence against Women in the field of Crime Prevention and Criminal Justice. These Model Strategies provided a new impetus for concrete reform and international cooperation in the area of elimination of violence against women.

The strategies are relevant to all aspects of the criminal justice system, from community based crime prevention to law enforcement, to courts, sentencing, and corrections. They also address several issues concerning research, the media, education and public awareness. The main focus of the Model Strategies are to ensure that criminal justice systems around the world provide a fair treatment response to all incidents of violence against women. They aim to provide de jure as well as de facto equality between women and men. The Strategies do not give preferential treatment to women but aim to ensure that any inequalities or forms of discrimination that women face in achieving access to justice, particularly in respects of acts of violence, are redressed. It is fair to say, therefore, that the Model Strategies do not emphasize the need to ensure that criminal justice institutions adopt strong measures to effectively protect women against gender-based exploitation and violence resulting from organized transnational criminal activities.

Transnational organized crime, by nature, calls for distinct and somewhat different responses from criminal justice systems. Among other things, it calls for a level of international cooperation that is not usually necessary in the control and prevention of other forms of crime. The same is true, needless to say, of certain forms of transnational crime which specifically targets women. As a result, the control and prevention of these crimes may require specific strategies which have not been sufficiently articulated in the Model Strategies adopted by the General Assembly.

REVIEWING LEGISLATION

The Beijing Platform for Action urged governments to consider enacting legislation aimed at preventing sex tourism and trafficking, giving special emphasis to the protection of young women and children {action no. 130 (e)}. Since then, a number of countries have enacted such legislation, each reflecting a different way of dealing with the problem of extra-territorial criminalization raised by this type of offense. The impact of these new law has not yet been evaluated systematically.

A recent resolution by the Commission on Human Rights (1999/40) urges Governments to take appropriate measures to address the root factors, including external factors, that encourage trafficking in women and girls for prostitution and other forms of commercialized sex, forced marriages and forced labour, so as to eliminate trafficking in women, including by strengthening existing legislation with a view to providing better protection of the rights of women and girls and to punishing perpetrators, through both criminal and civil measures. The resolution also urges Governments to criminalize trafficking in women and girls in all its forms, to condemn and penalize all the offenders involved, including intermediaries, whether their offence was committed in their own country or in a foreign country, while ensuring that the victims of those practices are not penalized.

In line with the Model Strategies, according to the 1999 Report of the Secretary General on the Elimination of Violence Against Women, some countries have recently reformed their laws and regulations or have adopted strategic plans, programmes and plans of action to reflect the issues addressed by that instrument. Major developments were prompted by it and new initiatives taken by States have related to review and reform of legislation (including criminal law and criminal procedure) by which acts of violence against women were criminalized; empowerment of the police and judiciary with authority to intervene in certain cases of domestic violence; and introduction of victim reconciliation and compensation, either by the offender or by the State.

In Austria, for example, a new law was introduced concerning sex offences, trafficking in human beings and pornographic presentations involving minors in electronic media. A new aliens law, which entered into force in 1998, offers protection to victims and witnesses of trafficking in human beings. In Germany, a working group on trafficking in women was established in 1998. An Interministerial Committee for Action to Combat Trafficking in Women and Children was established in Colombia. In Ukraine, 1997 amendments to the Criminal

Code and the Code of Criminal Procedure established trafficking in persons as a criminal offence.

In the United States, an Interagency Working Group on Worker Exploitation has recently proposed new legislation and sentencing guidelines relating to situations not yet adequately covered by existing federal laws. Legislation is proposed that would make it a crime to recruit or transport any person, knowing or having reason to know that the person will be subjected to unlawfully exploitative labor conditions. It would punish those who directly or indirectly profit from the fruits of involuntary servitude or debt bondage.

States of the Organization for Security and Cooperation in Europe (OSCE) concluded that there is currently is no unified approach to combating trafficking among OSCE destination countries. OSCE States lack an adequate legal framework to combat trafficking in human beings. Most of them rely on existing criminal law statutes usually dealing with prostitution. Few States have specific anti-trafficking laws. The few laws that exist tend to define the offence in terms of trafficking for prostitution or sexual exploitation and may, therefore, be inadequate to address trafficking for other forms of forced labour or contemporary forms of slavery.

A typical indictment to prostitute or procuring statute, for example, will not reach many of the actors involved in trafficking and does not carry penalties reflecting the serious and often brutal nature of trafficking crimes. The laws and policies (as well as the level of co-ordination and implementation vary considerably between major destination countries, even within the EU. In some countries, such as Germany, laws and policies are further decentralized, and vary even within the country .itself. Very few OSCE destination countries have established a national point person, agency, or task force to coordinate anti-trafficking strategies nationally and internationally.

Many slavery or servitude, or forced prostitution statutes tend to be defined or interpreted too narrowly to cover all frequent trafficking situations. Existing criminal code provisions concerning rape, assault, extortion, deceit, and unlawful confinement, as well as laws prohibiting labour exploitation and servitude are apparently rarely used in trafficking cases.

In some of the existing legislation, the crime of trafficking must involve an element of coercion, and that element is often too narrowly defined to include several trafficking situations where the threats are directed against the victim s family (in another country). The crime is also often defined in a way which takes into account the transnational nature of that form of exploitation and does not cover the behaviour of certain members of the transnational criminal network who aided, abetted or conspired to commit the crime of trafficking.

Immigration Policies and Procedures

Migrants who are or have been the victims of criminal exploitation in the source, transit or destination countries are even more vulnerable to further exploitation, victimization and violation of their rights. All States are under an obligation to ensure respect for and protection of the rights of illegal migrants, including victims of trafficking, which are owed to them under applicable international law. The High Commissioner for Human Rights has noted that the fact that national antitrafficking measures have been used in some situations to discriminate against women and other groups in a manner that amounts to a denial of their basic right to leave a country and to migrate legally.

Immigration laws, policies and procedures clearly require urgent attention to ensure that the victimization of trafficked persons is not compounded by the intervention of the destination, transit or source state. The vulnerability of migrants, in particular irregular migrants, as a result of their precarious situation in society often leads to violations of their most basic human rights. In many cases, it is clear that strict immigration laws and procedures relating to the deportation of illegal migrants or workers work at cross-purposes with efforts to prosecute trafficking crimes and to protect the human rights of victims. For instance,

— the threat of immediate deportation prevents victims from seeking help from police or other authorities;

— victims who are arrested or otherwise escape their traffickers do not receive the assistance or protection they need and entitled to under international human rights norms. In fact, most cases are further victimized by the State s criminal and immigration policies;

— NGOs attempting to assist victims of trafficking are reluctant to co-operate with law enforcement; and,

— effective law enforcement is severely undermined because victims are unwilling or unable to testify against traffickers.

In the case of the country of origin to which the victim is often returned, there usually is no ability to provide the victim with the necessary medical and psychological help, legal assistance or effective protection against reprisals or intimidation. For instance, it does not appear that any OSCE states have programs to protect trafficked persons from retribution by traffickers upon return to the country of origin. There are frequent cases of re-trafficking of the same victim upon her return to the country of origin and not infrequent reports of the presence of collusion between immigration officials and organized criminal elements to take advantage of returning victims. There are also many situations where the deportation of the trafficked person as illegal immigrants has serious and longlasting implications for the trafficked persons (e.g., victims may be prosecuted for leaving the country illegally, using false documents or engaging in prostitution, and they may be fined, jailed or charged for the costs of her repatriation, etc.). Law enforcement agencies have often argued that it is very difficult for them to prosecute trafficking offences under the current system in their countries. It is very difficult to convict a trafficker if the key witness has already been deported.

Law Enforcement

Codes and procedures related to violence against women are consistently enforced in such a way that all criminal acts of violence against women are recognized and responded to accordingly by the criminal justice system {article 8(a)}, to develop investigative techniques that do not degrade women subjected to violence and minimize intrusion {article 8(b)}, to ensure that police procedures, including decisions on the arrest, detention and terms of any form of release of the perpetrator, take into account the need for the safety of the victim and others related through family, socially or otherwise and that these procedures also prevent further acts of violence {article 8 (c)}, and to empower the police to respond promptly to incidents of violence against women (article 8(d)}.

Following are the main law enforcement problems:

— trafficking in human beings tends to be seen as a far less serious problem than trafficking in drugs or firearms;

— few law enforcement agencies seem to fully recognize the brutality of the crime or address the involvement of organized criminal groups;

— unspoken biases, confusion and disbelief over the issue contribute to a lack of determination to combat the phenomenon;

— trafficking is often characterized as nothing more than foreign prostitution or black-market labour rather than a form of slavery;

— the consent of the trafficked person is presumed;

— the problem is dismissed as an abuse by private individuals for which States have no responsibility;

— the laws that are enforced are far more likely to be enforced against the trafficked persons than the perpetrator of the trafficking crimes.

Victim Support and Assistance

The Beijing Platform for Action advocated the allocation of resources by Governments of countries of origin, transit and destination, regional and international organizations to provide comprehensive programmes designed to heal and rehabilitate into society victims of trafficking, including through job training, legal assistance and confidential health care, and take measures to cooperate with non governmental organizations to provide for the social, medical and psychological care of the victims of trafficking {action no. 130 (d)}. Victims of trafficking offences are all too often treated as offenders.

Victims who are arrested do not receive the assistance they need even though they are entitled to be treated in accordance with international human rights norms. Their almost automatic deportation as illegal migrants also compounds the problem. Many victims are deported without having even been identified as such. A few countries have specific legislation permitting a temporary stay for victims of trafficking. These provisions are meant to allow the victim of a trafficking crime to temporary reside and receive assistance while she is cooperating with law enforcement. A few countries (e.g. Belgium, Italy, and the Netherlands) have institutionalized policies for assisting victims of trafficking offences and offer a temporary stay of deportation while the victim decides whether to participate as a witness in criminal proceedings. Not surprisingly, these countries report significant increases in witness testimony and successful prosecution of traffickers. The High Commissioner for Human Rights has expressed the view that, at a very minimum, the identification of an individual as a trafficked person should be sufficient to ensure that immediate expulsion that goes against the will of the victim does not occur and that protection and assistance be offered.

Whereas the laws of many countries now recognize the rights of crime victims to redress or compensation, it would appear that that right is effectively denied in most cases to victims of trafficking. In the few countries where material assistance is offered to victims, that assistance is terminated as soon as they are returned to their original country. The current prevailing situation of forced deportation and repatriation of victims of trafficking is intolerable. It represents an unacceptable safety risk for the victims. This is why the High Commissioner for Human Rights has expressed the view that safe and, as far as possible, voluntary return must be at the core of any credible protection strategy for trafficked persons.

The recent resolution of the Commission on Human Rights concerning Traffic in Women and Girls calls upon concerned Governments to allocate resources to provide comprehensive programmes designed to heal and rehabilitate into society victims of trafficking, including through job training, legal assistance and health care and by taking measures to cooperate with non-governmental organizations to provide for the social, medical and psychological care to victims.

Crime Prevention Measures

Article 14 of the Model Strategies contains a list of general crime prevention measures which should be considered and implemented by many countries and various nongovernmental actors. Many of these measure focus on the provision of information to potential victims and measures to promote general awareness of the issue of discrimination and violence against women and their impact on society. Specific measures are certainly also required to raise public awareness of the seriousness of the impact of certain forms of organized transnational crime, in particular trafficking in women and children, on the lives of women and their families. Specific measures are also required in source countries to inform potential victims of trafficking of the risk they face.

In many source countries, young women and children still believe that there is a high demand for local girls to work abroad and are unaware of the suspect nature of advertised jobs or of other deceitful tactics. The Working Group on Contemporary Forms of Slavery recently urged States to initiate community-based prevention programmes, especially in high-risk areas, to educate people on the tactics of recruiters and traffickers and on the risks of sexual exploitation. According to the recent review of the situation in OSCE countries, it would appear that state-sponsored programmes are virtually non-existent in most countries of origin, and public awareness about trafficking remains very low.

The Beijing Platform for Action advocated stepped up cooperation and concerted action by all relevant law enforcement authorities and institutions with a view to dismantling national, regional and international networks in trafficking {action no. 130 (c)}. It also urged countries to ratify and enforce existing international conventions on trafficking in persons and slavery {action no. 130(a)}. Article 16 of the UN Convention to cooperate and collaborate at the regional and international levels with relevant entities to prevent violence against women and to promote measures to effectively bring perpetrators to justice, through mechanisms of international cooperation and assistance in accordance with national law.

The importance of fully implementing and achieving universal ratification of the Convention on the Elimination of All forms of Discrimination against Women was also emphasized. Some relevant regional instruments and initiatives can also play an important role in promoting international cooperation to eliminate violence against women and combating trafficking in particular. This is obviously the case, for instance, of the Inter-American Convention on the Prevention, Punishment, and Eradication of Violence against Women. However, the latter may also be in need of a careful reexamination to ensure that it addresses the growing amount of violence against women resulting from specific forms of transnational organized crime.

The Council of Europe formulated a Plan of Action for Combating Violence Against Women as well as a Plan of Action against Traffic in Women and Forced Prostitution. The Ministerial Conference of the European Union to prepare the European Code to Prevent and Combat Trafficking in Women adopted The Hague Ministerial Declaration on European Guidelines to Prevent and Combat Trafficking in Women for the Purpose of Sexual Exploitation. Furthermore, since the adoption of the Model Strategies, considerable progress has been achieved in developing a draft protocol to prevent, suppress and punish trafficking in women and children, supplementary to the proposed United Nations Convention Against Transnational Organized Crime.

9

Organised Crime in India

In India, organized crime is at its worst in Mumbai, the commercial capital of the country. The first well-known organized gang to emerge in recent times was that of Varadharajan Mudaliar in the early sixties. His illegal activities included illicit liquor, gold smuggling, gambling, extortion and contract murders. Three other gangs emerged shortly thereafter, namely, Haji Mastan (gold smuggling), Yusuf Patel (gold smuggling) and Karim Lala (drug smuggling). During the emergency in 1975, when there was a crackdown on the Indian Mafia, new gangs emerged. Dawood Ibrahim, the most successful, came in conflict with the Pathan gangs of Alamzeb and Amirzada which led to bitter internecine gang warfare.

The Pathan gangs were liquidated to leave the field free for Dawood Ibrahim. In 1985, there was increased police pressure which made Dawood Ibrahim flee the country. In March 1993, Dawood Ibrahim was behind the serial bomb blasts in Mumbai in which 257 persons died and 713 were maimed. Public and private property worth several million rupees was destroyed. Investigation revealed the transnational character of the conspiracy, the objective of which was to cripple the economy, create communal divide and spread terror in the commercial capital of India. Dawood Ibrahim, Tiger Memon and

Mohammed Dosa are presently reported to be operating from Dubai. Their field of activity primarily extends to extorting money from builders and film producers, mediating in monetary disputes, and undertaking contract killings.

The other major gangs of Mumbai indulging in organized crime are those of Chhota Rajan (Drug Trafficking and Contract Killings), Arun Gawli (Contract Killings and Protection Money), Late Amar Naik (Protection Money) and Choota Shakeel. Organized crime exists in other cities too, though not to the same extent as in Mumbai. There are several gangs operating in Delhi from neighboring State of Uttar Pradesh indulging in kidnapping for ransom. Om Prakash Srivastava, alias Babloo Gang of Uttar Pradesh, has been responsible for organizing kidnappings in Delhi and Mumbai in which ransom amounts were paid in foreign countr ies th rough "Hawala". Land Mafia has political connect ions and i ndul ges in land grabbing, intimidation, forcible vacation, etc. Of late, the ganglords of Mumbai have started using Delhi as a place for hiding and transit. Chhota Rajan group is strengthening its base in Delhi.

Ahmedabad city has been a hotbed of liquor Mafia because of a prohibition policy (banning of liquor). The Mafia became synonymous with the name of Latif, who started in the mid-seventies as a small time bootlegger and grew up to set up a 200 strong gang after eliminating rivals with intimidation, extortion, kidnappings and murders. He won municipal elections from five different constituencies with strong political patronage.

He was killed by the police in an encounter in 1997. A boom in construction activities in Bangalore city has provided a fertile breeding ground for the underworld. Builders are used for laundering black money. Forcible vacation of old disputed buildings is a popular side business for the underworld. The local gangsters in the

State of Karnataka have connections with the underworld of Mumbai. One of the Mumbai gang operations here is the Chhota Rajan gang.

Transnational Organized Criminal Groups

Following are the three major transnational organized criminal groups:

Dawood Ibrahim Gang

Dawood Ibrahim group is the most dreaded mafia gang with countrywide network and foreign connections. He has stationed himself in Dubai since 1985 and has indulged in drug and arms trafficking, smuggling, extortion and contract killings. His brother Anees Ibrahim looks after smuggling, drugs and contract killings, Noora looks after film financing and extortion; and Iqbal is in charge of the legitimate business which includes stock broking in Hong Kong. Anees is in legitimate business too, managing the Mohd. Anees Trading Company in Dubai. His business interests in India are shopping centres, hotels, airlines and travel agencies in Mumbai with an annual turnover of about Rs.20000 million. Extradition of offenders from Dubai has not been possible since there is no extradition treaty with Dubai. Moreover, some of these offenders have strong social links with politicians and other top personalities in Dubai.

Chhota Rajan Gang

Chhota Rajan was a member of the Dawood gang but parted company after the 1993 serial bomb blasts in Mumbai. He raised his own gang in 1994-95 which is reported to have a membership of several hundred persons today. Chhota Rajan himself is in a foreign country to avoid elimination by the Dawood gang. His gang indulges in drug trafficking and contract killings. In collaboration with another local gang, he organized the killing of a trusted leader of the Dawood Ibrahim gang, Mr. Sunil Samant, in Dubai in 1995.

Babloo Shrivastava Gang

Om Prakash Shrivastava in Babloo Shrivastava is facing 41 cases of murder, kidnappings for ransom, etc. He was arrested in Singapore in April 1995 on the basis of a Red Corner Notice issued by INTERPOL and extradited to India in August 1995. He has since been in jail but his gang continued to indulge in organized kidnappings and killings. The ransom amount is received by them in foreign countries through hawala (alternative non-banking remittance channel). The power of this gang has dwindled after his arrest.

Illicit Drug Trafficking

Illicit drug trafficking is the most significant transnational organized crime which has become a ser ious issue confronting both developing and developed countries. In most countries, despite years of drug suppression and prevention efforts, the cycle of drug trafficking and drug abuse continues. If allowed to remain unabated, the drug menace will considerably destroy the quality of life of people and hamper countries in their social, economic and cultural development. India is a vast country with land borders extending over more than 15000 kilometers and a sea coast line of over 7000 kilometers.

India's narcotic problem needs to be visualized from its geographical situation. India is flanked on either side by two regions which are internationally acknowledged as major sources of illicit opiates namely, South-West Asia (Afghanistan and Pakistan) and South-East Asia (Myanmar, Laos, Thailand). Additionally, Nepal, a traditional producer of cannabis, both herbal and resinous, fringes the country in the North. India is a traditional producer of licit opium for medicinal and scienti fic purposes. It is grown in three states, namely, Uttar Pradesh, Rajasthan and Madhya Pradesh under official control of Narcotics Commissioner. A part of the licit opium enters the illicit market in different forms. Although opium production is strictly under Government control in India, illicit poppy plantations have been reported in some places.

Besides, there is illicit cultivation of opium in the hill tracks of some states. India has a large presence of chemical industries producing precursor materials like acetic anhydride, acetyl anthranilic acid, etc. for lawful purposes. These chemicals are also utilized for processing and manufacturing heroin. The illicit cultivation of opium as well as the precursor chemicals can be used for the manufacture of heroin. For the last several years, India has also become a base for the manufacture of heroin, particularly in and around the opium producing districts of Uttar Pradesh, Madhya Pradesh and Rajasthan. The illicit drug trade in India has centered around f ive major narcotic substances namely heroin, hashish, opium, herbal cannabis and methaqualone. The Indo-Pak border has traditionally been the most vulnerable to drug trafficking.

Drug trafficking through India consists of hashish and heroin from Pakistan, hashish from Nepal, white heroin from Myanmar and heroin from Bangladesh. In the early eighties, the Border State of Punjab became affected with narco-terrorism with the smuggling of narcotic drugs and arms from across the border. This was also the time when the drug Mafia emerged in Golden Crescent countries. Although the use of India by the drug traffickers as a transit country has resulted in an increase in drug abuse due to the spill-over effect, drug addiction in India has not assumed such a serious magnitude as in some of the western countries, but there are no grounds for complacency. There have been reports of drug use among the students of universities in Delhi, Mumbai, Calcutta and Chandigarh. Indian society is not agitated too much. It is customary in some places to consume Bhang (crushed leaves of the cannabis plant) on the popular festival of Holi. There is no such tolerance for charas or ganja which also derived from the same cannabis plant.

1. Quantities of the most common drugs and precursors seized in India during the years 1997 to 2000

Name of the drug/precursor	Quantities seized in kilograms			
	1997	1998	1999	2000
Opium	3,316	2,031	1,635	2,524
Morphine	128	19	36	37
Heroin	1,332	655	861	1,198
Ganja	80,886	68,221	40,113	94,682
Hashish	3,281	10,106	3,391	4,923
Cocaine	24	1	1	0.08
Methaqualone	1,740	2,257	474	1,095
Acetic Anhydride	8,311	6,197	2,963	1,337

2. Details of significant seizures of narcotic drugs and psychotropic substances made during 2001

   (i) On 5 January 2001, the Directorate of Revenue Intelligence, Amritsar Regional Unit seized 17,900 kg heroin from a truck at octroi post. The suspected source of the seized drug was Pakistan and it was concealed in three packets kept in a cabinet in a driver's cabin and 15 packets in an LPG cylinder lying in the tool box on the roof of the truck.

   (ii) On 8 February 2001, the Narcotics Control Bureau, Mumbai Zonal Unit seized 1423.690 kg of mandrax tablets from a truck at the premises of M/s High Point Industries, MIDC, Taloja.

(iii) On 17 April 2001, the Directorate of Revenue Intelligence, New Delhi seized 17.000 kg of heroin at National Highway No.8, opposite Shiva temple, Delhi-Gurgaon Road when the occupants of two vehicles were transferring the drug from one vehicle to another. The suspected source of the seized heroin was South-West Asia.

(iv) In the first week of August, 2001, the Directorate of Revenue Intelligence, New Delhi seized two tonnes of hashi sh from two godowns in Mordabad, near Delhi. It is the biggest ever seizure in Northern India. The hashish was brought from Nepal, where it was processed initially for over a period of 2 to 3 months. The bundles of 200 to 300 kgs of hashish were brought hidden in a mini luxury bus over a period of 3 to 4 months, and stashed away in a godown in Mordabad. The bundles were then covered in polythene bags, wrapped wi th aluminum f o ils, vacuum-packed and the bundles shifted to another godown nearby. The machine used in vacuum packing was also recovered. A total of 4,000 packets, each containing 500 gms of hashish in cake form, were recovered. The vacuum-packed hashish concealed in packages of handicrafts was to be transported to Mumbai docks and then shipped to the United States.

The Government of India have taken various legislative, administrative and preventive measures to counter drug trafficking in the country. Among the prominent legislative measures are the provisions of deterrent punishment under the NDPS Act, 1985, applications of preventive detention of drug traffickers under the Conservation of Foreign Exchange and Prevention of Smuggling Activi ties Act, 1974 (COFEPOSA), notification of certain chemicals like

acetic anhydride as a 'specified item' under the Customs Act, 1962 and India's land border with Myanmar falling within the territories of the States of Arunachal Pradesh, Nagaland, Manipur and Mizoram having been declared as 'specified areas' under the said Act for the purpose of checking illegal trafficking across the border.

The creation of the Narcotics Control Bureau as an apex coordinating and enforcement agency at the national level is one of the prominent administrative measures taken by the Government. The Narcotic Drugs & Psychotropic Substances (NDPS) Act, 1985, which was enforced with effect from 14 November 1985, provides for a minimum punishment of 10 years ' rigorous imprisonment and a fine of one hundred thousand Rupees extendable to 20 years rigorous imprisonment and a fine of two hundred thousand Rupees. In respect of repeat offenses, the Act provides for the death sentence in certain circumstances. In remaining cases, a minimum punishment of 15 years rigorous imprisonment and a fine of Rs.1.5 hundred thousand, which is extendable up to 30 years rigorous imprisonment and fine of three hundred thousand Rupees. The courts have been empowered to impose fines exceeding the above limits for reasons to be recorded in their judgments.

The N.D.P.S. Act also provides for:

(i) Constitution of a National Fund for Control of Drug Abuse to meet the expenditure incurred in connection with the measures for combating illicit traffic and preventing drug abuse.

(ii) Control over chemical substances which can be used in the manufacture of narcotic drugs and psychotropic substances through appropriate licensing and deterrent punishment for violation thereof.

(iii) Total ban on suspension, remission or commutation of sentences under the penal provision.

(iv) Forfeiture of all illegally acquired properties derived from or attributable to illicit trafficking. All enforcement agencies have been empowered to trace and freeze/seize such property as are liable to forfeiture under the Act, subject to confirmation within a period of 30 days by the competent authority appointed under this Act. The law applies to all properties and assets of traffickers acquired within a period of six years immediately preceding the date on which such a trafficker is charged with an offense under this Act.

India is one of the few countries in which an adequately deterrent penal system has been developed with regard to drug trafficking. This is in conformity with the UN Resolutions of 1961, 1971 and 1988 on Narcotic Drugs and Psychotropic Substances.

FIREARMS TRAFFICKING

Firearms trafficking i s a global phenomenon and generally resorted to for generating profit, purchasing narcotics and supporting illegal activities of organized criminal groups. In India, the states of Punjab which were affected by terrorist activities during the 1980s and Jammu & Kashmir have been particularly vulnerable to arms trafficking across the border. India has a long border with Pakistan, Nepal, Bhutan, China, Myanmar and Bangladesh. The Border Security Force, which guards the borders, continues to seize large quantities of AK Series rifles, heavy machine guns, p istols and revolvers, rocket launchers, ri fles, magazines and ammunition.

In 1993, a consignment of AK-56 rifles, magazines, l ive r ounds and hand grenades was sent from a Gulf country by land at the cost of Dighi Jetti in the State of Gujarat. Subsequently, huge quantities of arms, ammunition and explosives were smuggled into India by sea route at Shekhadi in District Raigad. These were used for bomb blasts in Mumbai on 12 March 1993, which caused terror, widespread damage, loss of 257 lives and maiming of 713 persons. During investigation, some of the arms recovered included 62 AK-56 ri f les with 280 magazines and 38,888 rounds, 479 hand grenades, 12 pistols of 9 mm make with ammunition, 1100 electronic detonators, 2313 kgs. of RDX, etc.

The Police Authorities in the state of Madhya Pradesh in central India recovered 24 AK-56 ri f les, 5250 cartridges, 81 magazines and 27 hand grenades on 4 November 1995. On 17 February 1996, Delhi Police recovered 361 pistols of 0.30 caliber with the inscription "Made in China by Norinco", 728 magazines and 3738 live rounds in a cavity in the undercarriage of a caravan bus. In this case, a Swiss national and an Iranian national living in Pakistan since 1981, were detained and the investigation disclosed that this in fact was the second consignment, the first one having been successfully smuggled into India in 1995. 22 persons including f ive foreign nationals have been prosecuted in the court of law in this case.

A sensational case called the Purulia arms drop case was an example of illicit arms traf f i cking by air. On 17th December 1996, an Antonov 26 aircraft dropped over 300 AK47/56 rifles and 20,545 rounds of ammunition, dragnov sniper weapons, rocket launchers and night vision devices in Purulia village in West Bengal. The aircraft was bought from Latvia for US$2 mi l l i on and chartered by a Hong Kong registered company Carol Airlines. Payments were made mostly from foreign bank accounts. The aircraft picked up a consignment of arms from Bulgaria using end-users cert ificate issued by a neighboring country. The arms were airdropped over Purulia in the state of West Bengal. This case was investigated by the Central Bureau of Investigation and a charge sheeted in the City Sessions Court, Calcutta.

After trial, the court found the accused persons guilty of offenses under the Indian Penal Code, Explosive Substances Act, Arms Act, Explosives Act, and the Aircraft Act and sentenced Mr. Peter James Gifran Van Kalkstein Bleach (British National), Mr. Alexander Klichine, Mr. Igor Moskvitine, Mr. Oleg Gai dash, Mr. Evgueni Antimenko, Mr. Igor Timmerman (all Latvian nationals) and Mr. Vinay Kumar Singh (Indian national) to various terms of rigorous imprisonment on 2 February 2000.

Human (Women and Children) Trafficking

Emigration of human beings from one country to another for trade, commerce, religious and other purposes is as old as human civilization itself. However, the word 'traffic in human beings' implies illegal movement of people from one country to another in violation of existing national laws and procedures. The countries of the West have become highly vulnerable on this count as they are attracting hoards of illegal emigrants mainly because of their relative economic prosperity. Illiterate, innocent and gullible persons from under developed and developing countries, in their urge to earn more money from overseas employment, fal l easy prey to unscrupulous and unauthorised agents. Such activities in India have turned into lucrative business as the agents induce/ make the immigrants part with large sums of monies towards their commission/service charges, expenses on journeys as well as for arranging passports, visas and statutory clearance.

Often the travel documents are not valid and sometimes they are simply dumped into foreign lands without giving them promised employment. India has also been significantly affected by such immigrants. India is found to be both the country of origin and destination for trafficking in women. According to intelligence reports, about 1200 thousand emigrants from Bangladesh have settled in the border States of West Bengal and Assam after independence. The problem, however, has spread as far wide as Mumbai, Rajasthan and Delhi, which have an estimated 300 thousand emigrants from Bangladesh. Similarly, a large number of Indians are working abroad, particularly in the Gulf region. A number of young girls from southern India have been sent to the Gulf countries. There have also been reports that India has served as a transit point for trafficking of young virgins from Nepal, Myanmar and Bangladesh to the Middle East, mostly Dubai.

An estimated 5,000 to 7,000 Nepali girls are annually sold into brothels in India for prostitution. According to a press report, 9 Nepalese girls aged between 14 and 25 years, were rescued at Nepal-India border point at Kakarbhitta in Eastern Nepal in September, 2000. The rescued girls said that they were lured by the agents on the pretext of getting them married or obtaining jobs for them in India. According to another press report, the Nepal police arrested one Dhan Bahadur Gurung in November, 2000 on charges of selling more than 300 women and girls. He is accused of luring them into prost itution by falsely promising marriage and jobs in the circuses in India. In early 2001, an emigration racket, in which a nexus of policemen deployed at the Hyderabad airport and travel agents facilitated more than 3,000 people sneaking out on fake papers, came to light when nearly 40 women mostly illiterate were being sent to the Gulf countries from Hyderabad airport on fake papers.

Paedophiles now have a titillating new tool-the Internet. It allows them to access pornographic photographs of children, enter their homes, and 'groom' them for rape. The f irst case of paedophilia appears to have come to light in India in April, 1991 when the police raided the house of Father Freddy Peat, who had been running an orphanage in Goa, and recovered drugs and 2,305 photographs of children forced into sexual acts. Peat was arrested and la ter sentenced for life. It is believed that copies of a large number of pictures seized from Peat in 1991 have made their way onto the Web.

On December 16, 2000, a Swiss couple William and Loshier Marty, who were part of an international paedophile racket with operations in the West, Thailand, Sri Lanka and India were arrested at a resort in Madh Island, Mumbai with two minor girls. According to the police sources, photos of the couple's victims-some as young as seven-were supplied to paedophiles rings and were also posted on the Web. The internet has facilitated the organization of paedophiles, who can now easily down load pictures, forward them to friends, enter chat rooms and pick out targets and eventually lure them into a meeting. Another site came into the focus of CBI's Cyber Crime Investigation Cell during routine surfing. The site sold itself as a platform for those who would like to buy or sell sex slaves. In business since 1998, it offered members a sickening variety of slaves: virgin, black, teen, pregnant and more. A membership fee could be waived if a person tortured a slave and sent in photographs. The CBI set up a decoy customer and were promptly offered a teenage girl. The site's pimp was learnt to be operating from cybercafes in Delhi. At the last minute, however, he backed out of the deal and remained untraceable.

India's first case of child porn on the Net came to notice last year. The site in question had a deceptively innocent homepage. But persist with the links and the site brought out 27 files with titles such as "Little bitches on the beach" and "All in the family". By paying a little more one could watch the "VIP series" and customized videos. Most of the girls featured were under 10 and South Asian. Investigation reveals that the site was created in Lima, Peru. But its domain server was being provided by Arvind Shyam Jagdam from Hyderabad. Jagdam was arrested in September, 2000. Information was sought from Peru police but the response is still awaited. An interesting fact revealed during investigation was that the naked children shown on the site were missing from their homes.

Child-porn sites showcase India as a paedophile's paradise. However, most Indians still discount child porn on the net as a western perversion. Paedophilia and more so its prevalence online is still not a priority crime for the police in India. The Indian mind set is such that few are willing to accept that their children can be at such risk. India has sufficient legislation to deal e f fect ively with the problem of Suppression of Immoral Traffic as well as illegal emigration out of India. The Suppression of Immoral Traf fi c in Womens and Girls Act, 1956 to deal with these offenses, was re-enacted under the name of Immoral Traffic (Prevention) Act, 1986 to rectify some lacunae in the earlier Act.

The National Commission for Women reviews laws, conducts inquiries for redressal of complaints, undertakes promotional research for policies, advises the Government and ensures custodial justice for women. The Commission enjoys the powers of a Civil Court by virtue of Section 10(4) of National Commission for Women Act, 1992. It has formed an Expert Committee and has formulated a 10-year National Plan of Action (1997-2006) to coordinate with the 9th and 10th Indian Five Year Plans. The law relating to emigration of citizens of India was consolidated and amended by enacting the Emigration Act, 1983 which repealed the earlier Act of 1922. In order to protect and aid, with advice, al l in tending emigrants, a provision was made for the appointment of a Protector-General of Emigrants and Protector of Emigrants by the Central Government.

The Act prohibi ts a recruiting agent to commence or carry on the business of recruitment except under, and in accordance with, a certificate issued on that behalf by the Prosecutor-General of Emigrants or any other officer notified as registering authority under the Act. It further prohibited an employer to recruit any c itizen of India for employment in any country or place outside India except through a recruiting agent competent under the Act to make such recruitment or in accordance with a valid permit issued on this behalf under the Act.

The Act provides for a punishment of imprisonment for a term which may be extended to two years and with a fine which may extend to two thousand rupees for contravening the above provisions or col lecting, f rom an emigrant, any charges in excess of the limits prescribed under the Act or cheating any emigrants, etc. All offenses under the Emigration Act, 1983 are cognizable.

Money Laundering

Crime pays and criminals naturally want to be able to enjoy their profits without worrying about the police or the courts. This is not a new economic or sociological problem. However, geopolitical developments over the past 50 years together with economic globalization have meant that the international movement of money has increased. The rapid expansion of international financial activity has gone hand-in-hand with the development of transnational crime, which takes advantage of political borders and exploits the differences between legal systems in order to maximise profits. The groups involved are genuinely multinational and pose a direct threat to the financial stability of economic systems. They destabilise democracy because they are backed by clandestine networks subject to the law of the underworld.

Money laundering cannot be disassociated from other forms of crime. It is a fact that it thrives on corruption. Corrupt people use financial techniques to hide their fraudulently obtained assets and the continued successful application of these techniques depends on the involvement of influential accomplices. Money laundering is therefore at the centre of all criminal activity, because it is the common denominator of all other criminal acts, whether the aim is to make profits or hide them.

Laundering operations are, in fact, intended more to conceal the origin of the money than its criminal nature, in other words to hide the traffic from which it is derived rather than the general criminal activity which actually generated it. It is therefore essential to move the money in order to scramble the route it takes. The operation is wholly successful when the nature of the money is also concealed and it is impossible to establish a link with any criminal activity because the di fferent circuits taken give it the appearance of legitimate income. The Indian "Hawala" or "Hundi" system can be explained as a transfer of money through unofficial channels, normally outside the banking channels used by businessmen. The money so transferred often includes the money derived from criminal activities or in violation of the country's legislation.

Underground banking which conveys a sense of a system may not strictly cover misuse of banking channel. It may refer to, in a restricted manner, a system of rendering services which are similar to banking services, the most important in this context being the transmission of money. Hawala represents such services. As a developing nation, India feels seriously concerned not only because money laundering, including compensatory payments known as HAWALA transactions, have been threatening the economy but also because such practices contribute to the country's illicit drug trafficking and terrorist and subversive activities leading to large scale violence.

Of late, an impression is gaining ground that India is becoming increasingly vulnerable to money laundering activities and is becoming a transit point for drug traffickers and other criminals from the Golden Crescent i.e. Pakistan, Afghanistan and Iran and the Golden Triangle i.e. Burma, Thailand and Laos. The Economic Intelligence Council meeting of August, 1993 also observed that money laundering is now a major issue and has become a means of financial clout and strength of economic offenders and drug traffickers. India is fast becoming a conduit for the South East, Middle East, Far East and Latin American countries. The Indian hawala system or underground banking is used extensively for drug trafficking and remittances of money by both nonresident Indians and resident Indians.

In 1992-93, there were press reports on the U.S. State Department ' s investigations into the possible use of Indian Banking Channels for laundering drug money, including the possibility of links with the securities irregularities of 1992. An article in the London Times of May, 1993 had suggested that India, more specifically Bombay, was attracting huge amounts of Narcotics money from drug cartels in Columbia. There were also, in 1994, reports in the press that the private sector in India is making its presence felt in the area of quick transfer of cash across continents. Travel agents and courier companies are targeting Indians living abroad who want to repatriate money. As no minimum/ maximum limits are prescribed, the time taken to transfer money is much less. As such private companies do not fall within the direct control of the banking system, it could perhaps lead to the facility being used by money launderers, though there is no such case reported so far.

The high tax rate and the Exchange Control Regulations (though now considerably liberalised) have been the major reasons for hawala and other economic crimes in India. The Indian hawala system or underground banking is used extensively for drug trafficking and remittances of money by both nonresident and resident

Indians. It is the Hawala where the economic offenders and the launderers meet. These offenders easily become prey for money launderers, or it can be said that these offenders on the one side and the money launderers on the other side close the circle.

In India, money laundering is also indulged in by some corporate houses to evade taxes as well as by the organized criminal groups to launder dirty money. Money laundering techniques include smurf ing, establ ishment of front companies, acquisition of commercial and non-commercial properties, remittances through Hawala (non-banking channels), over-invoicing and double invoicing legi t imate business and foreign remittances. Non-resident Indians have been given some special banking facilities. These facilities are misused to bring back the money as white money. For example, a portfolio account is opened in a foreign country and the money is laundered back to be invested in the stock markets. Another modus operandi is to launder the money through bogus exports.

The conversion of black money is done by over-invoicing the products. Some shell companies are setup to issue bills or invoices accompanied by bogus transport receipts in order to obtain funds against these documents from bank/financial institutions and then divert major parts of such proceeds by issuing cheques in the names of nonexistent front companies of cheque discounters. The cheque discounters then hand over cash immediately to the party after deduction of their commission. The cheque discounte rs are generally associated with commodities markets where fake transactions in commodities can largely go unnoticed. The cheque discounters also issue fake Letters of Credit and false bills. The cheque discounters file income tax returns in which the commission is shown as taxable income.

Money laundering per se has not been made a criminal offence in India so far. Certain activities like diversion of funds, submitting false statements relating to inventories, multiple financing etc. which could serve as means towards the end of money laundering are also not considered as crimes. The problem had so far been dealt with mainly under the Foreign Exchange Regulation Act, 1973, but with effect from June 2000, FERA has been replaced by the Foreign Exchange Maintenance Act. A bill to enact a money laundering law to be named 'The Prevention of Money Laundering Bill' has been introduced in Parliament by the Government of India but the same still remains to be enacted as law.

Money laundering has been proposed as a cognizable crime punishable with rigorous imprisonment of 3-7 years which could be extended to 10 years and a fine of up to Rs. 0.5 mil lion. The acquisition, possession or owning of money, movable and immovable assets from crime, especially from drug and narcotic crimes, would be tantamount to money laundering. Concealment of information on proceeds or gains from crime made within India or abroad is proposed to be an offence. An adjudicating authority is proposed which would have powers to confiscate properties of money launderers. An administrator may be appointed to manage the confiscated assets. An appellate tribunal is proposed to be set up with three members to hear appeals from the orders of the adjudicating authority.

The rulings of the adjudicating authority would thus not be contestable in the local courts. Financial in stitutions are expected to maintain transaction records and furnish these to the adjudicating authority. Failure to do so would be punishable too. However, at present, there is certain legislation to deal with such offenders. Such legislation is specifically intended to deprive offenders of the proceeds and benefits derived from the commission of offences against the laws of the country. Besides, such legislation also provides for the confiscation or forfeiture of the proceeds or assets used in connection with the commission of certain crimes. In the offences relating to narcotic drugs and psychotropic substances in particular, the very act of acquisition of property derived from or used in illicit trade and in relat ion to which proceedings for forfeiture have been initiated has been made punishable, also as a distinct offence.

To deprive persons of the proceeds and benefits derived from the commission of an offence against the law of the land including forfeiture or confiscation of such property, Indian legislation also include the following Acts:

(i) Criminal Law (Amendment) Ordinance, 1944;

(ii) Customs Act, 1962 (Secs. 119 to 122);

(iii) Code of Criminal Procedure, 1973 (Sec.452);

(iv) Smugglers & Foreign Exchange Manipulators (Forfeiture of Property) Act, 1976;

(v) Narcotic Drugs & Psychotropic Substances Act, 1985 (Secs. 68-A to 68-Y);

(vi) In addition, Indian statutes also contain provisions for preventive detention of foreign exchange racketeers under the Conservation of Foreign Exchange and Prevention of Smuggling Activities (COFEPOSA) Act, 1974, and of the drug traffickers under the Prevention of Illicit Traffic in Narcotic Drugs and Psychotropic Substances (PITNDPS) Act, 1988.

In one of the cases of money laundering dealt with by the Central Bureau of Investigation, an organized group of Hawala dealers operating from London and Dubai used to receive remittances from foreign banks for transferring the same to India. A telephonic message in coded words would be passed to agents in India to pay money in Indian currency. The remittances so received by the above mentioned persons in Dollars or Pounds Sterling at

London and Dubai were used for purchase o f gold, drugs, arms, ammunitions and explosives through the underworld. The arms, ammunitions and explosives were used to be smuggled into India and sold to various criminal/ terrorist groups while the drug used to be distributed to the traffickers.

Cyber Crime

The exponential growth of computerrelated crime commensurate with the increasing dependence of computers in our day-to-day lives has posed new challenges to the law enforcement agencies in India. With the physical growth of the Internet over the past few years, a number of new generation crimes affecting the LAN, WAN and Internet have created extraordinary situations. Hacking, computer network breaches, copyright piracy, software piracy, child pornography, password sniffers, credit card frauds, cyber squatting are some of the new terms in the average criminal investigator's dictionary. Highly intelligent persons commit these new generation crimes leaving hardly any trace and making investigation highly difficult and complicated.

Recently, one of the hurdles in the investigation of computer-related crimes in India was overcome by the enactment of legislation in the form of the Information Technology Act, 2000, which came into force on October 17, 2000. The Act delineates two separate types of penal provisions: contraventions and information technology offences. While contravention results in monetary penalty, the IT offences may result in the offender being imprisoned or paying a fine or both. Tampering with computer source codes, obscenity, hacking, unauthorized access to a protected sys tem, misrepresentat ion before authorities, breach of confidentiality and privacy, publication of false particulars in digital signature certificates, etc. have been listed as criminal offences under this Act.

Amendments have also been made to the Indian Penal Code, Indian Evidence Act, the Bankers' Book Evidence Act and Reserve Bank of India Act to facilitate investigation and prosecution of cyber crime. The Central Bureau of Investigation has recently created a Cyber Crime Research & Development Unit which maintains close liaison with international agencies like the FBI, Interpol and other foreign police agencies to share skills and techniques in investigating cyber crimes. The officers of CBI associated in this exercise share their expertise with the State police forces through regional training programmes held periodically.

CURRENCY COUNTERFEITING

Currency counterfeiting is one of the organized white collar crimes which has assumed serious proportions globally. It not only causes serious setbacks to the world's economy but also jeopardizes the genuine business transact ions. Nowadays, the counterfeiting of currency notes is done with the help of modern equipment such as colour scanners, colour copiers and printers, as well as by offset process. Most of the security features are copies from genuine notes by using modern techniques to produce the counterfeit currency notes very close to genuine currency notes. For achieving the required finish in the art of counterfeiting, the advance computer technology provides them with sophistication and perfection.

There has been an upsurge in the incidents of supply of counterfeit Indian currency notes from across the border of India especially from the Indo-Pakistan border and Indo-Nepal border. During the year 1999, counterfeit Indian currency notes valued at Rs.18.4 million were seized as compared to Rs.6.5 million during 1998 indicating a threefold increase. During the year 1999, the three States of Uttar Pradesh, Bihar and West Bengal accounted for almost 40% of the total seizures. There are two recent cases of recovery of counterfeit Indian currency notes which have international ramifications:

(i) In January, 2001, the Uttar Pradesh Police, with the arrest of a suspected ISI agent, identified as Abal, from Muzaffarnagar District, busted a gang responsible for circulating fake currency notes across Western Uttar Pradesh, Delhi, Haryana, Rajasthan and Punjab. Currency notes worth Rs.17,000/- in the denominations of Rs.500/- and Rs.100/- were seized from Abal.

(ii) In March, 2001, the Mumbai Police, in one of the biggest hauls, seized counterfeit currency notes worth Rs.15 million in two separate cases. Ten persons linked to a Dubai-based notorious ISI agent Aftab Batki, were arrested. The counterfeit notes were of Rs.500/- denominat ion. The consignment had arrived from Dubai by air a couple of weeks ago. The notes were concealed in water dispensers and TV sets. After being smuggled into Mumbai, these were handed over to the Dawood gangsters for circulation. The interrogation of the arrested accused revealed that they worked for Aftab Batki. The police recovered from them a separate consignment o f fake currency notes worth Rs.9 million meant to be supplied to certain businessmen in Mumbai.

India, as a signatory to the Geneva Convention, 1929, is committed to extend full cooperation to all other countries for eliminating or containing to the furthest extent possible, the counterfeiting of domestic as well as foreign currencies. Indian laws and enforcement measures are in full conformity with the principles laid down in the Convention. The Indian Penal Code provides for punishment of life imprisonment or imprisonment for up to 10 years for counterfei t ing any currency note or bank note, using as genuine, forged or counterfeit currency notes or bank notes and making or possessing instruments or materials for forging or counterfeiting currency notes. It also provides for punishment of imprisonment up to 7 years for possession of forged or counterfeit currency notes or bank notes.

The making or using of documents resembling currency notes or bank notes is also an offence punishable with a fine. The investigation of cases involving counterfeit currency is done by specially trained staff of the State Police. At the national level, the Central Bureau of Investigation has created a separate unit to take up the investigation of offences of counterfeit currency which have inter-state or international ramifications.

Special Investigative Tools To Combat Transnational Organized Crime

The use of traditional investigative methods to combat transnational organized crime has proved to be both very difficult and ineffective. This demands that law enforcement agencies utilise special investigative tools such as control led delivery, undercover operations and electronic surveillance (wiretapping, communicat ions interception etc.) to effectively fight transnational organized crime. However, the use of these tools are often surrounded with controversy because there is always public fear that they might infringe on human rights to privacy or are likely to be misused by the government to oppress citizens.

Controlled Delivery

Controlled delivery techniques have proven an important enforcement tool in identifying the principles involved in drug t raf f icking and other major smuggling offences. It is particularly important in countering the criminal activities of drug traffickers who, by the use of couriers, creat ion of false documents and other deceptive practices, carefully disassociate themselves and try to be remote from the drug trafficking operations. The United Nations Conférence for the adoption of a Convention against illicit traffic in narcotic drugs and psychotropic substances has defined controlled delivery as follows:

> "Controlled delivery" means the technique of allowing illicit or suspect consignments of narcotic drugs, psychotropic substances, substances in Table-I and Table-II annexed to this Convention, or substances substituted for them, to pass out of, through or into the territory of one or more countries, with the knowledge and under the supervision of their competent authorities, with a view to identifying persons involved in the commission of offences established in a ccordance with Article 3, paragraph-1 of the Convention."

Further, Article 11 of the Convention, covering controlled delivery, reads as follows:

> "1. If permitted by the basic principles of the irrespective domestic legal systems, the Parties shall take the necessary measures, within their possibilities, to allow for the appropriate use of controlled delivery at the international level, on the basis of agreements or arrangements mutually consented to, with a view to identifying persons involved in offenses established in ac cordance wi .th Article 3, paragraph 1, and to taking legal action against them.
>
> 2. Decis ions to use controlled delivery shall be made on a case-bycase basis and may, when necessary, take into consideration financial arrangements and understandings with respect to the exercise of jurisdict ion by the Parties concerned."

Section 4 of the Indian Narcotic Drugs and Psychotropic Substances Act, 1985 provides:

1. Subject to the provisions of this Act, the Central Government shall take all such measures as it deems

necessary or expedient for the purpose of preventing and combating abuse of narcotic drugs and psychotropic substances and the illicit traffic therein.

2. In particular and without prejudice to the generality of the provisions of subsection (I), the measures which the Central Government may take under that subsection include measures with respect to all or any of the following matters, namely:

   a. ....

   b. Obligations under the International Conventions;

   c. Assistance to the concerned authorities in foreign countries and concerned international organisations with a view to facilitating coordination and universal action for prevention and suppression of illicit traffic in narcotic drugs and psychotropic substances.

The above provisions thus enable the drug law enforcement agencies in India to use the controlled delivery technique as an effective tool of investigation against organized syndicates, nationally and internationally. However, before adopting this technique, the originating country and the recipient country should discuss in detail the entire operation, maintain surveillance simultaneously in both the countries, keep close surveillance on the movement of drugs either through cargo or through couriers, and time the final strike operation simultaneously in both the countries to achieve maximum results. It will also be necessary to authenticate the evidence gathered in both the countries for successful prosecution of the traffickers.

In India, the Narcotics Control Bureau, the nodal agency for enforcement of laws concerning narcotic drugs and psychotropic substances, has undertaken controlled delivery operations with a number of countries from time to time both on its own initiative or when suitable cases are brought to its notice by other enforcement agencies. The operation of controlled delivery is very difficult and complicated, particularly when it involves many countries and there is a difference in their legal systems and practices. In using this technique, there is always a fear that the consignment of illicit drugs may be lost during transit. The uniformity of legislation and close cooperation amongst the law enforcement agencies of different countries are necessary make this technique effective.

Electronic Surveillance

Electronic surveillance covers wiretapping, communications interception, etc. Telephone interception and the monitoring of all electronic communications are the most controversial aspects of electronic surveillance. Yet these are very useful in assisting law enforcement agencies to combat transnational organized crime. Wiretapping or telephone interception is defined simply as the interception of a telephone conversation between parties without their knowledge, using equipment that is inserted into the electronic circuit between the transmitter and the receiver. In India, interception of messages, transmitted or received by any telegraph is covered under subsection 2 of section 5 of the Indian Telegraphic Act, 1885, when it is necessary or expedient to do so in the interests of the sovereignty and integrity of India, the security of the State, friendly relations with a foreign country or for preventing incitement to commission of an offence.

The issue of constitutional validity of this provision came under scrutiny of the Supreme Court of India in a writ petition filed by the People's Union for Civil Liberties. The Supreme Court passed a judgment on 18th December, 1996, upholding the constitutional validity of the Act but laid down certain guidelines prescribing that the order for interception will be issued by the Home Secretaries at the Centre and in the States. A copy of the order should be sent to the Review Committee within a week. The order will cease to have an effect after two months unless renewed. The Review Committee will review the order passed by the authority concerned within two months of the passing of the order. The total period shall not exceed six months.

The Government of India has made a legal provision in the licensing conditions formulated along with the cellular operators to make it mandatory on the part of the cellular companies to provide parallel monitoring facilities for all communications being received and emanating from a particular mobile set. Cellular operators operating in four metropolitan cities of Mumbai, Kolkata, Delhi and Chennai have made this facility available whereas others are bound to provide this facility within three years of the initiation of the mobile network.

Undercover Operations

The law enforcement agents, through undercover operations, are able to infiltrate the highest levels of organized crime groups by posing as criminals when real criminals discuss their plans and seek assistance in committing crimes. In India, there is no legislation or regulations to undertake undercover operations.

Immunity Systems

Immunity refers to the process of exempting from prosecution a co-accused, in order to maximise the potential of witness co-operat ion as a tool for combating transnational organized crime. The testimony of a person, who is party to a crime is very reliable because of his relationship to any co-accused. During investigation, a co-accused can reveal the true identities of other suspects, assist the police in locating the victim of a crime, or point out the corpus delicti or body of the crime. It is a very effective tool in prosecuting terrorists or members of criminal organisations.

Section 306 of Code of the Criminal Procedure, 1973, provides f o r the obtaining of evidence of an accomplice by tender of pardon subject to his voluntarily making a full disclosure of the facts and circumstances relevant to the offence for which the accomplice and co-accused are being charged with or investigated for. This provision is applicable in offences punishable with imprisonment of seven years or more.

Witness and Victim Protection Programmes

There is no legislation in India at present for protection of witnesses and the members of their families. Section 171 of the Criminal Procedure Code prohibits police officers to carry the complainant or witness to court. The intention of such legislation appears to be to ensure independence of evidence given by the witnesses without any influence from the police.

Law to Control Organized Crime

In India, there is no comprehensive law to control organized crime in all its dimensions and manifestations. There is, however, substantive law regarding criminal conspiracy There are also penal provisions in various statutes against specific violations of those statutes.

Criminal Conspiracy

Sec. 120-A of the Indian Penal Code defines criminal conspiracy as:

"When two or more persons agree to do, or cause to be done -

(1) An illegal act, or

(2) An Act which is not illegal by illegal means. Such an agreement is designated as criminal conspiracy: provided that no agreement except an agreement to commit an offence shall amount to a criminal conspiracy unless some act besides the agreement is done by one or more parties to such agreement in pursunce thereof Explanation: It is immaterial whether the illegal act is the ultimate object of such agreement, or is merely incidental to that object".

Section 120-B of the India Penal Code provides for punishment for criminal conspiracy. The punishment for the conspirator is the same as for the principal offender. It may, however, be emphasized that the criminal conspiracy by itself is a substantive offence. The conspiracy need not fructify and the mere proof of the existence of the criminal conspiracy is adequate to have the criminal punished for such criminal conspiracy

Dacoity and Related Offences

Dacoity is one of the oldest forms of crimes in India and is committed purely for the purpose of looting or extortion. Section 391 of the Penal Code defines dacoity as:

> "When five or more persons conjointly commit or attempt to commit a robbery, or where the whole number of persons conjointly committing or attempting to commit a robbery, and persons present and aiding such commission or attempt amount to five or more, every person so committing, attempting or aiding is said to commit 'dacoity'."

In other words, if five or more persons commit the offence of robbery, they commit 'dacoity'. Dacoity is punishable with imprisonment for life or rigorous imprisonment up to 10 years and five months (section 395). The Code also criminalizes preparation to commit dacoity (section 399) and assembly for the purpose of committing dacoity (section 402). Importantly, section 400 of the Code criminalizes the act of belonging to a 'gang' of persons associated for the purpose of habitually committing dacoities. The punishment is quite severe and may even extend to life imprisonment. Similarly, section 401 criminalizes the act of belonging to a gang of thieves. It would, thus, appear that adequate legislative tools are available to the law enforcement agencies to deal with gangs of dacoits and thieves, but the proof of existence of a gang in Court requires painstaking investigation.

In view of increasing incidents of kidnapping for ransom, the parliament inserted Section 364-A in the India Penal Code to provide for stringent punishment for such offences, further strengthened in 1995. The amended Section 364-A reads as follows:

> "Whoever kidnaps or abducts any person or keeps a person in detention after such kidnapping or abduction and threatens to cause death or hurt to such person, or by his conduct gives rise to a reasonable apprehension that such person may be put to death or hurt, or causes hurt or death to such person in order to compel the Government or any foreign State or international inter-governmental organization or to do or abstain from doing any act or to pay shall be punishable with death, or imprisonment for life, and shall also be liable to fine".

Law on Gangsters

There is no central legislation to suppress 'gang activity' having country-wide applicability. The State of Uttar Pradesha, most populous and politically most powerful (population: 139.1 million in 1991), enacted Uttar Pradesh Gangsters and Anti-Social Activities (Prevention) Act, 1986, which is applicable in that State only The gang has been defined as a group of persons, who, singly or collectively, indulge in anti-national activities by violence or threat of violence for gaining undue political, economic or physical advantages and includes, offences against the body, boot legging, forcible possession of immovable property, creating communal disturbances, obstructing public servants in the discharge of their duties, kidnapping for ransom, diverting an aircraft or public transport vehicle from its schedule path, etc16.

A gangster is punishable with minimum imprisonment of two years extendable up to 10 years (sec. 3). The rules of evidence have been modified and certain statutory presumptions can be raised against the gangsters by the trial court. Provision has also been made for the protection of witnesses. The trial may be held in-camera on the request of public prosecutor. The name and address of a witness can be omitted in the court records, if the Court so desires. The property of the gangster can be attached by the District Magistrate if satisfied that it was acquired through criminal activity This Act has a wide canvass and purports to cover large areas of organized criminal activity.

It is, however, different from laws enacted in foreign countries, in that, apart from criminalizing money making activities of the criminal gangs, it also criminalizes infringement of election laws, causing obstruction or disturbance in the pursuit of lawful trade, business or profession and incitement to violence and disturbance of communal harmony etc. It appears to be more comprehensive than RICO.

There is no firm data available to assess its effectiveness. It appears that due to inadequate investigations and inordinately delayed trials by the courts, this legislation has not been able to make any dent on the criminal landscape of the State.

Other Laws

There are several other central statutes which deal with specific facets of organized crime. Some of them are: the Customs Act, 1962; the Narcotics Drugs and Psychotropic Substances Act, 1884; the Immoral Traffic (Prevention) Act, 1956; the Foreign Exchange Regulation Act, 1973 and the Public Gambling Act, 1867 etc. Besides, the State Government have also legislated on subjects like excise, prohibition and gambling etc.

Preventive Action

The National Security Act 1980, provides for preventive detention by the Central Government or the State Government or by the officers designated by these Government. The detention order is issued for one year with a view to preventing a person from acting in any manner prejudicial to the defence of India or to the friendly relations with foreign powers. The detention has to be approved by an Advisory Board headed by a serving High Court judge. The expression 'security of India' is open to liberal interpretation and this Act has been used, though sparingly, against anti-national elements and hard core gangsters. Detention is an executive action and the case does not go to the court for trial.

The illicit trafficking in narcotic drugs and psychotropic substances poses a serious threat to the health and welfare of the people and the activities of persons engaged in such illicit traffic have a de-stablising effect on the national economy. The Prevention of Illicit Traffic in Narcotic Drugs and Psychotropic Substances Act 1988, provides for detention of such persons. The Central Government or the State Government or designated officers of these Government, can pass an order for detaining a person with a view to preventing him from engaging in illicit traffic in narcotic drugs. The detention can be made for one year but in certain circumstances it is extendable to two years.

Thus, India has laws scattered in various statutes to deal with various facets of organized crime. The existing laws, however, drastically fall short of the requirements to curb the menace. The Government of India is conscious of this and has drafted the Organized Crime Control Act. The draft Act defines 'Organized Criminal Gang' in a very comprehensive manner, incorporating most of the essential characteristics of organized crime. A gang is defined as:

> "A band of two or more persons who commit or attempt to commit or cause to be committed, either individually or collectively, in furtherance of a common object or objects and on a continuing basis, for material gains or otherwise, by taking recourse to use or show of violence or threat of violence, either direct or implied, or by fraudulent or dishonest means corrupting the public servants, any of the acts listed in Schedule I to this Act."

Schedule I includes most major criminal offences, including murder, bodily harm, smuggling, traffic in drugs, kidnapping for ransom, espionage, causing bomb blasts, aircraft hijacking, hostage taking, mass killing, contract killing, gang rapes, extortion etc. The draft Act specifically provides for admissibility of scientific expert evidence; computer print-outs of telephone calls, confession of the accused person made to a police officer; identification by videograph; evidence obtained through Interpol and protection of witnesses. It also provides for the setting up of a national body to co-ordinate effort against organized crime and the setting up of Organized Crime Cells at the State and District levels. The Act also criminalizes laundering the proceeds of crime.

The trial under the proposed Act is to be conducted by a Designated Court. The Act provides for stringent punishment to the accused. It is not known when the National Parliament will enact the law, but the above effort shows the government's deep concern and anxiety about the growing menace of organized crime and the need to curb it. The most significant aspect of the draft Act appears to be that continuing criminal activity, based on violence, even when not impelled by 'material gain', is proposed to be brought within the ambit of organized crime. This is an obvious departure from prevalent definitions of organized crime in other countries.

10

United Nations Convention against Transnational Organised Crime

Article 1
Statement of purpose

The purpose of this Convention is to promote cooperation to prevent and combat transnational organised crime more effectively.

Article 2
Use of terms

For the purposes of this Convention:

(a) "Organised criminal group" shall mean a structured group of three or more persons, existing for a period of time and acting in concert with the aim of committing one or more serious crimes or offences established in accordance with this Convention, in order to obtain, directly or indirectly, a financial or other material benefit;

(b) "Serious crime" shall mean conduct constituting an offence punishable by a maximum deprivation of liberty of at least four years or a more serious penalty;

(c) "Structured group" shall mean a group that is not randomly formed for the immediate commission of an offence and that does not need to have formally defined roles for its members, continuity of its membership or a developed structure;

(d) "Property" shall mean assets of every kind, whether corporeal or incorporeal, movable or immovable, tangible or intangible, and legal documents or instruments evidencing title to, or interest in, such assets;

(e) "Proceeds of crime" shall mean any property derived from or obtained, directly or indirectly, through the commission of an offence;

(f) "Freezing" or "seizure" shall mean temporarily prohibiting the transfer, conversion, disposition or movement of property or temporarily assuming custody or control of property on the basis of an order issued by a court or other competent authority;

(g) "Confiscation", which includes forfeiture where applicable, shall mean the permanent deprivation of property by order of a court or other competent authority;

(h) "Predicate offence" shall mean any offence as a result of which proceeds have been generated that may become the subject of an offence as defined in article 6 of this Convention;

(i) "Controlled delivery" shall mean the technique of allowing illicit or suspect consignments to pass out of, through or into the territory of one or more States, with the knowledge and under the supervision of their competent authorities, with a view to the investigation of an offence and the identification of persons involved in the commission of the offence;

(j) "Regional economic integration organisation" shall mean an organisation constituted by sovereign States of a given region, to which its member States have transferred competence in respect of matters governed by this Convention and which has been duly authorised, in accordance with its internal procedures, to sign, ratify, accept, approve or accede to it; references to "States Parties" under this Convention shall apply to such organisations within the limits of their competence.

ARTICLE 3
SCOPE OF APPLICATION

1. This Convention shall apply, except as otherwise stated herein, to the prevention, investigation and prosecution of:

   (a) The offences established in accordance with articles 5, 6, 8 and 23 of this Convention; and

   (b) Serious crime as defined in article 2 of this Convention; where the offence is transnational in nature and involves an organised criminal group.

2. For the purpose of paragraph 1 of this article, an offence is transnational in nature if:

   (a) It is committed in more than one State;

   (b) It is committed in one State but a substantial part of its preparation, planning, direction or control takes place in another State;

   (c) It is committed in one State but involves an organised criminal group that engages in criminal activities in more than one State; or

   (d) It is committed in one State but has substantial effects in another State.

Article 4
Protection of sovereignty

1. States Parties shall carry out their obligations under this Convention in a manner consistent with the principles of sovereign equality and territorial integrity of States and that of non-intervention in the domestic affairs of other States.

2. Nothing in this Convention entitles a State Party to undertake in the territory of another State the exercise of jurisdiction and performance of functions that are reserved exclusively for the authorities of that other State by its domestic law.

Article 5
Criminalisation of participation in an organised criminal group

1. Each State Party shall adopt such legislative and other measures as may be necessary to establish as criminal offences, when committed intentionally:

   (a) Either or both of the following as criminal offences distinct from those involving the attempt or completion of the criminal activity:

      (i) Agreeing with one or more other persons to commit a serious crime for a purpose relating directly or indirectly to the obtaining of a financial or other material benefit and, where required by domestic law, involving an act undertaken by one of the participants in furtherance of the agreement or involving an organised criminal group;

      (ii) Conduct by a person who, with knowledge of either the aim and general criminal activity of an organised criminal group or its

intention to commit the crimes in question, takes an active part in:

a. Criminal activities of the organised criminal group;

b. Other activities of the organised criminal group in the knowledge that his or her participation will contribute to the achievement of the above-described criminal aim;

(b) Organising, directing, aiding, abetting, facilitating or counselling the commission of serious crime involving an organised criminal group.

2. The knowledge, intent, aim, purpose or agreement referred to in paragraph 1 of this article may be inferred from objective factual circumstances.

3. States Parties whose domestic law requires involvement of an organised criminal group for purposes of the offences established in accordance with paragraph 1 (a) (i) of this article shall ensure that their domestic law covers all serious crimes involving organised criminal groups. Such States Parties, as well as States Parties whose domestic law requires an act in furtherance of the agreement for purposes of the offences established in accordance with paragraph 1 (a) (i) of this article, shall so inform the Secretary-General of the United Nations at the time of their signature or of deposit of their instrument of ratification, acceptance or approval of or accession to this Convention.

ARTICLE 6

CRIMINALISATION OF THE LAUNDERING OF PROCEEDS OF CRIME

1. Each State Party shall adopt, in accordance with

fundamental principles of its domestic law, such legislative and other measures as may be necessary to establish as criminal offences, when committed intentionally:

(a) (i) The conversion or transfer of property, knowing that such property is the proceeds of crime, for the purpose of concealing or disguising the illicit origin of the property or of helping any person who is involved in the commission of the predicate offence to evade the legal consequences of his or her action;

(ii) The concealment or disguise of the true nature, source, location, disposition, movement or ownership of or rights with respect to property, knowing that such property is the proceeds of crime;

(b) Subject to the basic concepts of its legal system:

(i) The acquisition, possession or use of property, knowing, at the time of receipt, that such property is the proceeds of crime;

(ii) Participation in, association with or conspiracy to commit, attempts to commit and aiding, abetting, facilitating and counselling the commission of any of the offences established in accordance with this article.

2. For purposes of implementing or applying paragraph 1 of this article:

(a) Each State Party shall seek to apply paragraph 1 of this article to the widest range of predicate offences;

(b) Each State Party shall include as predicate offences all serious crime as defined in article 2 of this Convention and the offences established in accordance with articles 5, 8 and 23 of this Convention. In the case of States Parties whose legislation sets out a list of specific predicate offences, they shall, at a minimum, include in such list a comprehensive range of offences associated with organised criminal groups;

(c) For the purposes of subparagraph (b), predicate offences shall include offences committed both within and outside the jurisdiction of the State Party in question. However, offences committed outside the jurisdiction of a State Party shall constitute predicate offences only when the relevant conduct is a criminal offence under the domestic law of the State where it is committed and would be a criminal offence under the domestic law of the State Party implementing or applying this article had it been committed there;

(d) Each State Party shall furnish copies of its laws that give effect to this article and of any subsequent changes to such laws or a description thereof to the Secretary-General of the United Nations;

(e) If required by fundamental principles of the domestic law of a State Party, it may be provided that the offences set forth in paragraph 1 of this article do not apply to the persons who committed the predicate offence;

(f) Knowledge, intent or purpose required as an element of an offence set forth in paragraph 1 of this article may be inferred from objective factual circumstances.

ARTICLE 7

MEASURES TO COMBAT MONEY-LAUNDERING

1. Each State Party:

(a) Shall institute a comprehensive domestic regulatory and supervisory regime for banks and non-bank financial institutions and, where appropriate, other bodies particularly susceptible to money-laundering, within its competence, in order to deter and detect all forms of money-laundering, which regime shall emphasise requirements for customer identification, record-keeping and the reporting of suspicious transactions;

(b) Shall, without prejudice to articles 18 and 27 of this Convention, ensure that administrative, regulatory, law enforcement and other authorities dedicated to combating money-laundering (including, where appropriate under domestic law, judicial authorities) have the ability to cooperate and exchange information at the national and international levels within the conditions prescribed by its domestic law and, to that end, shall consider the establishment of a financial intelligence unit to serve as a national centre for the collection, analysis and dissemination of information regarding potential money-laundering.

2. States Parties shall consider implementing feasible measures to detect and monitor the movement of cash and appropriate negotiable instruments across their borders, subject to safeguards to ensure proper use of information and without impeding in any way the movement of legitimate capital. Such measures may include a requirement that individuals and businesses report the cross-border transfer of substantial quantities of cash and appropriate negotiable instruments.

3. In establishing a domestic regulatory and supervisory regime under the terms of this article, and without prejudice to any other article of this Convention, States

Parties are called upon to use as a guideline the relevant initiatives of regional, interregional and multilateral organisations against money-laundering.

4. States Parties shall endeavour to develop and promote global, regional, subregional and bilateral cooperation among judicial, law enforcement and financial regulatory authorities in order to combat moneylaundering.

Article 8
Criminalisation of corruption

1. Each State Party shall adopt such legislative and other measures as may be necessary to establish as criminal offences, when committed intentionally:
   (a) The promise, offering or giving to a public official, directly or indirectly, of an undue advantage, for the official himself or herself or another person or entity, in order that the official act or refrain from acting in the exercise of his or her official duties;
   (b) The solicitation or acceptance by a public official, directly or indirectly, of an undue advantage, for the official himself or herself or another person or entity, in order that the official act or refrain from acting in the exercise of his or her official duties.
2. Each State Party shall consider adopting such legislative and other measures as may be necessary to establish as criminal offences conduct referred to in paragraph 1 of this article involving a foreign public official or international civil servant. Likewise, each State Party shall consider establishing as criminal offences other forms of corruption.
3. Each State Party shall also adopt such measures as may be necessary to establish as a criminal offence

participation as an accomplice in an offence established in accordance with this article.

4. For the purposes of paragraph 1 of this article and article 9 of this Convention, "public official" shall mean a public official or a person who provides a public service as defined in the domestic law and as applied in the criminal law of the State Party in which the person in question performs that function.

Article 9
Measures against corruption

1. In addition to the measures set forth in article 8 of this Convention, each State Party shall, to the extent appropriate and consistent with its legal system, adopt legislative, administrative or other effective measures to promote integrity and to prevent, detect and punish the corruption of public officials.

2. Each State Party shall take measures to ensure effective action by its authorities in the prevention, detection and punishment of the corruption of public officials, including providing such authorities with adequate independence to deter the exertion of inappropriate influence on their actions.

Article 10
Liability of legal persons

1. Each State Party shall adopt such measures as may be necessary, consistent with its legal principles, to establish the liability of legal persons for participation in serious crimes involving an organised criminal group and for the offences established in accordance with articles 5, 6, 8 and 23 of this Convention.

2. Subject to the legal principles of the State Party, the liability of legal persons may be criminal, civil or administrative.

3. Such liability shall be without prejudice to the criminal liability of the natural persons who have committed the offences.

4. Each State Party shall, in particular, ensure that legal persons held liable in accordance with this article are subject to effective, proportionate and dissuasive criminal or non-criminal sanctions, including monetary sanctions.

Article 11

Prosecution, adjudication and sanctions

1. Each State Party shall make the commission of an offence established in accordance with articles 5, 6, 8 and 23 of this Convention liable to sanctions that take into account the gravity of that offence.

2. Each State Party shall endeavour to ensure that any discretionary legal powers under its domestic law relating to the prosecution of persons for offences covered by this Convention are exercised to maximize the effectiveness of law enforcement measures in respect of those offences and with due regard to the need to deter the commission of such offences.

3. In the case of offences established in accordance with articles 5, 6, 8 and 23 of this Convention, each State Party shall take appropriate measures, in accordance with its domestic law and with due regard to the rights of the defence, to seek to ensure that conditions imposed in connection with decisions on release pending trial or appeal take into consideration the need to ensure the presence of the defendant at subsequent criminal proceedings.

4. Each State Party shall ensure that its courts or other competent authorities bear in mind the grave nature of the offences covered by this Convention when

considering the eventuality of early release or parole of persons convicted of such offences.

5. Each State Party shall, where appropriate, establish under its domestic law a long statute of limitations period in which to commence proceedings for any offence covered by this Convention and a longer period where the alleged offender has evaded the administration of justice.

6. Nothing contained in this Convention shall affect the principle that the description of the offences established in accordance with this Convention and of the applicable legal defences or other legal principles controlling the lawfulness of conduct is reserved to the domestic law of a State Party and that such offences shall be prosecuted and punished in accordance with that law.

Article 12

Confiscation and seizure

1. States Parties shall adopt, to the greatest extent possible within their domestic legal systems, such measures as may be necessary to enable confiscation of:

   (a) Proceeds of crime derived from offences covered by this Convention or property the value of which corresponds to that of such proceeds;

   (b) Property, equipment or other instrumentalities used in or destined for use in offences covered by this Convention.

2. States Parties shall adopt such measures as may be necessary to enable the identification, tracing, freezing or seizure of any item referred to in paragraph 1 of this article for the purpose of eventual confiscation.

3. If proceeds of crime have been transformed or converted, in part or in full, into other property, such property shall be liable to the measures referred to in this article instead of the proceeds.

4. If proceeds of crime have been intermingled with property acquired from legitimate sources, such property shall, without prejudice to any powers relating to freezing or seizure, be liable to confiscation up to the assessed value of the intermingled proceeds.

5. Income or other benefits derived from proceeds of crime, from property into which proceeds of crime have been transformed or converted or from property with which proceeds of crime have been intermingled shall also be liable to the measures referred to in this article, in the same manner and to the same extent as proceeds of crime.

6. For the purposes of this article and article 13 of this Convention, each State Party shall empower its courts or other competent authorities to order that bank, financial or commercial records be made available or be seized. States Parties shall not decline to act under the provisions of this paragraph on the ground of bank secrecy.

7. States Parties may consider the possibility of requiring that an offender demonstrate the lawful origin of alleged proceeds of crime or other property liable to confiscation, to the extent that such a requirement is consistent with the principles of their domestic law and with the nature of the judicial and other proceedings.

8. The provisions of this article shall not be construed to prejudice the rights of bona fide third parties.

9. Nothing contained in this article shall affect the principle that the measures to which it refers shall be

defined and implemented in accordance with and subject to the provisions of the domestic law of a State Party.

ARTICLE 13
INTERNATIONAL COOPERATION FOR PURPOSES OF CONFISCATION

1. A State Party that has received a request from another State Party having jurisdiction over an offence covered by this Convention for confiscation of proceeds of crime, property, equipment or other instrumentalities referred to in article 12, paragraph 1, of this Convention situated in its territory shall, to the greatest extent possible within its domestic legal system:

   (a) Submit the request to its competent authorities for the purpose of obtaining an order of confiscation and, if such an order is granted, give effect to it; or

   (b) Submit to its competent authorities, with a view to giving effect to it to the extent requested, an order of confiscation issued by a court in the territory of the requesting State Party in accordance with article 12, paragraph 1, of this Convention insofar as it relates to proceeds of crime, property, equipment or other instrumentalities referred to in article 12, paragraph 1, situated in the territory of the requested State Party.

2. Following a request made by another State Party having jurisdiction over an offence covered by this Convention, the requested State Party shall take measures to identify, trace and freeze or seize proceeds of crime, property, equipment or other instrumentalities referred to in article 12, paragraph

1, of this Convention for the purpose of eventual confiscation to be ordered either by the requesting State Party or, pursuant to a request under paragraph 1 of this article, by the requested State Party.

3. The provisions of article 18 of this Convention are applicable, mutatis mutandis, to this article. In addition to the information specified in article 18, paragraph 15, requests made pursuant to this article shall contain:

   (a) In the case of a request pertaining to paragraph 1 (a) of this article, a description of the property to be confiscated and a statement of the facts relied upon by the requesting State Party sufficient to enable the requested State Party to seek the order under its domestic law;

   (b) In the case of a request pertaining to paragraph 1 (b) of this article, a legally admissible copy of an order of confiscation upon which the request is based issued by the requesting State Party, a statement of the facts and information as to the extent to which execution of the order is requested;

   (c) In the case of a request pertaining to paragraph 2 of this article, a statement of the facts relied upon by the requesting State Party and a description of the actions requested.

4. The decisions or actions provided for in paragraphs 1 and 2 of this article shall be taken by the requested State Party in accordance with and subject to the provisions of its domestic law and its procedural rules or any bilateral or multilateral treaty, agreement or arrangement to which it may be bound in relation to the requesting State Party.

5. Each State Party shall furnish copies of its laws and regulations that give effect to this article and of any subsequent changes to such laws and regulations or

a description thereof to the Secretary-General of the United Nations.

6. If a State Party elects to make the taking of the measures referred to in paragraphs 1 and 2 of this article conditional on the existence of a relevant treaty, that State Party shall consider this Convention the necessary and sufficient treaty basis.

7. Cooperation under this article may be refused by a State Party if the offence to which the request relates is not an offence covered by this Convention.

8. The provisions of this article shall not be construed to prejudice the rights of bona fide third parties.

9. States Parties shall consider concluding bilateral or multilateral treaties, agreements or arrangements to enhance the effectiveness of international cooperation undertaken pursuant to this article.

ARTICLE 14

DISPOSAL OF CONFISCATED PROCEEDS OF CRIME OR PROPERTY

1. Proceeds of crime or property confiscated by a State Party pursuant to articles 12 or 13, paragraph 1, of this Convention shall be disposed of by that State Party in accordance with its domestic law and administrative procedures.

2. When acting on the request made by another State Party in accordance with article 13 of this Convention, States Parties shall, to the extent permitted by domestic law and if so requested, give priority consideration to returning the confiscated proceeds of crime or property to the requesting State Party so that it can give compensation to the victims of the crime or return such proceeds of crime or property to their legitimate owners.

3. When acting on the request made by another State Party in accordance with articles 12 and 13 of this Convention, a State Party may give special consideration to concluding agreements or arrangements on:

   (a) Contributing the value of such proceeds of crime or property or funds derived from the sale of such proceeds of crime or property or a part thereof to the account designated in accordance with article 30, paragraph 2 (c), of this Convention and to intergovernmental bodies specialising in the fight against organised crime;

   (b) Sharing with other States Parties, on a regular or case-by-case basis, such proceeds of crime or property, or funds derived from the sale of such proceeds of crime or property, in accordance with its domestic law or administrative procedures.

ARTICLE 15
JURISDICTION

1. Each State Party shall adopt such measures as may be necessary to establish its jurisdiction over the offences established in accordance with articles 5, 6, 8 and 23 of this Convention when:

   (a) The offence is committed in the territory of that State Party; or

   (b) The offence is committed on board a vessel that is flying the flag of that State Party or an aircraft that is registered under the laws of that State Party at the time that the offence is committed.

2. Subject to article 4 of this Convention, a State Party may also establish its jurisdiction over any such offence when:

(a) The offence is committed against a national of that State Party;

(b) The offence is committed by a national of that State Party or a stateless person who has his or her habitual residence in its territory; or

(c) The offence is:

(i) One of those established in accordance with article 5, paragraph 1, of this Convention and is committed outside its territory with a view to the commission of a serious crime within its territory;

(ii) One of those established in accordance with article 6, paragraph 1 (b) (ii), of this Convention and is committed outside its territory with a view to the commission of an offence established in accordance with article 6, paragraph 1 (a) (i) or (ii) or (b) (i), of this Convention within its territory.

3. For the purposes of article 16, paragraph 10, of this Convention, each State Party shall adopt such measures as may be necessary to establish its jurisdiction over the offences covered by this Convention when the alleged offender is present in its territory and it does not extradite such person solely on the ground that he or she is one of its nationals.

4. Each State Party may also adopt such measures as may be necessary to establish its jurisdiction over the offences covered by this Convention when the alleged offender is present in its territory and it does not extradite him or her.

5. If a State Party exercising its jurisdiction under paragraph 1 or 2 of this article has been notified, or has otherwise learned, that one or more other States

Parties are conducting an investigation, prosecution or judicial proceeding in respect of the same conduct, the competent authorities of those States Parties shall, as appropriate, consult one another with a view to coordinating their actions.

6. Without prejudice to norms of general international law, this Convention does not exclude the exercise of any criminal jurisdiction established by a State Party in accordance with its domestic law.

Article 16
Extradition

1. This article shall apply to the offences covered by this Convention or in cases where an offence referred to in article 3, paragraph 1 (a) or (b), involves an organised criminal group and the person who is the subject of the request for extradition is located in the territory of the requested State Party, provided that the offence for which extradition is sought is punishable under the domestic law of both the requesting State Party and the requested State Party.
2. If the request for extradition includes several separate serious crimes, some of which are not covered by this article, the requested State Party may apply this article also in respect of the latter offences.
3. Each of the offences to which this article applies shall be deemed to be included as an extraditable offence in any extradition treaty existing between States Parties. States Parties undertake to include such offences as extraditable offences in every extradition treaty to be concluded between them.
4. If a State Party that makes extradition conditional on the existence of a treaty receives a request for extradition from another State Party with which it has

no extradition treaty, it may consider this Convention the legal basis for extradition in respect of any offence to which this article applies.

5. States Parties that make extradition conditional on the existence of a treaty shall:

   (a) At the time of deposit of their instrument of ratification, acceptance, approval of or accession to this Convention, inform the Secretary-General of the United Nations whether they will take this Convention as the legal basis for cooperation on extradition with other States Parties to this Convention; and

   (b) If they do not take this Convention as the legal basis for cooperation on extradition, seek, where appropriate, to conclude treaties on extradition with other States Parties to this Convention in order to implement this article.

6. States Parties that do not make extradition conditional on the existence of a treaty shall recognise offences to which this article applies as extraditable offences between themselves.

7. Extradition shall be subject to the conditions provided for by the domestic law of the requested State Party or by applicable extradition treaties, including, inter alia, conditions in relation to the minimum penalty requirement for extradition and the grounds upon which the requested State Party may refuse extradition.

8. States Parties shall, subject to their domestic law, endeavour to expedite extradition procedures and to simplify evidentiary requirements relating thereto in respect of any offence to which this article applies.

9. Subject to the provisions of its domestic law and its extradition treaties, the requested State Party may, upon being satisfied that the circumstances so warrant

and are urgent and at the request of the requesting State Party, take a person whose extradition is sought and who is present in its territory into custody or take other appropriate measures to ensure his or her presence at extradition proceedings.

10. A State Party in whose territory an alleged offender is found, if it does not extradite such person in respect of an offence to which this article applies solely on the ground that he or she is one of its nationals, shall, at the request of the State Party seeking extradition, be obliged to submit the case without undue delay to its competent authorities for the purpose of prosecution. Those authorities shall take their decision and conduct their proceedings in the same manner as in the case of any other offence of a grave nature under the domestic law of that State Party. The States Parties concerned shall cooperate with each other, in particular on procedural and evidentiary aspects, to ensure the efficiency of such prosecution.
11. Whenever a State Party is permitted under its domestic law to extradite or otherwise surrender one of its nationals only upon the condition that the person will be returned to that State Party to serve the sentence imposed as a result of the trial or proceedings for which the extradition or surrender of the person was sought and that State Party and the State Party seeking the extradition of the person agree with this option and other terms that they may deem appropriate, such conditional extradition or surrender shall be sufficient to discharge the obligation set forth in paragraph 10 of this article.
12. If extradition, sought for purposes of enforcing a sentence, is refused because the person sought is a national of the requested State Party, the requested Party shall, if its domestic law so permits and in conformity with the requirements of such law, upon

application of the requesting Party, consider the enforcement of the sentence that has been imposed under the domestic law of the requesting Party or the remainder thereof.

13. Any person regarding whom proceedings are being carried out in connection with any of the offences to which this article applies shall be guaranteed fair treatment at all stages of the proceedings, including enjoyment of all the rights and guarantees provided by the domestic law of the State Party in the territory of which that person is present.

14. Nothing in this Convention shall be interpreted as imposing an obligation to extradite if the requested State Party has substantial grounds for believing that the request has been made for the purpose of prosecuting or punishing a person on account of that person's sex, race, religion, nationality, ethnic origin or political opinions or that compliance with the request would cause prejudice to that person's position for any one of these reasons.

15. States Parties may not refuse a request for extradition on the sole ground that the offence is also considered to involve fiscal matters.

16. Before refusing extradition, the requested State Party shall, where appropriate, consult with the requesting State Party to provide it with ample opportunity to present its opinions and to provide information relevant to its allegation.

17. States Parties shall seek to conclude bilateral and multilateral agreements or arrangements to carry out or to enhance the effectiveness of extradition.

Article 17

Transfer of sentenced persons

States Parties may consider entering into bilateral or

multilateral agreements or arrangements on the transfer to their territory of persons sentenced to imprisonment or other forms of deprivation of liberty for offences covered by this Convention, in order that they may complete their sentences there.

Article 18
Mutual legal assistance

1. States Parties shall afford one another the widest measure of mutual legal assistance in investigations, prosecutions and judicial proceedings in relation to the offences covered by this Convention as provided for in article 3 and shall reciprocally extend to one another similar assistance where the requesting State Party has reasonable grounds to suspect that the offence referred to in article 3, paragraph 1 (a) or (b), is transnational in nature, including that victims, witnesses, proceeds, instrumentalities or evidence of such offences are located in the requested State Party and that the offence involves an organised criminal group.
2. Mutual legal assistance shall be afforded to the fullest extent possible under relevant laws, treaties, agreements and arrangements of the requested State Party with respect to investigations, prosecutions and judicial proceedings in relation to the offences for which a legal person may be held liable in accordance with article 10 of this Convention in the requesting State Party.
3. Mutual legal assistance to be afforded in accordance with this article may be requested for any of the following purposes:

    (a) Taking evidence or statements from persons;

    (b) Effecting service of judicial documents;

    (c) Executing searches and seizures, and freezing;

(d) Examining objects and sites;

(e) Providing information, evidentiary items and expert evaluations;

(f) Providing originals or certified copies of relevant documents and records, including government, bank, financial, corporate or business records;

(g) Identifying or tracing proceeds of crime, property, instrumentalities or other things for evidentiary purposes;

(h) Facilitating the voluntary appearance of persons in the requesting State Party;

(i) Any other type of assistance that is not contrary to the domestic law of the requested State Party.

4. Without prejudice to domestic law, the competent authorities of a State Party may, without prior request, transmit information relating to criminal matters to a competent authority in another State Party where they believe that such information could assist the authority in undertaking or successfully concluding inquiries and criminal proceedings or could result in a request formulated by the latter State Party pursuant to this Convention.

5. The transmission of information pursuant to paragraph 4 of this article shall be without prejudice to inquiries and criminal proceedings in the State of the competent authorities providing the information. The competent authorities receiving the information shall comply with a request that said information remain confidential, even temporarily, or with restrictions on its use. However, this shall not prevent the receiving State Party from disclosing in its proceedings information that is exculpatory to an accused person. In such a case, the receiving State Party shall notify the transmitting State Party prior to

the disclosure and, if so requested, consult with the transmitting State Party. If, in an exceptional case, advance notice is not possible, the receiving State Party shall inform the transmitting State Party of the disclosure without delay.

6. The provisions of this article shall not affect the obligations under any other treaty, bilateral or multilateral, that governs or will govern, in whole or in part, mutual legal assistance.

7. Paragraphs 9 to 29 of this article shall apply to requests made pursuant to this article if the States Parties in question are not bound by a treaty of mutual legal assistance. If those States Parties are bound by such a treaty, the corresponding provisions of that treaty shall apply unless the States Parties agree to apply paragraphs 9 to 29 of this article in lieu thereof. States Parties are strongly encouraged to apply these paragraphs if they facilitate cooperation.

8. States Parties shall not decline to render mutual legal assistance pursuant to this article on the ground of bank secrecy.

9. States Parties may decline to render mutual legal assistance pursuant to this article on the ground of absence of dual criminality. However, the requested State Party may, when it deems appropriate, provide assistance, to the extent it decides at its discretion, irrespective of whether the conduct would constitute an offence under the domestic law of the requested State Party.

10. A person who is being detained or is serving a sentence in the territory of one State Party whose presence in another State Party is requested for purposes of identification, testimony or otherwise providing assistance in obtaining evidence for

investigations, prosecutions or judicial proceedings in relation to offences covered by this Convention may be transferred if the following conditions are met:

(a) The person freely gives his or her informed consent;

(b) The competent authorities of both States Parties agree, subject to such conditions as those States Parties may deem appropriate.

11. For the purposes of paragraph 10 of this article:

(a) The State Party to which the person is transferred shall have the authority and obligation to keep the person transferred in custody, unless otherwise requested or authorised by the State Party from which the person was transferred;

(b) The State Party to which the person is transferred shall without delay implement its obligation to return the person to the custody of the State Party from which the person was transferred as agreed beforehand, or as otherwise agreed, by the competent authorities of both States Parties;

(c) The State Party to which the person is transferred shall not require the State Party from which the person was transferred to initiate extradition proceedings for the return of the person;

(d) The person transferred shall receive credit for service of the sentence being served in the State from which he or she was transferred for time spent in the custody of the State Party to which he or she was transferred.

12. Unless the State Party from which a person is to be transferred in accordance with paragraphs 10 and 11 of this article so agrees, that person, whatever his or her nationality, shall not be prosecuted, detained,

punished or subjected to any other restriction of his or her personal liberty in the territory of the State to which that person is transferred in respect of acts, omissions or convictions prior to his or her departure from the territory of the State from which he or she was transferred.

13. Each State Party shall designate a central authority that shall have the responsibility and power to receive requests for mutual legal assistance and either to execute them or to transmit them to the competent authorities for execution. Where a State Party has a special region or territory with a separate system of mutual legal assistance, it may designate a distinct central authority that shall have the same function for that region or territory. Central authorities shall ensure the speedy and proper execution or transmission of the requests received. Where the central authority transmits the request to a competent authority for execution, it shall encourage the speedy and proper execution of the request by the competent authority. The Secretary-General of the United Nations shall be notified of the central authority designated for this purpose at the time each State Party deposits its instrument of ratification, acceptance or approval of or accession to this Convention. Requests for mutual legal assistance and any communication related thereto shall be transmitted to the central authorities designated by the States Parties. This requirement shall be without prejudice to the right of a State Party to require that such requests and communications be addressed to it through diplomatic channels and, in urgent circumstances, where the States Parties agree, through the International Criminal Police Organisation, if possible.

14. Requests shall be made in writing or, where possible, by any means capable of producing a written record,

in a language acceptable to the requested State Party, under conditions allowing that State Party to establish authenticity. The Secretary-General of the United Nations shall be notified of the language or languages acceptable to each State Party at the time it deposits its instrument of ratification, acceptance or approval of or accession to this Convention. In urgent circumstances and where agreed by the States Parties, requests may be made orally, but shall be confirmed in writing forthwith.

15. A request for mutual legal assistance shall contain:

    (a) The identity of the authority making the request;

    (b) The subject matter and nature of the investigation, prosecution or judicial proceeding to which the request relates and the name and functions of the authority conducting the investigation, prosecution or judicial proceeding;

    (c) A summary of the relevant facts, except in relation to requests for the purpose of service of judicial documents;

    (d) A description of the assistance sought and details of any particular procedure that the requesting State Party wishes to be followed;

    (e) Where possible, the identity, location and nationality of any person concerned; and

    (f) The purpose for which the evidence, information or action is sought.

16. The requested State Party may request additional information when it appears necessary for the execution of the request in accordance with its domestic law or when it can facilitate such execution.

17. A request shall be executed in accordance with the domestic law of the requested State Party and, to the

extent not contrary to the domestic law of the requested State Party and where possible, in accordance with the procedures specified in the request.

18. Wherever possible and consistent with fundamental principles of domestic law, when an individual is in the territory of a State Party and has to be heard as a witness or expert by the judicial authorities of another State Party, the first State Party may, at the request of the other, permit the hearing to take place by video conference if it is not possible or desirable for the individual in question to appear in person in the territory of the requesting State Party. States Parties may agree that the hearing shall be conducted by a judicial authority of the requesting State Party and attended by a judicial authority of the requested State Party.

19. The requesting State Party shall not transmit or use information or evidence furnished by the requested State Party for investigations, prosecutions or judicial proceedings other than those stated in the request without the prior consent of the requested State Party. Nothing in this paragraph shall prevent the requesting State Party from disclosing in its proceedings information or evidence that is exculpatory to an accused person. In the latter case, the requesting State Party shall notify the requested State Party prior to the disclosure and, if so requested, consult with the requested State Party. If, in an exceptional case, advance notice is not possible, the requesting State Party shall inform the requested State Party of the disclosure without delay.

20. The requesting State Party may require that the requested State Party keep confidential the fact and substance of the request, except to the extent necessary

to execute the request. If the requested State Party cannot comply with the requirement of confidentiality, it shall promptly inform the requesting State Party.

21. Mutual legal assistance may be refused:

    (a) If the request is not made in conformity with the provisions of this article;

    (b) If the requested State Party considers that execution of the request is likely to prejudice its sovereignty, security, ordre public or other essential interests;

    (c) If the authorities of the requested State Party would be prohibited by its domestic law from carrying out the action requested with regard to any similar offence, had it been subject to investigation, prosecution or judicial proceedings under their own jurisdiction;

    (d) If it would be contrary to the legal system of the requested State Party relating to mutual legal assistance for the request to be granted.

22. States Parties may not refuse a request for mutual legal assistance on the sole ground that the offence is also considered to involve fiscal matters.

23. Reasons shall be given for any refusal of mutual legal assistance.

24. The requested State Party shall execute the request for mutual legal assistance as soon as possible and shall take as full account as possible of any deadlines suggested by the requesting State Party and for which reasons are given, preferably in the request. The requested State Party shall respond to reasonable requests by the requesting State Party on progress of its handling of the request. The requesting State Party shall promptly inform the requested State Party when the assistance sought is no longer required.

25. Mutual legal assistance may be postponed by the requested State Party on the ground that it interferes with an ongoing investigation, prosecution or judicial proceeding.

26. Before refusing a request pursuant to paragraph 21 of this article or postponing its execution pursuant to paragraph 25 of this article, the requested State Party shall consult with the requesting State Party to consider whether assistance may be granted subject to such terms and conditions as it deems necessary. If the requesting State Party accepts assistance subject to those conditions, it shall comply with the conditions.

27. Without prejudice to the application of paragraph 12 of this article, a witness, expert or other person who, at the request of the requesting State Party, consents to give evidence in a proceeding or to assist in an investigation, prosecution or judicial proceeding in the territory of the requesting State Party shall not be prosecuted, detained, punished or subjected to any other restriction of his or her personal liberty in that territory in respect of acts, omissions or convictions prior to his or her departure from the territory of the requested State Party. Such safe conduct shall cease when the witness, expert or other person having had, for a period of fifteen consecutive days or for any period agreed upon by the States Parties from the date on which he or she has been officially informed that his or her presence is no longer required by the judicial authorities, an opportunity of leaving, has nevertheless remained voluntarily in the territory of the requesting State Party or, having left it, has returned of his or her own free will.

28. The ordinary costs of executing a request shall be borne by the requested State Party, unless otherwise

agreed by the States Parties concerned. If expenses of a substantial or extraordinary nature are or will be required to fulfil the request, the States Parties shall consult to determine the terms and conditions under which the request will be executed, as well as the manner in which the costs shall be borne.

29. The requested State Party:

    (a) Shall provide to the requesting State Party copies of government records, documents or information in its possession that under its domestic law are available to the general public;

    (b) May, at its discretion, provide to the requesting State Party in whole, in part or subject to such conditions as it deems appropriate, copies of any government records, documents or information in its possession that under its domestic law are not available to the general public.

30. States Parties shall consider, as may be necessary, the possibility of concluding bilateral or multilateral agreements or arrangements that would serve the purposes of, give practical effect to or enhance the provisions of this article.

Article 19
Joint investigations

States Parties shall consider concluding bilateral or multilateral agreements or arrangements whereby, in relation to matters that are the subject of investigations, prosecutions or judicial proceedings in one or more States, the competent authorities concerned may establish joint investigative bodies. In the absence of such agreements or arrangements, joint investigations may be undertaken by agreement on a case-by-case basis. The States Parties involved shall ensure that the sovereignty of the State

Party in whose territory such investigation is to take place is fully respected.

Article 20
Special investigative techniques

1. If permitted by the basic principles of its domestic legal system, each State Party shall, within its possibilities and under the conditions prescribed by its domestic law, take the necessary measures to allow for the appropriate use of controlled delivery and, where it deems appropriate, for the use of other special investigative techniques, such as electronic or other forms of surveillance and undercover operations, by its competent authorities in its territory for the purpose of effectively combating organised crime.
2. For the purpose of investigating the offences covered by this Convention, States Parties are encouraged to conclude, when necessary, appropriate bilateral or multilateral agreements or arrangements for using such special investigative techniques in the context of cooperation at the international level. Such agreements or arrangements shall be concluded and implemented in full compliance with the principle of sovereign equality of States and shall be carried out strictly in accordance with the terms of those agreements or arrangements.
3. In the absence of an agreement or arrangement as set forth in paragraph 2 of this article, decisions to use such special investigative techniques at the international level shall be made on a case-by-case basis and may, when necessary, take into consideration financial arrangements and understandings with respect to the exercise of jurisdiction by the States Parties concerned.

4. Decisions to use controlled delivery at the international level may, with the consent of the States Parties concerned, include methods such as intercepting and allowing the goods to continue intact or be removed or replaced in whole or in part.

ARTICLE 21
TRANSFER OF CRIMINAL PROCEEDINGS

States Parties shall consider the possibility of transferring to one another proceedings for the prosecution of an offence covered by this Convention in cases where such transfer is considered to be in the interests of the proper administration of justice, in particular in cases where several jurisdictions are involved, with a view to concentrating the prosecution.

ARTICLE 22
ESTABLISHMENT OF CRIMINAL RECORD

Each State Party may adopt such legislative or other measures as may be necessary to take into consideration, under such terms as and for the purpose that it deems appropriate, any previous conviction in another State of an alleged offender for the purpose of using such information in criminal proceedings relating to an offence covered by this Convention.

ARTICLE 23
CRIMINALISATION OF OBSTRUCTION OF JUSTICE

Each State Party shall adopt such legislative and other measures as may be necessary to establish as criminal offences, when committed intentionally:

(a) The use of physical force, threats or intimidation or the promise, offering or giving of an undue advantage to induce false testimony or to interfere in the giving of testimony or the production of evidence in a proceeding in relation to the commission of offences covered by this Convention;

(b) The use of physical force, threats or intimidation to interfere with the exercise of official duties by a justice or law enforcement official in relation to the commission of offences covered by this Convention. Nothing in this subparagraph shall prejudice the right of States Parties to have legislation that protects other categories of public officials.

ARTICLE 24
PROTECTION OF WITNESSES

1. Each State Party shall take appropriate measures within its means to provide effective protection from potential retaliation or intimidation for witnesses in criminal proceedings who give testimony concerning offences covered by this Convention and, as appropriate, for their relatives and other persons close to them.

2. The measures envisaged in paragraph 1 of this article may include, inter alia, without prejudice to the rights of the defendant, including the right to due process:

   (a) Establishing procedures for the physical protection of such persons, such as, to the extent necessary and feasible, relocating them and permitting, where appropriate, non-disclosure or limitations on the disclosure of information concerning the identity and whereabouts of such persons;

   (b) Providing evidentiary rules to permit witness testimony to be given in a manner that ensures the safety of the witness, such as permitting testimony to be given through the use of communications technology such as video links or other adequate means.

3. States Parties shall consider entering into agreements or arrangements with other States for the relocation of persons referred to in paragraph 1 of this article.

4. The provisions of this article shall also apply to victims insofar as they are witnesses.

Article 25

Assistance to and protection of victims

1. Each State Party shall take appropriate measures within its means to provide assistance and protection to victims of offences covered by this Convention, in particular in cases of threat of retaliation or intimidation.

2. Each State Party shall establish appropriate procedures to provide access to compensation and restitution for victims of offences covered by this Convention.

3. Each State Party shall, subject to its domestic law, enable views and concerns of victims to be presented and considered at appropriate stages of criminal proceedings against offenders in a manner not prejudicial to the rights of the defence.

Article 26

Measures to enhance cooperation with law enforcement authorities

1. Each State Party shall take appropriate measures to encourage persons who participate or who have participated in organised criminal groups:

   (a) To supply information useful to competent authorities for investigative and evidentiary purposes on such matters as:

(i) The identity, nature, composition, structure, location or activities of organised criminal groups;

(ii) Links, including international links, with other organised criminal groups;

(iii) Offences that organised criminal groups have committed or may commit;

(b) To provide factual, concrete help to competent authorities that may contribute to depriving organised criminal groups of their resources or of the proceeds of crime.

2. Each State Party shall consider providing for the possibility, in appropriate cases, of mitigating punishment of an accused person who provides substantial cooperation in the investigation or prosecution of an offence covered by this Convention.

3. Each State Party shall consider providing for the possibility, in accordance with fundamental principles of its domestic law, of granting immunity from prosecution to a person who provides substantial cooperation in the investigation or prosecution of an offence covered by this Convention.

4. Protection of such persons shall be as provided for in article 24 of this Convention.

5. Where a person referred to in paragraph 1 of this article located in one State Party can provide substantial cooperation to the competent authorities of another State Party, the States Parties concerned may consider entering into agreements or arrangements, in accordance with their domestic law, concerning the potential provision by the other State Party of the treatment set forth in paragraphs 2 and 3 of this article.

ARTICLE 27
LAW ENFORCEMENT COOPERATION

1. States Parties shall cooperate closely with one another, consistent with their respective domestic legal and administrative systems, to enhance the effectiveness of law enforcement action to combat the offences covered by this Convention. Each State Party shall, in particular, adopt effective measures:

   (a) To enhance and, where necessary, to establish channels of communication between their competent authorities, agencies and services in order to facilitate the secure and rapid exchange of information concerning all aspects of the offences covered by this Convention, including, if the States Parties concerned deem it appropriate, links with other criminal activities;

   (b) To cooperate with other States Parties in conducting inquiries with respect to offences covered by this Convention concerning:

      (i) The identity, whereabouts and activities of persons suspected of involvement in such offences or the location of other persons concerned;

      (ii) The movement of proceeds of crime or property derived from the commission of such offences;

      (iii) The movement of property, equipment or other instrumentalities used or intended for use in the commission of such offences;

   (c) To provide, when appropriate, necessary items or quantities of substances for analytical or investigative purposes;

(d) To facilitate effective coordination between their competent authorities, agencies and services and to promote the exchange of personnel and other experts, including, subject to bilateral agreements or arrangements between the States Parties concerned, the posting of liaison officers;

(e) To exchange information with other States Parties on specific means and methods used by organised criminal groups, including, where applicable, routes and conveyances and the use of false identities, altered or false documents or other means of concealing their activities;

(f) To exchange information and coordinate administrative and other measures taken as appropriate for the purpose of early identification of the offences covered by this Convention.

2. With a view to giving effect to this Convention, States Parties shall consider entering into bilateral or multilateral agreements or arrangements on direct cooperation between their law enforcement agencies and, where such agreements or arrangements already exist, amending them. In the absence of such agreements or arrangements between the States Parties concerned, the Parties may consider this Convention as the basis for mutual law enforcement cooperation in respect of the offences covered by this Convention. Whenever appropriate, States Parties shall make full use of agreements or arrangements, including international or regional organisations, to enhance the cooperation between their law enforcement agencies.

3. States Parties shall endeavour to cooperate within their means to respond to transnational organised crime committed through the use of modern technology.

ARTICLE 28

COLLECTION, EXCHANGE AND ANALYSIS OF INFORMATION ON THE NATURE OF ORGANISED CRIME

1. Each State Party shall consider analysing, in consultation with the scientific and academic communities, trends in organised crime in its territory, the circumstances in which organised crime operates, as well as the professional groups and technologies involved.
2. States Parties shall consider developing and sharing analytical expertise concerning organised criminal activities with each other and through international and regional organisations. For that purpose, common definitions, standards and methodologies should be developed and applied as appropriate.
3. Each State Party shall consider monitoring its policies and actual measures to combat organised crime and making assessments of their effectiveness and efficiency.

ARTICLE 29

TRAINING AND TECHNICAL ASSISTANCE

1. Each State Party shall, to the extent necessary, initiate, develop or improve specific training programmes for its law enforcement personnel, including prosecutors, investigating magistrates and customs personnel, and other personnel charged with the prevention, detection and control of the offences covered by this Convention. Such programmes may include secondments and exchanges of staff. Such programmes shall deal, in particular and to the extent permitted by domestic law, with the following:
   (a) Methods used in the prevention, detection and control of the offences covered by this Convention;

(b) Routes and techniques used by persons suspected of involvement in offences covered by this Convention, including in transit States, and appropriate countermeasures;

(c) Monitoring of the movement of contraband;

(d) Detection and monitoring of the movements of proceeds of crime, property, equipment or other instrumentalities and methods used for the transfer, concealment or disguise of such proceeds, property, equipment or other instrumentalities, as well as methods used in combating moneylaundering and other financial crimes;

(e) Collection of evidence;

(f) Control techniques in free trade zones and free ports;

(g) Modern law enforcement equipment and techniques, including electronic surveillance, controlled deliveries and undercover operations;

(h) Methods used in combating transnational organised crime committed through the use of computers, telecommunications networks or other forms of modern technology; and

(i) Methods used in the protection of victims and witnesses.

2. States Parties shall assist one another in planning and implementing research and training programmes designed to share expertise in the areas referred to in paragraph 1 of this article and to that end shall also, when appropriate, use regional and international conferences and seminars to promote cooperation and to stimulate discussion on problems of mutual concern, including the special problems and needs of transit States.

3. States Parties shall promote training and technical assistance that will facilitate extradition and mutual legal assistance. Such training and technical assistance may include language training, secondments and exchanges between personnel in central authorities or agencies with relevant responsibilities.

4. In the case of existing bilateral and multilateral agreements or arrangements, States Parties shall strengthen, to the extent necessary, efforts to maximize operational and training activities within international and regional organisations and within other relevant bilateral and multilateral agreements or arrangements.

Article 30

Other measures: implementation of the Convention through economic development and technical assistance

1. States Parties shall take measures conducive to the optimal implementation of this Convention to the extent possible, through international cooperation, taking into account the negative effects of organised crime on society in general, in particular on sustainable development.

2. States Parties shall make concrete efforts to the extent possible and in coordination with each other, as well as with international and regional organisations:

   (a) To enhance their cooperation at various levels with developing countries, with a view to strengthening the capacity of the latter to prevent and combat transnational organised crime;

   (b) To enhance financial and material assistance to support the efforts of developing countries to fight transnational organised crime effectively and to help them implement this Convention successfully;

(c) To provide technical assistance to developing countries and countries with economies in transition to assist them in meeting their needs for the implementation of this Convention. To that end, States Parties shall endeavour to make adequate and regular voluntary contributions to an account specifically designated for that purpose in a United Nations funding mechanism. States Parties may also give special consideration, in accordance with their domestic law and the provisions of this Convention, to contributing to the aforementioned account a percentage of the money or of the corresponding value of proceeds of crime or property confiscated in accordance with the provisions of this Convention;

(d) To encourage and persuade other States and financial institutions as appropriate to join them in efforts in accordance with this article, in particular by providing more training programmes and modern equipment to developing countries in order to assist them in achieving the objectives of this Convention.

3. To the extent possible, these measures shall be without prejudice to existing foreign assistance commitments or to other financial cooperation arrangements at the bilateral, regional or international level.

4. States Parties may conclude bilateral or multilateral agreements or arrangements on material and logistical assistance, taking into consideration the financial arrangements necessary for the means of international cooperation provided for by this Convention to be effective and for the prevention, detection and control of transnational organised crime.

Article 31
Prevention

1. States Parties shall endeavour to develop and evaluate national projects and to establish and promote best practices and policies aimed at the prevention of transnational organised crime.

2. States Parties shall endeavour, in accordance with fundamental principles of their domestic law, to reduce existing or future opportunities for organised criminal groups to participate in lawful markets with proceeds of crime, through appropriate legislative, administrative or other measures. These measures should focus on:

   (a) The strengthening of cooperation between law enforcement agencies or prosecutors and relevant private entities, including industry;

   (b) The promotion of the development of standards and procedures designed to safeguard the integrity of public and relevant private entities, as well as codes of conduct for relevant professions, in particular lawyers, notaries public, tax consultants and accountants;

   (c) The prevention of the misuse by organised criminal groups of tender procedures conducted by public authorities and of subsidies and licences granted by public authorities for commercial activity;

   (d) The prevention of the misuse of legal persons by organised criminal groups; such measures could include:

      (i) The establishment of public records on legal and natural persons involved in the establishment, management and funding of legal persons;

(ii) The introduction of the possibility of disqualifying by court order or any appropriate means for a reasonable period of time persons convicted of offences covered by this Convention from acting as directors of legal persons incorporated within their jurisdiction;

(iii) The establishment of national records of persons disqualified from acting as directors of legal persons; and

(iv) The exchange of information contained in the records referred to in sub-paragraphs (d) (i) and (iii) of this paragraph with the competent authorities of other States Parties.

3. States Parties shall endeavour to promote the reintegration into society of persons convicted of offences covered by this Convention.

4. States Parties shall endeavour to evaluate periodically existing relevant legal instruments and administrative practices with a view to detecting their vulnerability to misuse by organised criminal groups.

5. States Parties shall endeavour to promote public awareness regarding the existence, causes and gravity of and the threat posed by transnational organised crime. Information may be disseminated where appropriate through the mass media and shall include measures to promote public participation in preventing and combating such crime.

6. Each State Party shall inform the Secretary-General of the United Nations of the name and address of the authority or authorities that can assist other States Parties in developing measures to prevent transnational organised crime.

7. States Parties shall, as appropriate, collaborate with each other and relevant international and regional organisations in promoting and developing the measures referred to in this article. This includes participation in international projects aimed at the prevention of transnational organised crime, for example by alleviating the circumstances that render socially marginalised groups vulnerable to the action of transnational organised crime.

Article 32
Conference of the Parties to the Convention

1. A Conference of the Parties to the Convention is hereby established to improve the capacity of States Parties to combat transnational organised crime and to promote and review the implementation of this Convention.
2. The Secretary-General of the United Nations shall convene the Conference of the Parties not later than one year following the entry into force of this Convention. The Conference of the Parties shall adopt rules of procedure and rules governing the activities set forth in paragraphs 3 and 4 of this article (including rules concerning payment of expenses incurred in carrying out those activities).
3. The Conference of the Parties shall agree upon mechanisms for achieving the objectives mentioned in paragraph 1 of this article, including:
   (a) Facilitating activities by States Parties under articles 29, 30 and 31 of this Convention, including by encouraging the mobilisation of voluntary contributions;
   (b) Facilitating the exchange of information among States Parties on patterns and trends in